Reading Faces

New Directions in Social Psychology

Richard E. Nisbett, Series Editor

Social psychology is moving in new directions as the root questions of culture, group structure, communication, collective representations, and societal conflict are being answered in innovative ways. The new social psychology not only employs the conceptual and methodological tools of social cognition but in asking broader questions often draws on sociology, political science, history, philosophy, and anthropology. By using this interdisciplinary approach, social psychologists are mapping out ways to understand the role groups play in influencing individual minds. New Directions in Social Psychology brings the best of this work together in an effort to shape and advance these emerging trends.

Reading Faces: Window to the Soul? Leslie A. Zebrowitz

Culture of Honor: The Psychology of Violence in the South,
Richard E. Nisbett and Dov Cohen

Individualism and Collectivism, Harry C. Triandis

Justice, Liability, and Blame: Community Views and the Criminal Law,
Paul H. Robinson and John M. Darley

FORTHCOMING

Social Psychology and Law, Eugene Borgida

Cultural Psychology of African Americans, James M. Jones

Culture and Interpersonal Morality, Joan Miller

Reading Faces

Window to the Soul?

Leslie A. Zebrowitz

Westview Press
A Member of the Perseus Books Group

New Directions in Social Psychology

Copyright © 1998 by Westview Press, A Member of the Perseus Books Group

Published in 1997 in the United States of America by Westview Press, 5500 Central Avenue, Boulder, Colorado 80301-2877, and in the United Kingdom by Westview Press, 12 Hid's Copse Road, Cumnor Hill, Oxford OX2 9JJ

Library of Congress Cataloging-in-Publication Data
Zebrowitz, Leslie A., 1944–
   Reading faces : window to the soul? / Leslie A. Zebrowitz.
      p.   cm. —(New directions in social psychology)
   Includes bibliographical references and index.
   ISBN 0-8133-2746-6 (hc). —ISBN 0-8133-2747-4
(pb)
   1. Physiognomy.   2. Face—Social aspects.   3. Interpersonal
attraction.   I. Title.   II. Series.
BF859.Z43   1997
138—dc21   96-52663
                                                                                    CIP

The paper used in this publication meets the requirements of the American National Standard for Permanence of Paper for Printed Library Materials Z39.48-1984.

10   9   8   7   6   5

Contents

Illustrations

Preface

People often ask me how I became interested in faces, a topic of study that is not very popular among psychologists. This is a difficult question to answer. It is said that psychologists study their own problems. Perhaps, then, my interest in appearance began when I felt stigmatized by being the only child in my nursery school with glasses or the only child in my elementary school classes with red hair. Whatever the reason, I have long been both fascinated and puzzled by the trait impressions that faces can create. I knew that I formed very different initial impressions of people with different faces, but I didn't know why. What principles were governing these impressions? As a social psychologist, I was disappointed to discover that the research literature provided little insight into this phenomenon. For a while I tried to approach the question as an artist, taking up portrait painting and quizzing my teachers about the principles they followed when trying to portray a subject's character. To my disappointment, these artists were no more articulate about the problem than psychologists. Although they clearly did portray character in the faces they painted, they could not tell me what principles they followed, and some even claimed that what their portraits conveyed was all in the eye of the beholder.

I returned to psychology research, trying to make explicit the tacit knowledge that is expressed in artists' portraits and comprehended by face readers. This book is the product of that endeavor. It "unmasks" the face with a theoretical account of why we judge people by their appearance, and it provides an in-depth discussion of two facial qualities that influence our impressions of others: attractiveness, which has received the most attention from psychologists, and babyfaceness, which has been the focus of my own research. I hope that the insights this book provides will satisfy the curiosity of those who, like me, have wondered why they read traits in faces and what facial qualities give rise to particular trait impressions. I also hope that it will stimulate research that further unmasks the face. Finally, I hope that by making people aware of their tacit face-trait associations, this book will reduce the unwitting tendency to stereotype others on the basis of their appearance.

Leslie A. Zebrowitz

Acknowledgments

Portions of this book were written while I was supported by a research grant from the National Institute of Mental Health (MH42684) during a sabbatical leave as a Visiting Scholar at the Henry A. Murray Center at Radcliffe College. My own research reported in this book was also supported by that grant. This research benefited from stimulating collaborations with many students and colleagues: Carrie Andreoletti, Karen Apatow, Diane Berry, Jeremy Blumenthal, Sheila Brownlow, Mary Ann Collins, Ranjana Dutta, Jodie Fafel, Heidi Friedman, Lori Goldstein Rosenthal, Karen Hoffman, Don Kalick, Kathy Kendall-Tackett, Steve Kramer, Judith Langlois, Hoon-Koo Lee, Susan McDonald, Joann Montepare, Karen Olson, Kate Szymanski, Daniel Tenenbaum, and Luminita Voinescu. Some of these individuals also generously gave their time to critique one or more chapter drafts, and I am grateful to them as well as to Richard Ashmore, Regina Conti, Michael Cunningham, Richard Nisbett, and Elise Phillips, who also provided thoughtful and useful suggestions.

Nancy Carlston, formerly at Westview Press, provided extremely helpful feedback as well, and I want to thank her for unfailing support and encouragement and the many photographs she shot in order to provide appropriate faces to illustrate some of my points. Getting the photographs for this book in order was a major undertaking that was also aided by Mary Ann Collins, Joe Cunningham, Sallie Greenwood, Carrie Keating, Dave Jenemann, and Paul Vaughn whose help I greatly appreciate. Portions of this book are far more readable thanks to feedback I received from Caleb McArthur, Harry Zebrowitz, students working in my lab, and Brandeis first-year students who tested an early draft of the book in my University Seminar. Finally, the love and support of my family and friends meant much to me as I wrote this book.

L.A.Z.

1

Judging a Book by Its Cover

Afterwards on becoming very intimate with [the Captain], I heard that I had run a very narrow risk of being rejected on account of the shape of my nose! [He] was convinced that he could judge of a man's character by the outline of his features, and he doubted whether anyone with my nose could possess sufficient energy and determination for the voyage.[1]

The foregoing passage from Charles Darwin's autobiography reveals that the theory of evolution was almost lost for want of a proper nose: Darwin's nose practically cost him passage on the HMS *Beagle*, the ship from which he made many of the observations that spawned evolutionary theory. Darwin's anecdote illustrates the tendency to "judge a book by its cover," and the captain of the *Beagle* is by no means unique in this respect. After we had become best friends, my college roommate confessed her first impression of me. Jayne had perceived me to be the kind of person who would happily comply with all of her wishes. She expected to have the last word in decisions such as how to arrange the furniture in our room, when to have quiet times for study, and when to have "lights out." She even anticipated that I would be her "gofer": running to the candy machine to bring her a Clark bar or trudging to the laundry room to move the clothes from the washer to the dryer.

Although we may scoff at the judgments of the captain of the HMS *Beagle*, and I certainly laughed with Jayne about her erroneous first impression of me, one can't help but wonder where such impressions come from. We subscribe to maxims such as "don't judge a book by its cover"

1

FIGURE 1.1   *Fool in Profile. J. C. Lavater (1879). Essays in physiognomy (Plate II, Figure 2, p. 34a, Holcroft, 16th ed.). London: William Tegg.*

and "pretty is as pretty does," but the fact is that our views of other people are strongly influenced by superficial qualities, particularly their facial features. An honest appraisal of your reactions to the people you meet will surely reveal instances in which you had the immediate perception that someone was a "nice guy" or, to the contrary, that he was not to be trusted. You may or may not have wondered how you came to this conclusion. Was it something in his tone of voice? In his behavior? In his face? Although it may have been any one of these things, his face would have been sufficient. Consider the man in Figure 1.1. My tongue-in-cheek observation that he looks highly intelligent has elicited the same chuckles from U.S. and Korean audiences. The fact is that he looks quite simple-minded to all observers. Why is that so? This is one of the questions that will be addressed by this book.

Despite exhortations against the belief that character can be read from the face, you are in good company when you engage in face reading. This practice, called *physiognomy,* has persisted from ancient times to the present. In ancient Rome, the orator Cicero declared that "the countenance is the reflection of the soul." In ancient China, Confucius said, "Look into a person's pupils. He cannot hide himself." In ancient Greece, a lengthy treatise on physiognomy, which has been attributed to Aristotle, described facial signs of psychological traits, such as the following:

> Men with small foreheads are fickle, whereas if they are rounded or bulging out the owners are quick-tempered. Straight eyebrows indicate softness of disposition, those that curve out toward the temples, humor and dissimulation. The staring eye indicates impudence, the winking indecision. Large and outstanding ears indicate a tendency to irrelevant talk or chattering.[2]

Aristotle also drew analogies to animals, observing for example that "persons with hooked noses are ferocious; witness hawks."[3] Physiognomic principles, such as those espoused by Aristotle, were incorporated into Greek theater, where actors wore masks that represented certain types.

These masks depicted not only characteristic facial expressions, but also characteristic facial structures. A man of sorrows, such as Oedipus, would have a long face.[4] Clearly the ancient Greeks were able to use facial appearance as a basis for reading psychological traits, and many seem to have taken physiognomy very seriously. Indeed, the mathematician Pythagoras is reputed to have turned students away from his academy if their facial appearance was not suited to the profitable study of mathematics. One can only imagine the number of Euclids and Einsteins lost to civilization.

Darwin almost lost his passage on the Beagle because the captain was highly influenced by the Swiss physiognomist Johann Caspar Lavater (1741–1801), whose writings were widely read from the time his book *Essays on Physiognomy* was first published in 1772. This book was regularly reprinted for a hundred years in German, French, English, and Dutch, and two modern versions were published in Lavater's home country of Switzerland as late as 1940, bringing the grand total to 151 editions in various languages. The eighth edition of the *Encyclopaedia Britannica* documented the enormous impact of this book on social interactions: "In many places, where the study of human character from the face was an epidemic, the people went masked through the streets."[5]

Both the popularity of Lavater's writings and the fear they evoked attest to the appeal of physiognomy, an allure that persists in contemporary society, although there is ambivalence. Just as people hid from the scrutiny of physiognomists in the heyday of Lavater's influence, they remain wary of face-reading skills even today. Telling a stranger at a cocktail party that I study impressions of faces is a surefire way to end the conversation, even though studying impressions is not the same as actually reading character! A survey of university students suggested why people have this reaction: Over 90 percent believe that there are important facial guides to character.[6] The consensus regarding what psychological traits a face reveals is so strong that it can serve as a basis for humor, as in the cartoons shown in Figures 1.2, 1.3, and 1.4. Perhaps you can discern some common elements in the facial structure of the harmless-looking dog and man in two of these cartoons. Indeed, caricaturists work from the assumption that certain appearances can be manipulated as codes to create a psychological portrait that people can immediately recognize by reading elements of the code.

Daumier, one of the great masters of caricature, drew on the traditions of physiognomists to communicate the distinguishing traits of various social types among the bourgeoisie of nineteenth-century France—from the small shopkeeper and concierge to the politician, lawyer, and banker. Consider, for example, the banker shown in Figure 1.5. This caricature is meant to convey self-absorption and greed, as revealed by Daumier in the accompanying text: "He is the prototype of egoism, presumption and

4

FIGURE 1.2 *Garfield.* © 1984, 1993 Paws, Inc. Dist. by Universal Press Syndicate. *Reprinted with permission. All rights reserved.*

FIGURE 1.3 *Fred Basset. Reprinted by permission of Tribune Media Services.*

FIGURE 1.4 *Garfield.* © 1984, 1993, Paws, Inc. Dist. by Universal Press Syndicate. *Reprinted with permission. All rights reserved.*

pride. He loves luxury, and apes the aristocracy which he aspires to displace."[7] The appearance of this banker bears a close resemblance to Lavater's description of the appearance of selfish, greedy types as "large bulky persons, with small eyes, round full hanging cheeks, puffed lips, and a chin resembling a purse or bag; . . . who on every occasion consult their own ease without regard to others."[8]

Characteristic features recur in Daumier's caricatures, and their meaning is often metaphorical. The fullness of the banker's face and body represents the fullness of his coffers, and there may have been a kernel of truth in this representation in an era when corpulence was a sign of wealth. Similarly, the noses of Daumier's gluttonous types are full and bulbous, and "the poor and modest worker, spare and lean, is typically shown with

FIGURE 1.5   *Daumier, The Banker. French Types (D 263, 1835). Brandeis University Libraries, Waltham, Massachusetts, the Benjamin J. and Julia M. Trustman Collection (Photo credit: David Caras).*

cheek bone casting its shadows on the hollows, in contrast with the well rounded jowl of the bourgeois."[9] Daumier's use of metaphor is also shown in the lower foreheads of the lower classes and in the sharp noses of "sharp" critics and connoisseurs.

Comparisons of animals and humans codified by the seventeenth-century physiognomist Le Brun were also used by Daumier. Daumier's faces of clergy and government officials have features based on the crow, as do Le Brun's cheats, tricksters, and predators. Clergy were also depicted by Daumier as a cross between Le Brun's donkey (boorish) and his ram (stupid). As shown in Figure 1.6, butchers resembled oxen.

Fine artists, like caricaturists, exploit the ability of the face to convey psychological traits. In fact, Lavater viewed his work as a sourcebook for artists, saying of the painter, "his art too evidently reproves the childish and arrogant prejudices of those who pretend to disbelieve physiognomy."[10] An examination of portraits, such as those by Rembrandt and Gauguin shown in Figure 1.7, upholds this view. You don't merely perceive differences in face shape and feature size in these portraits; you also

FIGURE 1.6   *Metivet, Les Boeufs (1927)*. La Physionomie Humaine comparée à la Physionomie des animaux d'àpres les dessins de Le Brun. *Paris: Librairie Renouard.*

perceive differences in character. Rembrandt looks more approachable and flexible than Gauguin, a fact that must be somehow conveyed by facial structure, because the men wear similar facial expressions.

Leonardo da Vinci claimed that his portraits depicted "the motions of the mind."[11] His Mona Lisa, shown in Figure 1.8, is famous for the debates her face has inspired regarding what psychological machinations it reveals. Most have focused on her smile as the source of inferences about her psyche. The popular song asks is this a smile to charm a lover? to hide a broken heart? is it warm? is it real? Answers have ranged from the sublime to the ridiculous, but they reveal the range of information that people assume can be provided in a face. It has been said that the Mona Lisa is wearing the beatific smile of pregnancy, the smug smile of an unfaithful wife, the crooked smile of Bell's palsy, and even the satisfied smile of a burp. The Chinese artist, Song Bin, who has painted numerous replicas of the Mona Lisa affirms the connection between her smile and her character, noting that "the corners of her mouth are still the hardest to portray . . . You must understand her status in society, her personality."[12]

FIGURE 1.7   *Rembrandt (left), Self-Portrait (1661). Rijksmuseum, Amsterdam; Gauguin (right), Self-Portrait with Palette (1893–1894). Private collection, Acquavella Galleries, New York.*

Literature, like the graphic arts, conveys psychological traits through facial depictions. The nineteenth-century writer Balzac, like his contemporary Daumier, was concerned with the classification of Parisian types: the bureaucrat, the lawyer, the social climber, the banker. His verbal portrayals of physiognomy were as vivid as Daumier's pictorial ones. Balzac described the "idle rich" as follows:

> Unrelieved boredom, this inanity of mind, heart, and brain, this weariness with the unending round of Paris receptions, all leave their mark on the features and produce these paste-board faces, those premature wrinkles, that rich man's physiognomy on which impotence has set its grimace.[13]

His description of lawyers is not far removed from the current flurry of negative stereotypes:

> What countenance can retain its beauty in the debasing exercise of a profession which compels a man to bear the burden of public miseries . . . they no longer feel, they merely apply rules which are stultified by particular cases . . . And so their faces present the raw pallor, the unnatural colouring, the lack-lustre eyes with rings around them, the sensual, babbling mouths by which an observant person recognizes the symptoms of the deterioration of thought.[14]

Other authors who are acclaimed for their psychological portrayals, such as Shakespeare and Dickens, are also masters at physical portrayals.

FIGURE 1.8 *Leonardo da Vinci, Mona Lisa (c. 1503–1505). The Louvre, Paris.*

Thus, the physical description of Miss Murdstone in Dickens's *David Copperfield* provides an immediate grasp of her character:

> It was Miss Murdstone who was arrived, and a gloomy-looking lady she was; dark, like her brother . . . and with very heavy eyebrows, nearly meeting over her large nose, as if, being disabled by the wrongs of her sex from wearing whiskers, she had carried them to that account.[15]

Similarly, the following description makes readers feel that they have gotten to know something more than the body build, hairstyle, and face shape of Mr. Benjamin Allen in Dickens's *The Pickwick Papers*: "Mr. Benjamin Allen was a coarse, stout, thickset young man, with black hair cut rather short, and a white face cut rather long."[16]

Of course not all authors paint detailed word portraits. However, when they fail to do so, we automatically fill in the blanks, inferring face from character, perhaps in part because faces help us to remember who said what.[17] Testimony to this phenomenon is provided when we are jarred by the appearance of a character in a movie based on a book that we've read. An otherwise excellent movie can be spoiled when the actor doesn't look at all like the image of the character we had constructed while reading the book. Such a reaction reveals that it is not only the artist and the author who use physical appearance to communicate character. The layperson does so as well. Indeed, qualities of appearance are typically the first thing people mention when they are asked to describe a stranger or even their friends and family members. Moreover, the tendency to begin by describing someone in terms of appearance occurs even when people are asked for a description that will help others to know what it is like to be around that person. This reliance on physical appearance in descriptions of others is present from an early age. In fact very young children rely almost solely on physical qualities. The primacy of appearance suggests that it is seen as conveying other information about a person.[18]

The power of facial appearance to convey other information is confirmed by evidence that people's appearance affects impressions of their personality traits. Observers show high agreement when asked to judge the traits of people depicted in facial photographs. The person who looks honest or warm or intelligent to one observer also looks honest or warm or intelligent to another. Observers may show almost as much agreement when judging traits as when judging more "objective" physiognomic qualities, such as wideness of eyes or fullness of lips. In fact, people seem to find it much easier to make trait judgments than physiognomic judgments.

One interesting consequence of the relationship between facial appearance and personality impressions is that people who physically resemble each other are perceived to have similar traits and those who look different from one another are perceived to have different traits. These effects do *not* merely reflect racial, sex, or age stereotypes; that is, they do not reflect a tendency to attribute the same traits to people who resemble one another because they are of the same race, sex, or age group. The propensity to believe that people who look similar on the outside also have inner similarities is found even when the people being compared are the same race, the same sex, and approximately the same age. Another intriguing finding regarding face-trait correspondences is that people whose facial appearance deviates a lot from average—for example, very wide eyes or very thin lips—are also perceived to have more extreme personality traits than those with a more average appearance.[19]

People's faces influence perceptions of their motives as well as their traits. Consider the following scenario:

> A secretary has just been assigned for the first time to the vice president of the company, who is a young, dynamic, fast-rising, married man. He has just thanked her for taking dictation. The woman, standing at the door, asks, "Is there anything else you would like?"

When people are shown a photograph of the secretary and asked what she really meant by this question, their perception of her intentions depends on her face. Some faces are likely to be perceived as suggesting the woman's availability for a more personal and intimate relationship. Others are perceived as communicating the woman's skill in all aspects of secretarial service, not merely stenography. Some faces convey seductive intentions, whereas others convey ambitious intentions. Faces also vary in the extent to which they convey criminal intentions. Consider a second scenario:

A social worker interviews a woman on welfare whom she has discovered is holding a job while receiving payments. She has also discovered that the woman has acquired a modest set of investments. Outlining the penalties for such fraud, the social worker says to the client (who is in tears), "It doesn't have to be as bad as that. You seem to be an intelligent woman, and I like you. Let's talk about it some more."

When people are shown a photograph of the social worker and asked what she really meant by this statement, their perception of her intentions again depends on her face. Some faces are likely to be perceived as intimating willingness to cover up the fraud, if given a sufficient bribe. Others are perceived as simply being kind and reassuring.[20]

Not only does appearance convey character, but also stability in appearance facilitates the perception of a constant character. When a person shows constancy in his appearance, he is perceived to have a more invariant disposition than if his appearance noticeably changes. Thus, people who always look the same may be described as either energetic or relaxed, quiet or talkative, dominant or deferential, depending on their particular appearance. However, stable traits such as these are not attributed to people whose appearance varies. When asked to describe someone who looks different in different photographs—who in one photo is clean-shaven, with neat, medium-length hair; in another photo is unshaven with glasses and has messy, long hair; and in still another is moustached with neat, short hair—people are apt to say that such a person does not act consistently at different times and that whether he is energetic or relaxed, quiet or talkative, dominant or deferential "depends on the situation."[21]

Novelists often capitalize on the tendency to associate an unstable appearance with inconstancy of character. Flaubert's depiction of the "inconstant" Madam Bovary shows her "changing colors." At her sexual awakening, Madam Bovary's eyes are described as "dark in the shadows and blue in daylight," an inconstancy that corresponds to her double life. "Blue in daylight" evokes her normal open life as the wife of a doctor. "Dark in the shadows" conveys her shadowy, secret life as an adulteress.[22] Novelists also link a changed appearance with personality changes, a prime example being Oscar Wilde's *The Picture of Dorian Gray*, in which the life experiences of the protagonist are etched into his portrait:

The expression looked different . . . sunlight showed him the lines of cruelty round the mouth as clearly as if he had been looking into a mirror after he had done some dreadful thing. . . . Suddenly . . . he remembered it perfectly. He had uttered a mad wish that he himself might remain young, and the portrait grow old; that his own beauty might be untarnished, and the face on the canvas bear the burden of his passions and his sins. . . . It had altered already, and would alter more.[23]

Research indicates that the literary device of changing appearance to convey changes in character should be highly effective. Someone who behaves in a nervous and timid manner in a first encounter is, not surprisingly, perceived as low in confidence, aggressiveness, and forcefulness. When his behavior shows a drastic change in a second encounter, becoming much more aggressive and forward, impressions of his personality show a greater corresponding change if his haircut has also changed than if his haircut has remained constant. Whether the haircut has changed from short to long or from long to short doesn't matter. It is a change in appearance itself that facilitates changed impressions.[24] Therefore, those who want to "turn over a new leaf" would be well advised to change their appearance as well as their behavior.

The prominent role of facial appearance in impressions of others is paralleled by its role in attraction to others. It is perhaps not surprising that research has shown that people prefer to socialize with members of the opposite sex who are physically attractive rather than unattractive. What is more surprising is that the reasons people give for wanting or not wanting to get to know someone of either sex whom they have briefly seen on videotape include liking or disliking for a variety of facial features such as something about the person's eyes or mouth. Moreover, these and other appearance qualities are more important determinants of the desire to get to know someone than are the person's facial expressions and gestures or judgments of the person's humor, intelligence, or friendliness.[25]

It is interesting that "face readers" cannot clearly articulate the bases for their judgments. When asked the reasons for their personality ratings, they say things such as "I say that he looks intelligent because of something about his eyes" or "I don't know why he looks kind; there's just something about him."[26] On the occasion when some definite reason is given, it often cannot account for the findings. For example, after giving their impressions of schematic faces that varied in eye size, nose length, or placement of the features, people were asked what physical differences among these faces they had been responding to. Differences that were not even present, such as in hairstyles, mouth shapes, and facial expressions, were mentioned more frequently than the actual differences among the faces. Although the people knew that there was something different about the faces, and the impressions they formed were systematically related to the actual differences, they were not consciously aware of what those differences were. Despite this inability to pinpoint the source of their impressions, observers agree with one another when judging psychological traits from the face, which implies that there are some observable facial characteristics that convey these impressions, be they right or wrong. The questions remain, "What might these facial characteristics be, and why do they elicit the impressions they do?"

The answers that are provided in this book derive from a functional approach to social perception: "perceiving is for doing."[27] It is assumed that impressions of people that are based on their appearance must be useful inasmuch as these impressions guide our social behavior, which, more often than not, is relatively effective in achieving our social goals. Therefore, face reading either should be accurate or should reflect perceptual biases that serve some general adaptive function.[28] In particular, the evolutionary importance of detecting attributes like a person's identity, age, or genetic fitness may have produced such a strong tendency to respond to the facial qualities that reveal these attributes that our responses are overgeneralized to people whose faces merely resemble people we know or people of a certain age or fitness level. If so, the facial characteristics that influence impressions of people's traits will be related to those that reveal useful information, such as people's age, identity, or fitness.

In accordance with this functional approach to the question of why perceivers associate certain traits with certain facial qualities, Chapter 2 examines the useful information in faces that could give rise to trait impressions via overgeneralization effects, and Chapter 3 describes various overgeneralization effects that may occur. Chapter 3 also reviews evidence that appearance-based trait impressions may occur because they are in fact accurate, and it suggests how such accuracy may be explained. Two of the overgeneralization effects described in Chapter 3 are considered in depth in subsequent chapters: the babyface overgeneralization effect and the attractiveness halo effect, which are the only two facial stereotypes that have been the subject of extensive research. Chapter 4 examines the facial qualities that can produce a babyface overgeneralization effect, contrasting the appearance of infants with that of adults, documenting the power of infantile facial qualities to elicit certain responses from adults, and demonstrating the potential for these responses to be overgeneralized to babyfaced individuals who are not actually babies. Chapter 6 examines the facial qualities that can produce an attractiveness halo effect, identifying the appearance qualities that make a face attractive and considering evolutionary explanations for why these qualities are perceived as attractive. Chapters 5 and 7 document the environmental consequences, respectively, of a babyface and an attractive face—both the trait impressions that they create and, following the tenet that "perceiving is for doing," their more tangible social outcomes. Chapter 8 examines links between "attractiveness" or "babyfaceness" and behavior. In particular, this chapter considers whether perceivers' expectations may produce self-fulfilling prophecy effects, such that babyfaced or attractive people develop the traits they are expected to have. It also considers the possibility that people's personality traits may influence their appearance. Finally, Chapter 9 considers what kinds of individual and social changes might foster greater adherence to the adage "don't judge a book by its cover," and Chapter 10 provides some general conclusions regarding the phenomenon of face reading.

As the research literature is reviewed, particularly in Chapters 5–8, reference will be made to the size of the appearance effects that are reported. The reported effect sizes will be described as small/weak, medium/moderate, or large/strong, following conventions suggested by the statistician Jacob Cohen. A small effect is one that would not be discerned by perceivers unless they made use of statistical comparisons. To give a concrete example, the half inch average difference in height between 15- and 16-year-old girls is a small effect. A medium effect is large enough to be visible to the naked eye, for example, the 1 inch average difference in height between 14- and 18-year-old girls. A large effect occurs when there is little overlap between two groups in the phenomenon of interest. An example of a large effect is the average difference in height between 13- and 18-year-old girls.[29] These different effect sizes tell us that the difference in age between 13- and 18-year-old girls is a very important determinant of their height, whereas age differences are less important determinants of the differences in height between 15- and 16-year-old girls, which may depend as much on other factors such as genetic endowment. The same reasoning applies to small versus large effect sizes for facial appearance. A large effect means that appearance is a very important determinant of trait impressions, social outcomes, or behavior, and a small effect means that influences other than appearance play a relatively greater role.

2

What's in a Face?

As a rule a man's face says more of interest than does his tongue . . . it is the monogram of all his thoughts and aspirations.

—Schopenhauer, "On Physiognomy," 1851

Although many would dispute the claim that thoughts and aspirations are imprinted on the face, there is much that *is* reflected in the face, and the attempt to discover why people persist in using the face as a key to psychological traits may be advanced by considering what a person's face does reveal. Various facial qualities can tell us a lot about a person. Some of these qualities are structural, like the shape and size of the head and face; the color, lines, blotches, texture, and sagging of the skin; the size, shape, and location of the eyes, nose, mouth, and ears; and the amount and color of scalp and facial hair. Other diagnostic facial qualities are dynamic, like muscular movements, changes in coloration (e.g., blushing and blanching), gaze direction, and pupil dilation and contraction. Still other facial qualities are "artificial," like hairstyle, glasses, and makeup.

Through innate associations, evolutionarily prepared learning, and culturally specific learning, these facial qualities can reveal the stable personal attributes of sex, race, and identity; the rapidly changing attribute of emotion; and the more slowly changing attributes of age and physical and mental fitness.[1] Detecting each of these attributes is important for adaptive behavior, be it to promote species survival or to attain individual goals. We could not function well in this world if we were unable to differentiate men from women, friends from strangers, the angered from the happy, the healthy from the unfit, or children from adults. For this reason, the tendency to respond to the facial qualities that reveal these attributes may be so strong that it is overgeneralized to people whose faces

14

merely resemble those who actually have the attribute. In this chapter, I consider the ability of facial cues to reveal various adaptively significant attributes, and in Chapter 3 I demonstrate how overgeneralized responses to some of these facial cues may serve as a foundation for reading traits in faces.

Facial Cues to Age

The growth process from birth to maturity is accompanied by changes in the face that are reliable cues to age. These changes, which are described in more detail in Chapter 4, yield a relatively smaller, more backward-sloping forehead; relatively smaller, higher placed eyes; and a relatively bigger, more protrusive chin in the adult face. The head is also smaller relative to the body in an adult than in a child, and an adult's skin is darker than that of a child. Like maturation, the aging process also produces facial changes, most notably in the quality of the skin, which becomes progressively more leathery, crinkled, open-pored, and blemished. Age-related changes in connective tissue, bone loss, and the resorption of fatty tissue also yield a less angular jaw, pouches, sagging skin, and a double chin.[2] Some of these changes cause the elderly face to revert to a more infantile appearance.

In addition to the foregoing static cues to age provided by facial structure and skin quality, there are also dynamic cues to age provided by facial movements. The point-light technique has been used to reveal the information provided by facial movement that is independent of structure. People's faces are videotaped with small pieces of reflective tape affixed to them. When these tapes are played with the brightness reduced and the contrast maximized, what one sees is the movement of small luminous dots. When viewers are asked to guess the age of a particular face, their guesses are much more accurate when they see the video than when they are shown only a freeze-frame of it, thereby demonstrating that the facial movements are adding information about age over and above whatever structural information the dots provide. What has not yet been determined is the nature of the age differences in facial movement—whether, for example, there are differences in the amount of movement, in the symmetry of movement, or in the abruptness of movement onset and offset.[3]

Not only does the face change with age, but also there is a good deal of consensus and accuracy in guessing people's age from their facial appearance. Research has shown that people show high agreement with one another in their estimates of the ages of men and women who ranged from their mid 20s to their late 60s. In most cases, these estimates were quite accurate, missing the mark by no more than 3 to 7 years.[4] The ability to discern age from facial cues develops early. By the preschool years, children are proficient at using age category labels to identify people pictured in facial photographs and to rank in terms of age faces of people who range from infancy to over 70 years.[5] Moreover, children base their judgments on the same information that adults use, such as head shape and facial wrinkling.[6] One young child, when asked how he knew that a particular face was a baby, observed: "He's a baby because he's got a big forehead. It's bigger for his face than mine is or yours is."[7]

Research has not firmly established whether the ability to differentiate younger from older faces has a specific neural locus, but there is some evidence that individuals with particular types of brain damage have difficulty identifying people's ages from their faces.[8] There is also evidence for the development of age recognition very early in life. Even infants as young as 4 months of age can discriminate faces of different ages.[9] When a strange child approaches a baby, the most common response is a smile, and negative reactions are virtually nonexistent. Quite the opposite occurs when a strange adult approaches a baby. By 9 or 10 months of age, most babies exhibit some negative reaction, either frowning, looking away, moving away, or crying. A baby's more positive reaction to children does not reflect merely their smaller stature. Babies also show negative reactions when they are approached by a midget, who has the face of an adult and the size of a child. Thus, babies appear to find the faces of strange children less threatening than those of strange adults, a reaction that may have had evolutionary adaptive value.[10]

Although people's age estimates are quite accurate, we do sometimes misjudge, and there are some people whose ages are consistently over- or underestimated. Some people are "carded" at bars and liquor stores until they are well past the legal drinking age, and I can vividly remember the embarrassment of mistaking a toddler's father for her grandfather. It is interesting that age estimates that deviate from someone's true chronological age may correspond to that person's biological age. Thus, there may be a bit of truth in what appear to be mistaken age perceptions. Men between the ages of 17 and 97 who look old for their age to physicians who know nothing about them show responses typical of people older than themselves on subsequent examination. For example, their lung capacity and blood pressure are at levels that would be expected for somewhat older men. In contrast, those who look young for their age show responses typical of people younger than themselves. Moreover, older appearing men between the ages of 45 and 75 died sooner than their younger looking peers. Whether facial cues to age are critical to these effects remains to be determined, since the whole range of appearance information was available to the doctors making the age estimates.[11]

Facial Cues to Sex

People readily identify a person's sex from facial cues. Facial hair and smoothness of skin are the most obvious indicators, although this sex difference is more marked among Caucasians than other racial groups. Scalp hair is also used as a cue to sex, despite cultural and historical variations in this marker. Another, more subtle indicator is skin tone. Women from a wide range of cultures and racial backgrounds are lighter skinned than men of the same group, even when skin tone is assessed in parts of the body that have little exposure to the sun.[12] Other subtle markers of a person's sex are structural differences between male and female faces. Although people may not be aware of responding to these subtle cues to sex, they are described here because their interesting parallels to age cues have implications for the understanding of sex stereotypes, as is shown in Chapter 5. The structure of the female face is, in many respects, similar to that of the infantile face, whereas the male facial structure is more similar to that of the mature face.

Because males generally have a larger body size and correspondingly bigger lungs and larger airways, they tend to have proportionately larger noses than females do. As shown in Figure 2.1, the male nose is generally more protrusive, ranging from a straight to a convex profile, whereas the female nose tends to range from a straight to a somewhat concave profile. The male nose is also longer and wider, with larger and more flaring nostrils and a higher nasal bridge. The upshot of these sex differences is that men are more apt to have a roman nose, and women are more apt to have a pug nose. Men are also more apt to have a Neanderthal forehead. As shown in Figure 2.1, a man's forehead tends to protrude just above the nose and eyes and then to slope backward, whereas the forehead of a woman is more upright. The appearance of the eyes also tends to differ for men and women. A man's eyes appear more deep set owing to the protrusiveness of his nose and forehead, whereas a woman's eyes look more prominent. For the same reason, a woman's cheekbones tend to look more prominent than a man's. Finally, a man's jaw tends to be proportionately larger than a woman's.[13] It is surprising that sex can even be discriminated from the face of a young infant, an achievement that may reflect sensitivity to the fact that male neonates have larger heads and faces than females. They also have somewhat smaller eyes and lower eyebrows.[14]

In addition to sex differences in facial structure, there are also differences in the way the facial muscles move. The point-light technique, which was mentioned earlier, has shown that movements add information about sex over and above whatever structural information the dots

FIGURE 2.1   *Sex differences in facial structure. D. H. Enlow (1982).* Handbook of facial growth *(Figures 1–5, 1–6). Philadelphia: Saunders.*

provide. The precise nature of sex differences in facial movement remains to be discovered.[15]

Although research has not established whether the ability to differentiate male and female faces has a specific neural locus, there is some evidence that individuals with particular types of brain damage have difficulty identifying people's sex from their faces.[16] There is also evidence that sex identification develops very early in life. After looking at a pair of identical faces, 5-month-old infants take more notice when one of them is replaced with a face of a different sex than when it is replaced with a face of the same sex,[17] and children as young as 19 months of age are able to apply appropriate sex labels to photographs of adult faces.[18] Despite the sex differences in facial structure and movement and the evidence for early sensitivity to this information, people can be fooled: There is evidence that the Mona Lisa may be a self-portrait of Leonardo da Vinci;[19] the members of the Billy Tipton Trio of jazz musicians, shown in Figure 2.2, all passed for males, yet one is a female.

Facial Cues to Ethnicity and Race

I had just purchased a beautiful carved woodpecker from a crusty, 87-year-old man in Nova Scotia when he began a conversation that made me wish I had never set foot in his house.

FIGURE 2.2   *The Billy Tipton Trio. AP/Wide World Photos.*

"Are you from Boston?" he asked. "Yes," I replied. "I knew it," he said. "I can always tell where someone is from by their face. I can always spot those Jews from New York when they come in here with their big noses, like that Jewish actor on TV, Telly Savalas."

Although this man expressed a commonly held assumption about the recognizability of Jews, his powers of discernment were not so keen as he thought. *I* was a Jew of New York origin, having lived in the Boston area only a half dozen years at that time, and Savalas is of Greek heritage. The old man's errors are not uncommon. Indeed, over the years I have been privy to many anti-Semitic remarks uttered by people who assumed from my appearance that I was not Jewish. Judging someone's religious or ethnic background from facial appearance is commonplace (and not always tinged with religious or ethnic slurs). Although most of us are wise enough to know that appearance is not always a reliable predictor of ethnicity, it is the rare person who has not at one time or another said, "Gee, she doesn't look Jewish [or Irish or Italian or Swedish]." Perhaps this derives from a kernel of truth to ethnic appearance stereotypes. Indeed, although ethnic identification from appearance is subject to error, there is some evidence for above-chance performance in identifying Jews from physiognomy alone, although they tend to be confused with Italians.[20]

Such confusion may reflect similarities in the appearance of certain Jews and others of Mediterranean origin, a finding that recalls the old wood-carver's assertion that Telly Savalas is Jewish.

The fact is that there is a relationship between ethnicity and facial appearance, although the correlation is certainly not perfect. Certain ethnic groups differ in the predominance of two major facial types that have been identified by physical anthropologists. One facial type accompanies a long narrow head form, called dolichocephalic (DC). The other type accompanies a wide, short, globular head form, called brachycephalic (BC). To get a sense of how the DC and BC face types differ, imagine that the head is like a rubber balloon that can be squeezed or stretched, as shown in Figure 2.3. The extreme version of a squeezed, dolichocephalic balloon head yields a face with a convex profile, like profile b in Figure 2.3. It is a relatively angular face, narrow, long, and protrusive, with close-set eyes; a relatively thin, longish, and protrusive nose with a high bridge; and a relatively receding chin. The forehead in this face tends to slope backward and to jut out over the eyes, which consequently appear deep set. The extreme version of the stretched BC balloon head yields a face with a concave profile, like profile d in Figure 2.3. It is short, broad, and flat with wide-set eyes, a short, puglike nose, and a prominent chin. The forehead in this face tends to be upright, the eyes are bulging, and the cheekbones are squared and prominent. There is, of course, a range of face types within any given ethnic group, with many faces being a mixture of types, called mesocephalic. Nevertheless, one or the other type of face tends to predominate in different groups. The DC face tends to be more prevalent than the BC face in Great Britain, Scandinavia, northern Africa, India, and the Middle Eastern countries of Iran, Afghanistan, Iraq, and Saudi Arabia. The BC face tends to predominate in middle Europe and the Far East.[21] It is interesting that the BC head type is in many respects similar to the infantile head, whereas the DC head type is more similar to the mature head. Indeed, an anatomy textbook states that the brachycephalic type of face "appears more juvenile-like because it resembles the wide-face configuration characterizing a child. A dolichocephalic adult face 'looks' more mature because the nasal region is vertically longer."[22]

Like ethnicity, race is typically identified from facial cues. Although physical anthropologists agree that common racial groupings are not valid scientific categories, such groups are nevertheless identified by laypersons. The primary basis of identification is skin color, although facial features may also be used. People with broad noses and thick lips tend to be categorized as members of the Negroid race. People with small-bridged noses and slanted eyes tend to be categorized as members of the Mongoloid race. People with hairy faces (if male) and protruding noses tend to be categorized as members of the Caucasian race. Indeed,

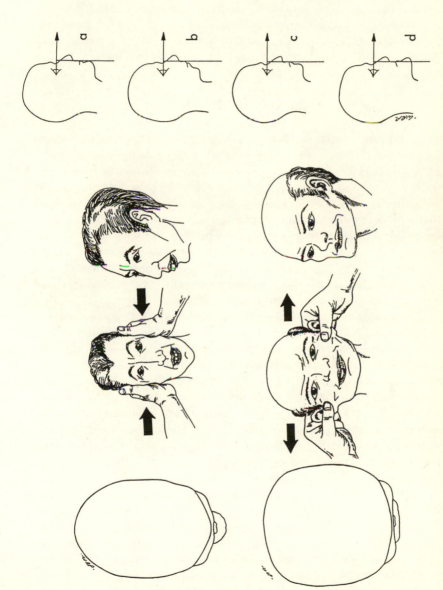

FIGURE 2.3 *Views of the dolichocephalic head (top row and b) and the brachycephalic head (bottom row and a or d). D. H. Enlow (1982). Handbook of facial growth (Figures 1–2, 1–3, 5–5). Philadelphia: Saunders.*

the first Western visitors to Korea were dubbed "bignoses" by their Asian hosts, and the word for both foreigner and westerner in Chinese is *dazi*, which literally means "big nose." Finally, it is also possible that variations in muscular movements can be used to identify race, since some differences in the facial musculature of racial groups have been noted.[23]

It is interesting to consider how people come to discern ethnicity and race from facial appearance. Researchers have not investigated at what age this ability is acquired nor how it is influenced by experience.

Facial Cues to Identity

Like snowflakes, no two faces are alike. Imagine that snowflakes were large enough that you could readily see their unique design and that you are given the task of recognizing hundreds or thousands of them—not only recognizing which ones you had seen before but also attaching a distinctive name to each one. This sounds like an impossible task or at least one that would require a great deal of effort, yet we automatically and effortlessly accomplish such recognition of human faces. Moreover, once we have learned a face, we rarely forget it. Fifty years after graduating from high school, people showed almost perfect accuracy in identifying faces taken from their own high school yearbooks as opposed to those taken from other yearbooks of the same era.[24]

The particular facial characteristics that enable us to recognize someone are difficult to describe, for it is the entire gestalt, or facial configuration, that matters rather than individual features. The gestalt is drastically altered when faces are inverted, and this transformation makes recognition extremely difficult. On the other hand, we can still recognize people after they've cut their hair, shaved their beard, or switched from glasses to contact lenses. We can recognize people whether they're smiling or crying. We can even recognize people after they've had their nose "fixed" or their jaw enhanced, and all of the sagging and bagging and wrinkling in an aging face doesn't prevent us from recognizing an old friend whom we haven't seen for many years. The continuity of identity in the face over time can be seen in the individuals depicted in Figure 2.4.

Whatever it is about a face that conveys a person's identity may also enable us to recognize kin. Indeed, one of the first questions asked about a newborn baby is, "Whom does she look like?" Although some may notice that baby's fingers are long and slender like grandma's, most of us focus on facial resemblances. Written under the newborn photo in my son's baby album is a detailed analysis of whose eyes, whose nose, whose mouth, and even whose earlobes he had inherited. A biological anthropologist has suggested that this fascination with identifying kinship re-

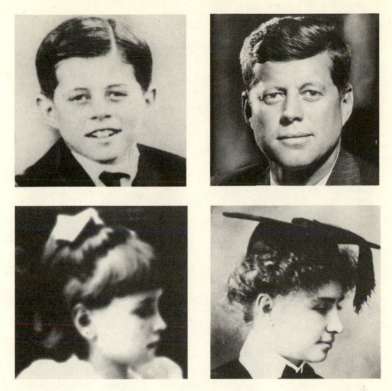

FIGURE 2.4 *John F. Kennedy in childhood and adulthood (top); Helen Keller in childhood and adulthood (bottom). AP/Wide World Photos.*

semblances may reflect our biological heritage and men's interest in detecting the legitimacy of their alleged offspring. Although kinship resemblances are often subtle, a discerning perceiver can often identify them, as the reader may be able to for the faces depicted in Figure 2.5.

The theme of physical resemblance as a marker of a genetic relation can be found in child and adult literature. The classic tale of the Ugly Duckling teaches children not only that the unfortunate among them may be late bloomers, who will come into their own, but also that the belief in family resemblances is a valid one. The sibling who looked different was not, after all, a sibling. The son who does not resemble his father in Emily Bronte's *Wuthering Heights* is also an outcast. The light-haired, fair-skinned Linton Heathcliff learns to his dismay that he is physically quite different from his black-haired, dark-eyed father. Disappointed by the physical appearance of his son, Heathcliff's dislike of the boy becomes more and more apparent with the passage of time.[25]

FIGURE 2.5 *Clockwise from upper left are three sisters, Sylvia Warren, Lisa Zebro, and Leslie Zebrowitz, and an unrelated friend, Joann Montepare.*

It is interesting that people's striking ability to identify faces is considerably weakened when the faces are not of their own race. Research on cross-race face recognition, in which people are asked to identify faces they have seen before, indicates that people have more difficulty recognizing faces of a race other than their own, an effect that can have adverse social consequences ranging from the wrongful conviction of misidentified defendants to the embarrassing confusion of people in social settings.[26] There is also anecdotal evidence to indicate that people have more difficulty differentiating ethnicities that are unfamiliar to them than those that are more familiar. For example, Westerners often report more difficulty differentiating Japanese from Chinese or Korean faces than differentiating Italian from Irish or Swedish faces. Although this fact suggests that perceptual experiences other than exposure to a particular face play a significant role in identity recognition, research has not shown a strong, consistent relationship between the debility in cross-race face recognition and prejudice or cross-racial experience—at least within the range of such experiences that have been studied.[27] However, it is possible that the quality of cross-racial experience is crucial. Immersion in another racial group, experiences that demand attention to other race faces, or perceptual experiences very early in life may be critical to the ability to identify faces of another race with the same facility that one identifies own-race faces. Perhaps extracting identity information from faces is like language acquisition: Just as experience with a particular language very early in life is necessary to become truly fluent, so may early experience with a particular set of faces be essential to facile recognition.

There is considerable evidence that face recognition has a specific neural locus. Electrophysiological recordings made from the brains of monkeys while they are viewing various visual stimuli reveal that certain neurons respond specifically to faces—either human faces or monkey faces. Moreover, some of these neurons respond more to certain faces than to others, thereby providing a basis for the recognition of different individuals.[28] Even sheep brains show specialization of certain cells for face recognition, a finding that is consistent with the importance to a sheep of accurate facial recognition. Sheep prefer to interact with members of their own breed, and information about breed is conveyed by the face. Sheep also recognize their offspring by their faces rather than by other features. Furthermore, sheep know to whom they should submit and whom they can dominate by the size of each other's horns. The activity of the specialized face-recognition cells in the sheep's brain reflect these various functions. Some cells respond strongly to faces from a familiar breed and very little to other animal faces. Other cells respond more to animals with large horns than those with small or no horns. Still another group of cells respond more to faces of humans and sheepdogs than to sheep or other animal faces.[29] It appears, therefore, that there is a specific neural locus for species recognition as well as for the recognition of individuals within a given species.

Although invasive electrophysiological recordings cannot be performed on humans, developmental and clinical evidence does indicate a specific neurological basis of face recognition. Newborn infants, 9 minutes old, show rapt attention to a moving schematic face but not to other moving patterns, and newborns who are only hours old are capable of recognizing their mother's face, preferring to look at their mother or a still video image of her rather than a stranger.[30] Other evidence of neural wiring specific to face recognition in humans is provided by a disorder called *prosopagnosia*, which means "not knowing people." This deficit results from a particular type of brain damage: bilateral lesions that involve the occipitotemporal sector of the central visual system.[31] People with such lesions show a perceptual deficit in face recognition. Consider the following case recounted by Oliver Sacks in his best-selling book *The Man Who Mistook His Wife for a Hat*:

Following a severe automobile accident, with unconsciousness for three weeks, [a man of 32] complained, exclusively, of an inability to recognise faces, even those of his wife and children. Not a single face was "familiar" to him, but there were three he could identify; . . . one with an eye-blinking tic, one with a large mole on his cheek, and a third because he was so tall and thin that no one else was like him. Each of these . . . was recognized solely by the single prominent feature mentioned. In general [the patient] recognised familiars only by their voices. He had difficulty even recognizing himself in a mirror. . . . On the other hand, simple schematic objects—scissors, watch, key—presented no difficulties.[32]

The deficits that prosopagnosics show in face perception are quite specific. These individuals are able to say which two faces are the same and which are different. They are also able to identify correctly facial expressions of emotion. What they cannot do is perceive the identity of a face that should be familiar to them. They may also have difficulty identifying the age and sex of persons from their faces, although like emotion perception, these abilities can remain intact even in the absence of obvious cues such as hair length. Generally speaking, people with prosopagnosia have no impairment in intelligence and no language deficits. They may also have no difficulty recognizing colors, pictures, objects, voices, or melodies. However, the loss of face recognition sometimes co-occurs with other recognition deficits, including animal recognition, probably because the brain areas in which face-recognition cells are found also contain cells responsive to these stimuli.[33]

Facial Cues to Emotion and Deception

In contrast to the warning "don't judge a book by its cover," which is invoked when we form impressions of people's character, we speak quite comfortably about "reading" someone's emotions or of fear being "written" on the face. The fact is that a person's emotional state *is* revealed in the face. Considerable research has demonstrated that at least seven basic emotions can be accurately communicated by facial expressions: happiness, fear, surprise, anger, sadness, disgust, and contempt.[34] One can easily recognize the expressions shown in Figure 2.6. The knitted eyebrows of sadness and the wide eyes of surprise are familiar to all, as is, of course, the smile of happiness. Whereas these photos identify static facial qualities that communicate various emotions, there are also dynamic, movement cues. Indeed, people are more accurate at guessing the emotion someone has reported experiencing when they view film clips of the facial expression than when they view slides of the same expressions taken from the films.[35] Moreover, the point-light technique has demonstrated

that movement information itself is sufficient for the accurate identification of
emotions even when no information
about the shape and position of facial features is discernible. For example, anger is
conveyed by downward movement in the
forehead area and compression in the
mouth area, whereas surprise is conveyed
by strong upward movement in the brow
area coupled with strong downward
movement in the jaw area.[36]

Whereas the static and dynamic qualities that have been described involve specific, local changes in the face for each expression, a more abstract characterization
of anger has been determined in an inge-
nious study of primitive masks from a variety of cultures. Compared with nonthreatening masks, those known to have a
threatening social function contain more
diagonal and angular features, such as
vertical lines between the eyebrows, diagonal cheekbone lines, triangular eyes and
nose, and pointed chin, beard, and ears.
Nonthreatening masks had more curvilinear features. Therefore, diagonal and
angular facial qualities communicate
anger.[37]

The fact that primitive masks have the
same meaning to modern observers as
they do in their cultures of origin supports Darwin's thesis that the basic expressions of emotion are universal to the
human species. Further support for the
pancultural generality of emotion reading
is provided by evidence that people from
North American, South American, Euro-

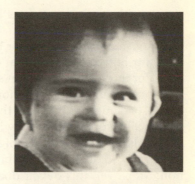

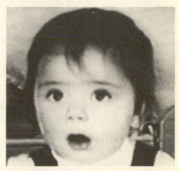

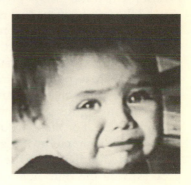

FIGURE 2.6 *Happiness, surprise,
and sadness. Photos courtesy of
Julie Riess and Joseph Cunningham.*

pean, African, and Asian countries, including those from an isolated New
Guinea tribe, all see the same emotion in particular facial expressions.[38]
At the same time, there are also some cultural differences in emotion
recognition, particularly for negative emotions.[39] In particular, Japanese
people have more difficulty than others recognizing negative facial expressions of emotion, an effect that may reflect a lack of perceptual expe-

rience with such expressions because of cultural proscriptions against displaying them. There is also some evidence that emotion recognition by African Americans is superior to that shown by whites, an effect that has been attributed to the fact that expressive information has greater importance for those who are low in social power.

Insofar as emotion perception from facial expressions is culturally universal, one might expect that this faculty has a specific neural basis. Some evidence to support this view is provided by cases of brain-damaged individuals. Patients with damage to certain areas of the right hemisphere show marked deficits in the ability to recognize facial expressions of emotion. Moreover, this deficit does not merely reflect difficulties in understanding emotional stimuli but rather is specific to faces. These patients show little impairment in their ability to read vocal or postural cues to emotion.[40] Research with normal populations also localizes the reading of facial expressions in the right hemisphere. This research uses what is called a *divided visual field technique*, in which facial stimuli are presented very briefly to either the right or the left visual field. Because of crisscrossing of neural pathways, images projected to the right visual field are received first by the left hemisphere of the brain, whereas those projected to the left visual field are received first by the right hemisphere. People are able to judge more quickly whether a face has a happy or a sad facial expression when the face is presented first to the right hemisphere rather than to the left, whereas this right hemisphere advantage is weak or absent in the case of neutral expressions.[41] Other evidence indicates that the neural basis of face identification, which was discussed previously, is independent of the neural basis of emotion recognition. One can identify faces but fail to recognize their emotional expressions and vice versa.[42]

The right hemisphere advantage in processing facial expressions is illustrated in Figure 2.7, which depicts mirror images of the same schematic face. For those who are right-handed, a quick glance at these faces reveals a happier expression on the bottom face. This is because, for right-handed individuals, the upturned mouth in the left visual field is processed by the right hemisphere, whereas the downturned mouth in the right visual field is processed by the left hemisphere. Because the right hemisphere dominates in right-handed people, this face looks happier than the top one, for which right hemisphere dominance emphasizes the downturned mouth. Those who are left-handed may perceive a happier expression on the top face. This is because the brain organization of many left-handed people differs from that of right-handers.

Like studies of brain-damaged individuals, studies of infants could conceivably shed light on the question of whether we are "wired" to perceive particular emotions in particular facial expressions. However, it is difficult to discover exactly what a particular emotional expression means to infants. One cannot simply query them about their perceptions. One approach has been to see whether infants can at least discriminate among different emotional expressions. What researchers have determined is whether infants show increased attention to one emotional expression after they have viewed another one to the point of bored inattention. If they perk up when a new expression appears but not when the old one reappears, this indicates that they can tell the two apart, and indeed, it turns out that they can.[43]

The question remains concerning what meaning the different expressions have for infants. Do they understand that a smile means happy, that a frown means sad, and that a scowl means angry? Since infants don't talk, we are forced to devise clever ways of answering this question by observing an infant's behavioral reactions. One ploy has been to see how different facial expressions affect an infant's reactions to loud noises. From early infancy, there is a tendency to blink in response to an unexpected loud noise. This blink reflex is stronger in adults when they are looking at slides that have negative emotional meaning, such as a snarling dog, than when they are looking at slides that have positive emotional meaning, such as a smiling baby. A similar effect has been shown in 5-month-old infants. They show a stronger startle response to

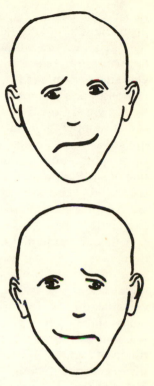

FIGURE 2.7 *Left side of the face dominates emotion perception by the right-handed. From* About Faces *by Terry Landau. [Copyright] 1989 by Terry Landau. Used by permission of Doubleday, a division of Bantam Doubleday Dell Publishing.*

noise when looking at an angry face than when looking at a happy face, which suggests that they grasp the dangerous meaning of the angry face.[44] Similarly, by 5 months of age, infants can communicate a dislike for angry expressions by turning away from them,[45] and crawling infants tell us that they understand the meaning of a smile, a scowl, and a frown by varying their willingness to cross a "visual cliff."

The visual cliff is a plexiglass-covered table divided into two halves. One half can look like a drop-off, depending on how far below the surface a pattern is placed. Infants will not cross to the deep side if their mother stands there with a posed fearful expression, whereas the vast majority do so if she poses a happy expression. Anger and, to a lesser extent, sad expressions also deter infants from crossing the cliff, which suggests that they may interpret all negative expressions as a warning.[46] Infants also take cues from the facial expressions of people other than their mothers. One study examined the influence of a stranger's facial expression on the responses of a 12-month-old infant to a remote-controlled beeping robot that emerged from a concealed spot under a table and moved toward him or her, stopping just out of reach. What infants tended to do was to look toward a woman seated nearby. If she was smiling, the infant was much more apt to approach and touch the robot and even to smile and kiss it than if she looked afraid. Indeed, when she looked afraid, infants tended to cry and to approach their mothers across the room.[47] The ability to read facial expressions of emotion is clearly present at a very early age, if not from birth.

Although emotional expressions are readily identified, facial cues to deception are more elusive despite the fact that detecting deception often requires reading subtle emotional expressions. In particular, it may require picking up "leakage" of hidden emotions that are being masked or detecting the "falsity" of emotions that are being expressed. Indeed, truth tellers show more "enjoyment smiles," whereas liars show more "masking smiles." The difference between these two types of smiles is illustrated in Figure 2.8. Both the mouth and the eyes are involved in a genuine "enjoyment smile," which lasts less than 5 seconds. The zygomatic major muscle around the mouth pulls the lip corners upward, and the obicularis oculi muscles around the eyes raise the cheek and crinkle the skin around the eye, creating crow's-feet. The false "masking smile" does not involve the eyes. Rather, it combines the smiling action around the mouth, which is part of the enjoyment smile, with traces of the muscle movements from a negative emotion. Such a feigned smile may also last longer than a genuine one does; it may stop more abruptly; and it may be crooked: stronger on one side of the face than the other.[48]

Although the face does provide clues to deception for the canny observer, the fact is that liars are good at falsifying their facial expressions. The notion that the dishonest person shows "shifty eyes" and a lot of nervous smiling is wrong. In fact, liars often show more eye contact and less smiling than truth tellers.[49] Consequently, when untrained people are asked to judge whether individuals shown on videotape are lying or telling the truth, they do not do much better than chance. The same is true for a variety of trained professionals, such as customs officials, judges, and psychiatrists.[50] Because the face is so easily controlled, lie detection is often more accurate when people rely on "leakier" channels of communication: the voice and the body.[51] It seems that Ovid was overly pessimistic when he lamented, "Alas, how hard it is not to betray a guilty conscience

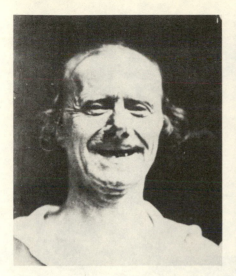

FIGURE 2.8 *Spontaneous smile (left) and fake smile (right). G. B. Duchenne (1990). The mechanism of human facial expression (Plates 31, 32, pp. 157–158). Translated by R. A. Cuthbertson. New York: Cambridge University Press. © Cambridge University Press, 1990. Reprinted with permission of Cambridge University Press.*

in the face!"[52] It is our voice or body that more often betrays us, and an obvious facial cue to deception like Pinocchio's nose is not to be found.

Facial Cues to Fitness

The face provides a wide variety of cues to intellectual, psychological, and physical fitness, a few examples of which are provided in the following sections. Although these examples show that the specific cues to fitness are diverse, there are also some commonalities that may underlie one of the overgeneralization effects proposed in Chapter 3 to account for the tendency to read psychological traits in faces. In particular, facial asymmetry and a facial structure that deviates markedly from the population average signify a lack of fitness in the intellectual, psychological, and physical realms.

Intellectual Fitness

Although variations in intelligence within the normal range cannot usually be detected, some forms of mental retardation are accompanied by a distinctive facial appearance. People with Down syndrome, caused by an

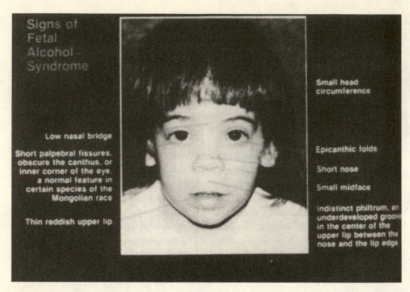

FIGURE 2.9 *The fetal alcohol syndrome. S. K. Clarren & D. W. Smith (1978).* New England Journal of Medicine, 298, *1063–1067. [Copyright] 1978, Massachusetts Medical Society. Reprinted by permission of* The New England Journal of Medicine.

extra chromosome, are readily recognized by their distinctive appearance: round heads with sparse, fine hair; almond-shaped, slanting eyes with thick eyelids; a flat nose; a small mouth with fissured lips; and a short neck. Cretinism, resulting from deficient thyroid secretion, is marked by a large head with abundant black, wiry hair; thick, dry skin; a broad, flat nose; and large flabby ears. The failure of the cranium to attain normal size owing to impaired brain development produces microcephaly, or "small-headedness." The heads of the mentally retarded individuals with this anomaly not only are small but also are cone-shaped with a receding chin and forehead. Hydrocephaly is another cause of mental retardation that is revealed in the face. The accumulation of cerebrospinal fluid in the cranium causes brain damage and enlargement of the cranium. Although the face remains relatively normal, the protruding skull is unmistakable.

Numerous other genetic and congenital anomalies that affect intellectual functioning also have facial markers. Among these is fetal alcohol syndrome (FAS), suffered by children born to alcoholic mothers. As shown in Figure 2.9, FAS is characterized by a pattern of facial malformations, including a small head circumference; a flattened midface, which is also elongated, making the nose appear short; a sunken nasal bridge; horizontally narrow eyes; epicanthic folds in the eyelids, resembling those in normal individuals of the Mongolian race; a thin, reddish upper lip; a smoothed and elongated groove between the nose and upper lip; and a small jaw.[53] Although these facial abnormalities are relatively minor, expert physicians are able to identify FAS children by their looks alone.[54] These looks signify mild mental retardation, even when FAS children are raised in stable, adoptive homes rather than by their alcoholic mothers.[55]

The more minor intellectual impairments suffered by the learning disabled may also have visible manifestations, although this is not universally true. In particular, learning-disabled persons may manifest a number of aberrations in facial structure that are called "minor physical anomalies." These anomalies, which are not typically noticed by untrained observers, include widely spaced eyes, atypical head circumference, multiple hair whorls, and ears that are asymmetrical, soft and pliable, malformed, and low-seated or that have attached lobes.[56]

The facial characteristics that mark severe intellectual retardation, such as Down syndrome, as well those that mark minor intellectual impairments, such as minor physical anomalies, yield an appearance that not only deviates significantly from the population average but also is characterized by asymmetry.[57]

Psychological Fitness

During the trial of Jeffrey Dahmer, murderer and cannibalistic sex offender, residents of Milwaukee lined up at 2 a.m. to secure one of the 34 courtroom seats reserved for the general public. Their loss of sleep was not in the service of hearing the gory details of Dahmer's crimes, which were amply provided on TV and radio. Rather, these people wanted to see the face of the man who could commit such atrocities. There is a long history to the view that emotional fitness is manifested in appearance. In classical Greek medical theories of the four humors (blood, yellow bile, phlegm, and black bile), melancholics were held to suffer from an excess of black bile, and they were described as bloated and swarthy. Other pathologies attributed to a predominance of black bile were hypochondriasis, epilepsy, and hysteria, and each was associated with specific physical signs.

Although the theory of the four humors did not endure, the assumed connection between psychopathology and appearance has persisted, and outward manifestations of insanity can be seen in art throughout the centuries, as shown in Figures 2.10 through 2.12. Images of insanity were as much a part of the medicine of the day as of the art. A nineteenth-century psychiatry textbook stated that "every psychopathic state, like the physiologic states of emotion, has its own peculiar facial expression and gen-

FIGURE 2.10 *Girolamo di Benvenuto*, St. Catherine of Siena Exorcising a Possessed Woman *(fifteenth century). Denver Art Museum, Samuel H. Kress Foundation collection.*

FIGURE 2.11 Bedlam, *from* A Rake's Progress *by William Hogarth. (eighteenth century) National Library of Medicine.*

FIGURE 2.12   *Louis Leopold Boilly,* Reunion of Thirty-five Diverse Heads, *a colored lithograph from the first half of the nineteenth century. Clements Fry Print Collection, Yale University, Harvey Cushing/John Hay Whitney Medical Library.*

eral manner of movement which, for the experienced, on superficial observation, makes a probable diagnosis possible."[58] Early medical texts used artists' renditions of various pathologies. In the mid 1850s, the superintendent of the women's department of a British lunatic asylum argued that textbook illustrations be replaced with photographs; later, in the nineteenth century, William Noyes endeavored to separate the appearance of specific pathologies from the appearance of specific individuals by making composite photographs through a series of multiple exposures of people with a particular pathology.

Photographs of the insane were scrutinized by Darwin in his seminal study of emotional expressions, and he came to view insanity as characterized by the loss of the ability to control the expression of emotion. Photographs were also used by Charcot, an influential French psychiatrist of the late 1800s, who founded a photographic journal devoted to the documentation of his findings concerning the visual appearance of the hysterical patient. Even in the twentieth century, psychiatrists continued the tradition of identifying differences in facial structure between patients with different mental illnesses. Kretschmer conducted an extensive study of

the facial and bodily proportions of mental patients depicted in photographs and concluded that those suffering from schizophrenia were
characterized by an egg-shaped face, a sharp and angular profile, and a
long and narrow nose, recalling the DC facial type described earlier.
Those suffering from depression had a broader, shieldlike facial form,
with softer outlines, and a medium-sized nose with a straight or convex
bridge, recalling the BC facial type.[59]

In modern psychiatry, the facial appearance of the patient plays only a
minor role in diagnosis. Still, the "bible" of practicing psychiatrists, the
Diagnostic and Statistical Manual (DSM IV), gives it some attention. For
example, the criteria for diagnosing schizophrenia include the facial manifestations of "affective flattening" and "prominent grimacing."[60] Recent
research indicates that schizophrenia has additional visible signs that are
not mentioned in DSM IV. Compared with mentally healthy individuals,
schizophrenics show not only less facial expression in general but also
fewer genuine smiles. The false smiles that schizophrenics more often
show are more crooked than genuine ones.[61] Schizophrenics also are
more likely to show a number of the minor physical anomalies that were
earlier noted as correlates of learning disabilities, such as widely spaced
eyes and malformed ears.[62] These anomalies, together with the false
smiles of schizophrenics, make facial asymmetry a marker of this disorder. Facial asymmetry is also a marker of milder psychological disorders,
such as the hyperactive behavior shown by those with fetal alcohol syndrome.

Physical Fitness

When we tell someone he doesn't look well, we are using facial cues to
detect his state of health. Although we may practice such diagnosis without a clear awareness of what facial qualities we are responding to, some
medical experts have been quite specific concerning the meaning of certain facial signs. Hippocrates, considered the "father of Western medicine," described the drawn and pinched face of those about to die: a
"death mask" marked by a sharp nose, hollow eyes, shrunken temples,
cold and contracted ears with their lobes turned outward, and yellow or
dark coloring with hard and tense skin. The traditional medicine of
China, Japan, and other Far Eastern cultures also emphasizes the face,
with physiognomy serving as a principal diagnostic tool. For example, as
shown in Figure 2.13, the area around the eye is believed to reflect the
state of the kidneys. If the kidneys are overworked and cannot discharge
properly, liquid accumulates under the eyes causing bags to form.

Modern research has provided evidence for a kernel of truth to ancient
wisdom regarding the diagnostic potential of the face. As shown in some
of the following examples, the signs are as varied as possible health prob-

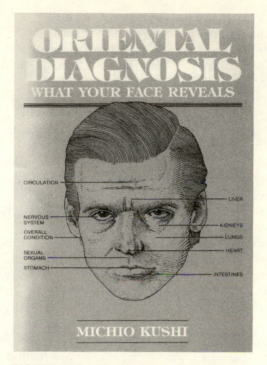

FIGURE 2.13   *The face in Oriental diagnosis.*
M. Kushi (1978). Introduction to Oriental diagnosis. *London: Sunwheel Publications. Cover
design by Peter Harris.*

lems. However, evolutionary theorists have argued that facial asymmetry
may be a marker of general susceptibility to disease, be it disease caused
by lack of resistance to infectious agents or disease caused by genetic sus-
ceptibilities. Whether this is true remains to be determined. Most of the
evidence bearing on asymmetry and physical fitness pertains either to
lower animals or to nonfacial, body asymmetries in humans, and one recent study examining the relationship between human facial asymmetry
and self-reports of infectious ailments found inconsistent effects.[63] However, other facial markers of susceptibility to disease have been found, although unlike asymmetry, each is tied to a specific vulnerability.

One recent example is an association between male pattern baldness
and heart disease, which was widely reported in the press. Other facial
cues may also aid the identification of individuals who are prone to coro-
nary artery disease. Such individuals, called Type A, are hard driving,
hostile, and competitive. They are the ones who honk their horns impa-
tiently in traffic jams or yell at the clerk who has misplaced their order.
Type B individuals, on the other hand, are more apt to "go with the flow."

These two types of people can be differentiated by their characteristic facial expressions. Type A people are more likely than Type B people to glare at an interviewer, lowering their brows, raising their upper eyelid, and tensing their lower eyes. They are also more likely to have a look of disgust on their face.[64]

In keeping with the thesis that suppressed emotion may be a contributing factor to poor health, the *lack* of facial expressivity can also be diagnostic of impending illness. The less facial expressivity people show while recounting events that elicited strong sadness, fear, or anger, the more somatic symptoms they report on an inventory that is a good predictor of future health status. In particular, people who show low facial expressivity when they are angry show symptoms diagnostic of future arthritis, and those who show low facial expressivity when they are sad show symptoms indicative of skin problems.[65]

Facial structure as well as expressivity may signal vulnerability to particular diseases. The symptoms of upper midriff pain, belching, and constipation are more likely to signal an ulcer in a patient who has a small head, a narrow face, a narrow nose, and a long jaw (recalling the DC facial type), and they are more likely to signal a diseased gall bladder in a patient who has a large head, a broad face, a medium-width nose, and a medium-length jaw (recalling the BC facial type). Just as those susceptible to ulcer and gall bladder problems seem to have a distinctive appearance, so do those susceptible to the polio virus. Polio patients are more likely than unaffected individuals to have large central incisor teeth; long, curved eyelashes; irregular pigmentation, dubbed "black spots," and signs of facial immaturity such as epicanthal eye folds, a flat nose bridge, and wide-set eyes.[66] Why facial features such as these should co-occur with greater susceptibility to a virus remains an open question.

In addition to facial cues that mark susceptibility to one or more physical ailments, facial signs may also signal a current illness. At the extreme is the facial appearance that Hippocrates attributed to those about to die. Minor health problems are also shown in the face. Pale lips can indicate anemia. Flushed cheeks may indicate a fever. Extreme pallor accompanies low blood pressure. In yellow fever and jaundice, the face has a yellow cast. Hyperthyroidism, or goiter, is marked by bulging eyes. Bloodshot eyes and a runny nose suggest a cold, allergies, or even drug use. A florid red nose also suggests a cold, or it may suggest alcoholism. Although observers may correctly discern some illnesses from facial qualities such as these, they may be mistaken about the particular illness inasmuch as one facial quality can signal various disorders. A man suffering from rosacea, a disfiguring skin disease, reported the following: "When I had a flareup, I avoided people. My nose would be cherry red. Coworkers would ask,

'Do you have a drinking problem?'"[67] Errors such as these may play a role in one of the overgeneralization effects discussed in Chapter 3.

Despite the possibility of error, there is evidence that laypersons can accurately detect people's physical health from their facial appearance. When college students were shown black and white portrait photos of 18-year-old men and women and asked to rate their health on a scale that ranged from poor to excellent, their judgments showed significant agreement with an index of the health of those individuals derived from their medical records.[68] Although this accuracy in detecting health was only a small effect, one would expect accuracy to be considerably greater when judges are provided with more realistic facial information that includes color and movement or when they are judging the health of older individuals, who show more variation in physical fitness.

Summary

A person's face can reveal age, sex, race, identity, emotion, and fitness. Although learning can play a role in our ability to extract this adaptively significant information from faces, developmental, cross-cultural, and neurological research indicates that there also is a specific neural component to this ability. The strength, universality, and adaptive value of the tendency to read these qualities in the face can provide a basis for the propensity to read psychological traits there as well. In particular, trait impressions can derive from a tendency for our reactions to facial markers of adaptively significant attributes, like age, to be overgeneralized to faces that show some resemblance to these markers. Such overgeneralization effects are considered in the next chapter.

3

The Bases of Reading Faces

There's no art
To find the mind's construction in the face.

—Shakespeare, *Macbeth*

This quotation from Shakespeare suggests that anyone can read psychological characteristics in faces and that such face reading is accurate. In the present chapter, I consider whether Shakespeare was right about the accuracy of face reading. I also consider what "constructions of the mind" people's facial qualities reveal as evidenced by links between particular facial qualities and particular psychological traits. Finally, I consider bases for face reading other than accuracy: the overgeneralization of reactions to facial qualities that convey the adaptively significant attributes that were discussed in Chapter 2.

What You See Is What You Get

It is possible that we read psychological traits in faces for the same reason that we read sex or age or emotions. Just as a frown reveals anger, which it is socially adaptive to detect, so does a particular facial structure reveal an aggressive personality or other traits. This view, implicit in Shakespeare's quotation, was espoused by physiognomists of the eighteenth and nineteenth centuries. Lavater, for example, said the following:

Does not reason tell us that . . . an exact relationship exists between the soul and the body, between the internal and the external of man, that the infinite variety of the souls or the internal nature of man creates an infinite variety in his body or externality . . . If such differences exist then they must be recognizable; they must also be the basis for an exact science.[1]

In considering what psychological traits we see in various facial qualities, Lavater and other physiognomists generated many colorful hypotheses. Consider, for example, the following pronouncements on lips and eyes:

Well-defined, large, and proportionate lips . . . are never seen in a bad, mean, common, false, crouching, vicious countenance. A lipless mouth, resembling a single line, denotes coldness, industry, a lover of order, precision . . . .[2]

Blue eyes are, generally, more significant of weakness, effeminacy, and yielding, than brown and black.[3]

The view that the face provides an accurate reflection of personality is not restricted to eighteenth-century physiognomists. Placards advertising face reading are commonplace in the storefronts on California city streets, and face readers are more abundant than palm readers in the market-places of Hong Kong. There, for a small fee, we were told that my son's ears revealed an orderly nature and that his eyebrows and eyes revealed a gentle, nonthreatening disposition. Even scientific psychology gives credence to the assumption that facial qualities may reveal psychological ones. The functionalist view that "perceiving is for doing," coupled with the relative effectiveness of social behavior, suggests that there is considerable accuracy in impressions of people that are based on their appearance.[4] Although a belief in the accuracy of face reading transcends time, culture, and profession, assessing the validity of that belief is not an easy task.

Assessing the Accuracy of Face Reading

A significant obstacle to determining whether facial qualities accurately specify traits is presented by the need to measure the facial qualities and traits of interest. The assessment of some facial qualities can be complicated. For example, a particular face may contain a mixture of the dolichocephalic and brachycephalic features described in Chapter 2, which makes it difficult to categorize. Measuring other facial qualities, like eye color, is more straightforward, but there is still the problem of how to measure the predicted traits.

To test Lavater's physiognomic principle that people with blue eyes are weaker and more yielding than those with brown eyes, we must have some objective measure of people's weakness and yielding. Physical weakness could be measured by objective tests, although even this is not a simple task. There are many ways to measure physical strength, and they may not all converge. For example, people who show the highest physical stamina (as in long-distance running) may not show the greatest physical force (as in bench pressing). If blue-eyed people show less force but more stamina than brown-eyed ones, what shall we conclude regarding Lavater's principle?

Things get even more complicated when one tries to assess psychological qualities, like yielding. One could consider judgments made by acquaintances of blue-eyed and brown-eyed people. But if blue-eyed people are judged to be more yielding, as Lavater predicted, it could be that these acquaintances are vulnerable to the same stereotypical misconceptions as Lavater. Alternatively, one could ask brown- and blue-eyed people how yielding they are. But this self-report criterion is problematic: People may not realize how yielding they are; people may be unwilling to acknowledge a negative trait; and self-descriptions may also be vulnerable to stereotypes. Another possibility is to administer personality tests to blue- and brown-eyed people. Unfortunately, personality tests can also be flawed. Even clinicians, who have been trained to make judgments about people's personalities, can disagree with one another or be vulnerable to perceiving erroneously the traits they expect. For example, in one study, clinicians perceived a person they were interviewing to be more maladjusted when they were told he was an ex-mental patient than when they were told he was a job interviewee.[5] A final criterion for assessing the accuracy of trait impressions is behavioral observations. A shortcoming of this method is that such observations are laborious to collect and may capture only a small segment of the trait in question. Given the weaknesses inherent in any one measure of psychological traits, it is important to use a variety of measures when testing hypotheses concerning links between appearance and personality. The message to be taken from the foregoing considerations is that testing hypotheses about the links between facial appearance and personality traits is a difficult enterprise and that the results are subject to various interpretations. With these caveats in mind, I now consider some of the existing research evidence on this subject.

Accuracy Evidence

There is considerable research bearing on the general question of whether people can accurately judge others' traits from their appearance. Although these investigations rarely tell us what appearance qualities people use to make their judgments, they have provided some evidence of accuracy. Much of this evidence is based on the finding of consensual agreement in trait judgments. For example, several researchers have asked college students to rate one another as well as themselves after spending a short time together in small groups with no opportunity to talk. In other studies, strangers' ratings of people have been based only on facial photographs or brief videotapes. These studies have revealed that strangers agree with one another in some of their trait judgments, an effect that has been dubbed "consensus at zero acquaintance." For example, the person who is rated as very sociable by one stranger is also rated as highly sociable by the other strangers, and the person who is rated as reclusive by one stranger is similarly rated by others. There is a danger in using the consensus data alone as an indicator of accuracy in judging personality from appearance since, as suggested earlier, consensual judgments could reflect shared appearance stereotypes rather than revealing perceivers' accurate perceptions of people's traits. Additional evidence for the accuracy of these consensual judgments is needed, and it has been provided by their agreement with people's self-ratings, ratings by acquaintances, personality test scores, and behavioral observations.

In considering what trait judgments are likely to show the highest consensus, researchers have taken two approaches. Some have examined personality traits known as the Big Five: extraversion, conscientiousness, agreeableness, emotional stability, and culture. These traits are of interest because they appear to capture both the organization of people's perceptions of others and the organization of self-perceptions. This suggests that people not only are perceived to differ along these dimensions but also do differ in these ways, and the Big Five have therefore have been viewed by many theorists as *the* fundamental traits. Other researchers have taken a functional approach in selecting trait perceptions to study, arguing that people should be most attuned to traits whose correct or incorrect identification had implications for survival and reproduction in our evolutionary past. Such traits include social dominance, sexual availability, intelligence, and honesty.

Judgments of the Big Five trait of extraversion show considerable accuracy. Not only is there moderate consensus in judging extraversion—how talkative, open, adventurous, and sociable a person is—but also there is corroboration of these judgments from several sources.[6] People who are consensually perceived as more extraverted at zero acquaintance show a moderate-to-strong tendency to exhibit more extraverted behaviors, such as a lot of talking, smiling, gesturing, and enthusiasm. They also show a moderate tendency to be judged by their friends and by themselves as more extraverted. Moreover, self-ratings of extraversion and friendliness appear to be an accurate reflection of extraverted behavior, yielding moderate-to-strong prediction of the frequency of initiating acts in a free-ranging conversation, the number of questions asked, smiling, laughing, and joking.

Judgments of the Big Five trait of conscientiousness—how tidy, responsible, scrupulous, and persevering a person is—also elicit significant agreement, but the consensus is small. Judgments of a stranger's conscientiousness also show small-to-medium agreement with the person's self-ratings. Agreement is even more elusive in judging the trait of agreeableness—how good-natured, nonjealous, and cooperative a person is—although weak agreement has been found when clear facial cues are provided.[7] Emotional stability (how nervous, excitable, and hypochondriacal a person is) and culture (how artistically sensitive, polished, and intellectual a person is) elicit no significant consensus in strangers' judgments and no consistent agreement between self-ratings and strangers' ratings.[8]

Judgments of dominance, like those of extraversion, show considerable accuracy, perhaps because these two traits are closely related.[9] Consistent with the functionalist position, which argues for the evolutionary adaptive value of identifying dominance, consensus in children's judgments of who is "tougher" than whom develops earlier and shows greater strength than does consensus in judgments of other attributes, such as smartness or niceness. Judgments of who is tougher than whom also show greater accuracy than other trait judgments, a strong effect assessed by agreement of toughness judgments with the self-evaluations of those being judged.[10] Of course, the children's judgments were not made at zero acquaintance, and behavioral as well as appearance information was available to them. However, other research has shown considerable accuracy in adults' judgments of the dominance of strangers. We know a leader when we see one.

People show a moderate consensus when rating the dominance of unknown individuals depicted in photographs, and these ratings have been validated by evidence from several sources, including personality and behavioral measures and self-ratings.[11] People also can accurately identify strangers who score high on a test of Machiavellianism, a personality type that encompasses traits such as dominance, persuasiveness, and boldness. Correct identification of Machiavellian men was accomplished either on the basis of photographs, which yielded 57 percent correct identifications (slightly more than the chance level of 50 percent correct), or on the basis of brief, silent videotape clips, which yielded 66 percent correct identifications.[12] Accuracy in judging dominance is also shown in people's ratings of the leadership status of students depicted in high school yearbook photos. There was a strong tendency for people to identify correctly those who held positions of responsibility in student government, clubs, and sports teams.[13] People not only are accurate in their identification of strangers who have dominant personality traits and social roles, but also they can accurately predict dominant behavior. "First-glance" ratings of a person's dominance following a brief encounter moderately predicted dominant behavior in a problem-solving situation as shown in the relative amount of talking by that person.[14] Also, ratings of a brief videoclip of a stranger's behavior can predict the social consequences of that behavior, such as a teacher's effectiveness or a newscaster's influence on viewers' voting behavior.[15] Finally, ratings of the dominance of strangers show a moderate correspondence with their self-ratings, which, in turn, strongly predict the frequency of dominant behaviors in a problem-solving situation, such as making suggestions, giving commands, providing information, and taking over the problem-solving task.[16]

Not only do we recognize leaders, but also we are able to recognize available sexual partners. Accuracy in judging sexual availability is shown by a moderate correspondence between strangers' ratings and self-ratings on traits such as "sexually permissive" and "sexually active." This stranger-self agreement has been found to be larger than for other traits, including emotional stability, extraversion, and dominance.[17] Although these findings indicate that perceivers can accurately judge sexual availability, additional research is needed before one concludes that this is in fact the easiest trait to identify. It is possible that the relatively high accuracy judges showed in the study cited derived from the fact that their judgments were based on a videotape on which they saw (but could not hear) targets talking with someone of the opposite sex about a possible lunch date. If targets had been debating some controversial issue, dominance cues might have been more salient, and social dominance may have been the trait most accurately perceived.

Intelligence is another trait for which accurate detection would seem to be functional, since it is useful to know whose advice to follow and whose to eschew. Although there is not much research on this trait, an early study found a moderate relationship between ratings of the intelligence of executives that were based on facial photos and the executives' IQ scores.[18] However, this relationship may be overestimated, since it was calculated for executives in the top and bottom of the IQ score distribution. Although a more recent study also found moderate accuracy in judging the intelligence of people whose IQs spanned a somewhat broader range, accuracy required that perceivers see a sound film rather than a silent film. Further research is needed to resolve the question of whether appearance alone can accurately communicate intelligence.[19]

It would certainly be useful to be able to identify honest individuals. On the other hand, it is also adaptive to be able to conceal one's dishonesty, and it is therefore difficult to predict from a functional perspective whether honesty can be accurately perceived. As I discussed in Chapter 2, people are poor at detecting deception when asked to judge whether a person is lying or telling the truth in a particular instance. However, there is a robust demeanor bias, whereby some people are consistently suspected of lying and others are perceived as telling the truth.[20] Moreover, the demeanor bias is sometimes accurate. Strangers' judgments of college students' dispositional dishonesty from facial photographs show a small-to-moderate tendency to predict honesty ratings of the same students by their acquaintances as well as a small tendency to predict a students' willingness to participate in a study that would require lying to peers.[21] Judgments of honesty from facial photos also has shown a strong positive relationship with a personality measure of honesty for men in their 30s and 50s, albeit only men who had looked honest since childhood. On the other hand, judgments of honesty were inaccurate for women who had been stable in real honesty since childhood: Those who looked more honest were actually more dishonest.[22] These discrepant results suggest that the accuracy of honesty perceptions may depend on particular life experiences of the individuals being judged as well the particular way in which honesty is assessed.

If accuracy in reading faces depends on the usefulness of the trait information to the perceiver, as suggested by a functional perspective, then experience reading particular cues and the motivation to read certain cues may enhance accuracy. Evidence for the effects of experience is provided in a study that found that Americans showed small but significant accuracy in detecting lies told by Americans, correctly identifying lying 55 percent of the time, whereas they did no better than chance accuracy of 50 percent in detecting lies told by Jordanians. Jordanians correctly identified lying by Jordanians 57 percent of the time but did no better than chance in detecting lies told by Americans.[23] Evidence for the effects of motivation is provided in a study that found that perceivers with a dependent personality were more likely than those with a dominant personality to notice how affiliative people are. This small effect is consistent with a dependent person's goal of eliciting approval and support in social interactions. Dominant perceivers, on the other hand, have shown a small tendency to notice more than others how assertive people are, information that is more pertinent to the interpersonal goals of dominant individuals.[24] The more general motivation to be accurate also increases accuracy: Feeling accountable for judgments about a target person increases perceivers' accuracy as does the expectation of checking their impressions against accurate information and having their own outcomes depend on an accurate reading of the target person.[25] These influences on accuracy are discussed further in Chapter 9.

Physiognomic and Expressive Cues

It is important to know what specific aspects of appearance enable judges to perceive a person's traits accurately. Much of the work establishing the accuracy of trait impressions at zero acquaintance has provided access to cues in addition to those available in the face; judges often have viewed the whole body of the person being "read," either live or on videotape. Although static photographs also have yielded strong consensual judgments, there is less evidence concerning whether these judgments are consistently accurate. As such, it is unclear to what extent accuracy at zero acquaintance derives from the reading of facial cues as opposed to bodily cues. Furthermore, to the extent that facial cues are implicated, it is unclear whether facial physiognomy or expressive facial movement is critical. Although evidence for the role of facial cues in generating accurate judgments is scarce, there is some. In particular, the facial qualities that communicate various traits have been investigated by examining static and expressive features that are correlated both with actual traits, as revealed in self-reports, and with strangers' trait judgments.[26] The results of these analyses are difficult to assimilate because there is no guiding theory to tie them together and there are often inconsistencies across studies. Still, they are worth considering for their possible contribution to identifying the principles that underlie the ability to read personality in the face.

Valid cues to extraversion include attractiveness, use of makeup, and stylish hair, as well as frequent head movements; a friendly, self-assured expression; and extensive smiling. These qualities are associated both with how extraverted a person is according to self-reports and with how extraverted he or she is perceived to be. The average correlation with ratings by self and others was moderate for all cues. There is also evidence that agreeableness may be accurately communicated by some facial features, although other cues mislead judges, often yielding inaccurate judgments overall. Valid cues to agreeableness can include an attractive, refined appearance; soft facial lineaments; a babyface; and a friendly expression. Valid cues to conscientiousness may include an attractive, refined appearance and short hair. An attractive, refined appearance may also provide valid cues to emotional stability, as does a friendly expression. None of the facial qualities measured to date have been found to communicate accurately the remaining Big Five trait of culture. However, a self-assured facial expression may accurately communicate intelligence, and attractiveness may accurately communicate sexual availability.

Whereas the studies that yielded the foregoing results sampled an array of physiognomic cues with no particular theoretical rationale, other research on appearance-trait relations has been related to specific hypotheses found in folklore and physiognomic treatises as well as to more recent theoretical hypotheses. Although this research addresses the question of whether particular facial cues are accurate indicators of psychological traits, it does not always address the question of whether people use these cues when making trait judgments.

Is there any accuracy to the popular stereotype that the bespectacled are brainy? The answer is *yes* and *no*. Myopic (nearsighted) children do score higher on tests of intelligence. However, the difference between the IQ scores of these children and those with normal vision amounts to only a small-to-medium effect that would probably not be detected by perceivers who didn't have access to the test results. Moreover, visual defects other than myopia are either unrelated to intelligence or associated with lower intelligence. It appears, therefore, that there is no general validity to the stereotype of the bespectacled "brain."[27] The highbrow stereotype also appears to be without foundation. Indeed, it may be the lowbrows who are smarter. Contrary to the popular notion that a large forehead signifies intelligence, "highbrow" first-year engineering students tended to receive slightly lower grades than the "lowbrows."[28] Similarly, convicts with higher foreheads had lower intelligence, although they were seen as smarter by raters who had assigned each to an occupational task.[29]

Do blonds have more fun? Are they dumb? Early studies of trait differences between blonds and brunettes found negligible differences despite popular stereotypes.[30] Are the wide-eyed innocent and the "crooked" dishonest, as well-known aphorisms suggest? Larger eyes and a more symmetrical face do in fact have a small-to-moderate positive effect on judgments of honesty. However, these facial qualities are not related to people's actual honesty as assessed by personality measures. Indeed, the relations that have been found run counter to popular wisdom. Boys with big eyes and girls with symmetrical faces are less honest than their more beady-eyed or crooked-faced peers, findings that are consistent with the hypothesis that people with honest-looking faces lie more because they can get away with it.[31]

Although thin-lipped people were described as industrious by the eighteenth-century physiognomist Lavater, and they also tend to be perceived as conscientious by twentieth-century college students, personality measures do not corroborate this impression.[32] On the other hand, a larger body of research provides some support for Lavater's claim that blue-eyed people are weaker and more yielding than the brown-eyed. Young children with blue eyes are overrepresented among children whom we call shy: Over 60 percent of shy children were blue-eyed in one study, whereas only 40 percent of all children in that population had blue eyes. These shy children showed a more inhibited temperament than those with brown eyes. They were more likely to be fearful in new situations, to hesitate in their approach to objects, to remain quiet with new people, and to stay close to their mother. Those who were brown-eyed, on the other hand, were more likely to approach objects without hesitation, to talk spontaneously to unfamiliar persons, and to spend little time in proximity to their mother.[33]

Elementary school teachers also detect differences in the temperament of blue- and brown-eyed children. When 133 teachers in grades K through

3 were asked to nominate the one Caucasian child in their class who was the most timid, shy, and inhibited, 60 percent of the children selected were blue-eyed, significantly more than the 50 percent expected by chance in that population. Brown-eyed children were overrepresented in these teachers' selections of the one Caucasian child who was the most sociable, outgoing, and uninhibited. Although the evidence for differences between blue- and brown-eyed adults is mixed, there is also some indication of more behavioral inhibition in the blue-eyed.[34] The correlation between eye color and personality suggests that the accuracy in judging extraversion that was discussed earlier could be enhanced by showing color videotapes or photographs of those being judged, provided, of course, that perceivers use the valid cue of eye color when judging strangers' extraversion.

Facial shape may also predict temperament, as Chinese theories of yin and yang faces would suggest. People with yang faces, which correspond in most respects to the brachycephalic facial type that was described in Chapter 2, are said to be more strong, active, and extraverted than people with yin faces, which correspond to the dolichocephalic facial type.[35] Consistent with this assertion, young children with more yin-like, narrow upper faces showed a greater predisposition to develop an inhibited temperament than those with yang-like, broader faces, an effect attributed to biochemical influences on upper jaw growth and emotional reactivity during embryonic development.[36] Unfortunately, researchers examining the physiognomic cues that yield accurate judgments of extraversion have not considered this particular facial cue.

Other research findings bearing on yin versus yang faces do not provide a very coherent picture, in part because different investigators have taken different facial measures. One study compared the personality traits of adults with long, yin-like faces and short yang-like faces. Long-faced people showed a moderate-to-large tendency to be more naive, cheerful, active, impulsive, and independent than those with short, yang-like faces, who were more likely to be shrewd, moody, passive, self-disciplined, and dependent.[37] These results do not jive with the predictions of Chinese physiognomists. Neither do investigations of the relationship between profile convexity and personality. As shown in Figure 2.3, a convex profile is like the yin face and the dolichocephalic head, whereas a concave profile is like the yang face and the brachycephalic head. Researchers in one study precisely measured the degree of profile convexity of each of 25 members of a university sorority and correlated these measurements with trait ratings made by each woman's sorority sisters. There was a small-to-moderate tendency for more convex, yin-like profiles to be associated with greater activity, ambition, and dominance, which is opposite to the predictions of Chinese physiognomists.[38] A final verdict on the validity of these predictions must await research that assesses the entire configuration of features that compose a yin or a yang face: width and length and profile convexity.

In addition to research investigating links between psychological traits and individual facial qualities, such as face width or lip thickness, there also has been research on links between traits and configural facial qualities. Two such qualities are attractiveness and babyfaceness, whose links to personality are discussed in detail in Chapter 8. A third configural quality of interest is minor physical anomalies, which include widely spaced eyes, atypical head circumference, multiple hair whorls, and ears that are asymmetrical, soft and pliable, malformed, or low-seated or that have attached lobes. I discussed in Chapter 2 the fact that these anomalies are associated with various mental disorders. It has been found that they also predict temperament in normal individuals, particularly males. Male college students with more minor physical anomalies show a small-to-moderate tendency to be more active, aggressive, and clumsy, and young boys show a similar pattern of behavior. Those with more minor physical anomalies also show moderately more Type A behavior, a syndrome marked by hard-driving, hostile, and competitive behavior.[39] Although minor physical anomalies provide accurate physiognomic cues to personality traits, it is not known whether perceivers use these cues.

There are expressive indicators of psychological traits in a person's appearance in addition to structural ones. As noted previously, various expressive behaviors communicate extraversion. Also, as discussed in Chapter 2, there is a strong tendency for Type A people to glare more at an interviewer, lowering their brows, raising their upper eyelid, and tensing their lower eyes. They are also more likely to have a look of disgust on their face, another strong effect.[40] In short, they look hostile, and they are hostile. There is also some cross-cultural evidence for judging traits from expressive indicators, although researchers have not investigated the accuracy of these judgments. In particular, nonsmiling mouths in individuals from a variety of ethnic backgrounds weakly communicate dominance to judges from a variety of cultural groups. Lowered brows also communicate dominance, an effect that is moderate for judges from Western cultures but weak or absent for less westernized judges.[41] An understanding of the causes of these cultural differences, as well as an assessment of the accuracy of cross-cultural judgments, awaits further research.

Although the available evidence indicates that one reason we may read psychological traits in faces is that they provide accurate information, the research evidence concerning physiognomic and expressive cues to psychological traits is rather muddled and leaves much to learn regarding the facial qualities that enable strangers to identify people's traits accurately. What is sorely lacking in the available research is a theoretical basis for predicting what qualities of appearance communicate what traits. Certainly, the physiognomists did not provide such a theory; they provided only a lot of assertions that have no logical coherence. A coherent theory must address two questions: (a) why various traits are manifested in facial appearance, with predictions regarding particular face-trait associations following from this explanation, and (b) how people discern these relations.

A Model of Appearance-Trait Relations

The question of why traits are manifested in the face is addressed in Figure 3.1, which illustrates four possible causal routes to actual appearance-trait relations.[42] First, as shown in Path A, appearance and psychological traits may be related because both are influenced by the same biological factors. For example, just as genes cause eye color and hair color to go together, so may they cause a relationship between eye color and temperament. Indeed, the gene that produces albinism in mice also causes the animals to have difficulty learning to escape from a noxious stimulus.[43] The genes that produce blue versus brown eyes in humans may also cause differences in behavior, an effect that may be due to the fact that the hormone that influences eye color (alpha-melanocyte-stimulating hormone) also affects arousal level and emotional reactivity.[44] The biological anomalies that produce the intellectual impairments associated with Down syndrome, cretinism, and fetal alcohol syndrome also produce distinctive facial markers. Another example of a biological influence on appearance and psychological traits is the recently discovered Bloom's syndrome. This syndrome is caused by a rare mutant gene that produces both a distinctive facial appearance (large, sun-sensitive red markings on the face and a small narrow head) as well as distinctive personality traits (a charming, pleasant personality; inordinate optimism; and a failure to mature from childlike judgment and gullibility).[45] With Path A as the route to accuracy, the task becomes to discover biological factors that influence both facial appearance and psychological traits. Researchers can then determine whether perceivers are sensitive to these true relations between appearance and traits.

A second possible link between appearance and psychological traits is that both may be influenced by the same environmental factors, as shown in Path B. The person who has a thin, bony face owing to poor nutrition may also have psychological traits that derive from food deprivation. Like the physical environment, the social environment may have an effect on both appearance and traits. As suggested by the cartoon shown in Figure 3.2, a person's physical and psychological qualities both may be

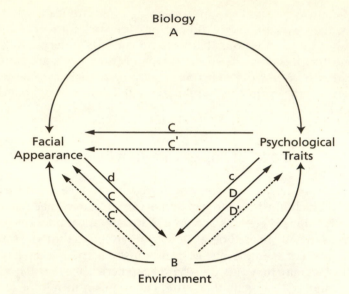

FIGURE 3.1   *A model of appearance-trait relations. Biology can*
influence both appearance and traits (Path A) as can environment
(Path B). Traits can produce a congruent appearance (Path C, Do-
rian Gray effect) or an incongruent appearance (Path C', artifice
effect). Appearance can produce congruent traits (Path D, self-ful-
filling prophecy effect) or incongruent traits (Path D', self-defeat-
ing prophecy effect).

influenced by the people with whom they routinely interact. Indeed, sci-
entists have suggested that kin resemblance may not simply be a matter
of common genes; it may also be a matter of prolonged social contact,
with the tendency for husbands and wives to become more similar in facial appearance over time, reflecting repeated empathic mimicry of each
other's facial expressions. Similarity in spouses' traits may also reflect
common social factors.[46] Another example of the influence of the social
environment on appearance and psychological traits is provided by the
tendency for people to groom themselves in distinctive ways and to develop distinctive behavior patterns that differ. If Path B is the route to accurate trait perceptions, the task becomes to discover environmental factors that influence both facial appearance and psychological traits and to
determine whether perceivers are sensitive to these true relations.

A third possible link between appearance and psychological traits is
that differences in personality cause differences in facial appearance. Although we tend to think of facial structure as fixed, this is not so. For example, people with an irritable temperament may tense certain facial

FIGURE 3.2   *On the Fastrack.* © 11/11/94. *Reprinted with special permission of King Features Syndicate.*

muscles in a way that yields different jaw development from that in people who are more easygoing. Similarly, over the years a person's temperament may become etched in the pattern of wrinkles on the face. In the words of George Orwell, "at 50, everyone has the face he deserves."[47] Indeed, elderly people whose facial appearance resembles a particular emotional expression have been found to have a related personality disposition.[48] Those whose neutral faces look angry have a more hostile disposition; that is, they are frequently angry. Those whose neutral faces look sad have more depressive tendencies, and those whose neutral faces look guilty tend to feel guilty a lot. The tendency for personality to produce a congruent facial appearance is represented by the solid Paths C in Figure 3.1. This is called the "Dorian Gray" effect after the novel by Oscar Wilde in which the portrait of the protagonist changed over time, registering an increasingly menacing visage with his increasingly dastardly deeds. The Dorian Gray effect can be a direct effect of personality on appearance or it can be mediated through the environment, as shown by Path C in Figure 3.1. For example, individuals with a hostile temperament may be more likely to choose activities that have a deleterious effect on their appearance, such as boxing or alcohol abuse, and those who are highly sociable may choose grooming aids that have a beneficial effect on their appearance.[49]

Another possible effect of personality on appearance is an artifice effect, whereby personality produces an *incongruent* facial appearance. This effect is shown by the broken Paths C' in Figure 3.1. It can be direct, as when a liar smiles and looks people in the eye, or it can be mediated by the environment, as when a con artist uses grooming aids, clothing, or even cosmetic surgery to portray the image of an upstanding individual, the wolf in sheep's clothing. Evidence that individuals can indeed manipulate their facial appearance to convey certain psychological qualities is provided by the finding that people are seen as more powerful when they are attempting to look dominant than when they are attempting to look submissive even when they have an emotionally neutral facial expression in both cases.[50] It should be noted that such projection of psychological qualities requires the existence of strong physical-psychological associations that can be exploited. To the extent that such artifice effects occur, the information provided by facial qualities yields inaccurate social perceptions. If Path C is the route to accurate trait perceptions, the task becomes to discover personality traits that influence facial qualities, what the direction of the influence is, and whether perceivers are sensitive to the resultant relations between appearance and personality.

A final causal path is one in which different facial qualities cause people to experience different environments, as shown in Path D, and these divergent environments in turn cause differences in the traits of those who look one way versus another. There are two ways in which appearance may exert a causal influence on the environment. First, a person's appearance may lead her actively to *select* a particular type of environment. For example, an extremely fair-skinned person may avoid activities in the sun. Second, the extremely fair-skinned person may *evoke* a certain kind of environment; she may be viewed and treated by others as if she were sickly and fragile.[51] Such environmental effects of appearance may produce one of two effects on behavior. They may produce a self-fulfilling prophecy effect in which the fair-skinned person becomes less active than someone who spends a lot of time outdoors or someone who is treated by others as if she were robust. This effect is illustrated by the solid Path D in Figure 3.1. Alternatively, these experiences may produce a self-defeating prophecy effect in which the fair-skinned person compensates for the deprivation of outdoor activities or for others' negative expectations by becoming even more robust than someone who does not experience these environmental consequences of appearance. This possibility is illustrated by the broken Path D' in Figure 3.1. Like artifice effects, self-defeating prophecy effects yield inaccurate judgments of traits from facial appearance. If Path D is the route to accurate trait perceptions, the task becomes to discover appearance qualities that influence the social environment and to learn how the environment in turn influences personality development. Chapter 8 provides a more extensive discussion of the possible effects of appearance on personality and vice versa, with attention to the conditions conducive to each of the various paths.

Origins of Appearance-Based Trait Expectations

We have seen that there are several plausible routes to true relationships between appearance and psychological traits that could account for the evidence of accurate impressions at zero acquaintance. However, a significant question that remains is how perceivers come to discern the true correlations that exist. Four possibilities are considered here: direct instruction; direct experiences; an innate preparedness for certain correlations; and overgeneralization effects that produce self-fulfilling prophecies.

Direct instruction regarding appearance-trait links is unlikely to be provided by socializing agents, such as parents or teachers, with the possible exception of links that are associated with stereotyped social groups, such as women, blacks, or old people. However, direct instruction regarding these groups may be biased rather than accurate. Instruction of doubtful accuracy may also occur through exposure to aphorisms such as "blonds have more fun," "redheads are hot-tempered," or "fat people are jolly." All in all, direct instruction seems an unlikely source of accurate trait perceptions. A more likely source is direct experience with people in whom certain facial qualities are associated with certain observed behaviors. If people who vary in appearance also vary in their behavior, perceivers may learn these associations. Exposure to associations between appearance and behavior may occur if there is a correlation owing to biological or environmental influences on both; if people with particular traits have developed distinctive facial qualities by virtue of expressive mannerisms or intentional efforts to modify these qualities; or if people with particular facial qualities have developed particular traits by virtue of self-fulfilling or self-defeating prophecy effects. The media may also provide exposure to associations between appearance and traits, although the accuracy of these correlations is unknown. For example, the media regularly pair attractive faces with behaviors that are different from those paired with unattractive ones. Heroes and heroines are rarely ugly. Villains are rarely attractive. More subtle pairings may also be prevalent in the media or in real life, and people are very sensitive to correspondences between facial features and personality traits.

After being exposed to photos of a few short-faced professors who were known to be fair and a few long-faced professors who were unfair, college students subsequently judged an unknown short-faced professor to be more fair than an unknown long-faced one. They showed this strong effect even though they were not consciously aware of the correspondence between facial length and fairness among the professors to whom they initially were exposed. Indeed, when asked why they had made a particular fairness judgment, students typically mentioned facial expression or gaze. This experiment shows how readily we can acquire a tacit rule about the correspondence between a particular facial feature and a particular personality trait. Moreover, use of such rules can increase over time even when no confirmatory feedback is provided.[52]

The fact that perceivers do not seem to need much experience to learn correlations between appearance and traits suggests a third possible explanation for perceivers' ability to detect true correlations: There may be an evolutionary preparedness to extract certain correlations from the wealth of information available. Without such a selective mechanism, many false correlations would be detected, and learning through exposure would not yield accurate perceptions. A preparedness for certain correlations is equally important to discern accurately associations between appearance and traits that are too rare for perceivers to learn through direct exposure. For example, the correlation between the physical and psychological manifestations of cretinism is unlikely to be learned by exposure to people with this syndrome, since it is so rare. If this correlation can be detected by perceivers who have had no direct instruction about the syndrome, then it is likely to reflect some innate preparedness. Evidence consistent with the argument that perceivers are "prepared" for certain correlations between appearance and behavioral events has been provided by research using classical conditioning paradigms to show that facial expressions are more readily associated with events of a similar valence by both infants and adults. For example, negative events are more readily associated with fearful or angry faces than with happy ones.[53]

A fourth possible origin of perceivers' ability to discern true appearance-trait correlations is the self-fulfilling prophecy effect. To the extent that Path D in the model of appearance-trait relations is operative (Figure 3.1), perceivers' trait perceptions may be accurate because their own expectancies make them accurate: They evoke the behavior they expect. For this explanation to be noncircular, the expectancies cannot be attributed to expectancy-induced correlations that have been detected in the past, and it is necessary to specify their origin. The next section of this chapter proposes overgeneralization effects that can yield expectancies that contribute to the development of actual appearance-trait relations via self-fulfilling prophecies. These overgeneralization effects may also contribute to self-defeating prophecies or artifice effects, or they may simply produce stereotypes.

Overgeneralization Effects

The proposed overgeneralization effects all derive from the adaptive value of responding to the information that appearance qualities provide. The evolutionary importance of detecting identity, species, fitness, emotion, or age may have produced such a strong preparedness to respond to the facial qualities that reveal these attributes that our responses are overgeneralized to individuals whose appearance merely resembles them.

Whereas the evolutionary origin of overgeneralization effects cannot be proved, the evidence cited earlier of specific neural mechanisms for identifying the attributes from which overgeneralization is predicted affirms the adaptive significance of perceiving these attributes. Although overgeneralization may not seem particularly adaptive, the errors that result from overresponding to facial qualities that suggest a particular age, or emotion, or species may be less maladaptive than errors that would result from failure to respond to these qualities. The proposed overgeneralization effects not only provide an explanation for the strong tendency to read faces but also specify particular facial qualities that will be associated with particular traits. The resemblance on which these overgeneralization effects is based is a *configuration* of facial qualities, not the isolated features that have often been examined in past research on physiognomic correlates of traits. Finally, as noted previously, overgeneralization effects can contribute to the accuracy of face reading insofar as they create self-fulfilling prophecy effects.

The Case of Mistaken Identity

Strangers may be perceived to have the same traits as the significant others or archetypes whom they resemble. This overgeneralization effect may be rooted in the adaptive value of the appearance markers of identity for avoiding potentially dangerous strangers and approaching safe, familiar people. A historical illustration of the mistaken identity effect is provided by an account of the first reactions of the Mexican Indians to the Spanish explorers of the sixteenth century. They initially viewed the Spaniards as gods, and it has been suggested that they mistook these white-skinned explorers for a white-skinned legendary god, Quetzalcoatl, who may have been an early Viking explorer. This example illustrates the potential for overgeneralization effects to influence impressions of people whose facial appearance resembles a particular ethnic or racial group, regardless of whether they are members of that group.

Although the Spaniards profited from their resemblance to Quetzalcoatl, a Hitler look-alike would have a difficult time convincing people of his warm and nurturant qualities. Similarly, the woman who resembles Marilyn Monroe will find it hard to convince people of her intellect, and the man who matches people's image of a sleazy politician will have a harder time convincing people of his fitness for elective office. Some of the traits that students have attributed to a typical politician include the following: "smiles all the time . . . tends to pose, concerned with appearances and putting on a front . . . does only what is expected . . . vain and very ambitious . . . opinions are noncommittal . . . often swayed by pressure."[54] Looking like a politician emphasizes such negative impressions.

When an unknown politician was described in a personality profile as having both stereotypical politician traits and nonpolitician traits, students' evaluations of him were much more negative if his physical appearance matched their politician image than if it did not.

The transfer of traits from a significant person to another individual may occur when the person is significant only to you. The Freudian concept of *transference* concerns this phenomenon. According to Freud, childhood fantasies about one's mother or father are superimposed onto the analyst during therapy. Others have found transference to be a more general phenomenon. Although such transfer effects are frequently elicited by similarities in the roles or traits of a significant other and a stranger, similarities in their appearance may also be effective. Indeed, men showed a moderate tendency to attribute their own mother's traits to young women who look like "good mother types" but not to wanton-looking women.[55] Similarly, men were more likely to attribute the traits of a good friend to a woman who physically resembles her than to an equally attractive woman who does not.[56] Additionally, college women expressed more positive emotions about a man if he was physically similar to the type of man they had been attracted to in the past than if he did not physically resemble an old flame, although he might be quite attractive.[57]

Even a brief encounter with someone may be sufficient to set in motion the "mistaken identify" effect. When people were asked to choose one of two women, A or B, for a job requiring a kind and friendly person, they were more likely to choose Woman A if they had just been treated kindly by someone who resembled her than if they had not had such an interaction. Similarly, when others were required to interact with either A or B, people were more likely to approach B if they had just been treated irritably by someone who resembled A.[58] The earlier example of the ease with which college students came to associate certain facial qualities, such as short faces, with certain traits, such as fairness, is another example of the mistaken identity effect. In that study, an unknown professor was perceived to have the same traits as known professors whose facial structure his resembled.[59]

Animal Analogies

People may be perceived to have traits that are associated with the animals that their features resemble: an animal overgeneralization effect. Although this principle may seem a bit far-fetched, it could be rooted in our evolutionary history, since differences in appearance among species provide information that facilitates adaptive actions, such as running from dangerous lions but not from harmless rabbits. Moreover, as noted in

Chapter 2, animal research showing the differential reactivity of various neurons to faces of different species suggests that there is a specific neural locus for species identification just as there is for the identification of different individuals within a species. The loss of the particular ability to identify animals in some individuals suffering from prosopagnosia suggests a specific neural locus in humans as well.

Associations between particular animal features and particular traits are clearly seen in classical writings. Aristotle argued that just as animals with coarse hair are brave—the lion, the wild boar, the wolf—so are people with coarse hair. People with smooth, silky hair, on the other hand, Aristotle thought timid as lambs. In the seventeenth century, Della Porta expressed the logic of animal analogies in the following syllogism: "All parrots are talkers, all men with such noses are like parrots, therefore all such men are talkers."[60] Lavater, the prominent physiognomist of that era, also endorsed this view, stating the following:

> If any one would endeavor to discover the signs of bravery in man, he would act wisely to collect all the signs of bravery in animated nature, by which courageous animals are distinguished from others . . . were the lion and lamb, for the first time, placed before us, had we never known such animals, never heard their names, still we could not resist the impression of the courage and strength of the one, or of the weakness and sufference of the other.[61]

As noted in Chapter 1, the seventeenth-century French painter Charles Le Brun captured on canvas intriguing similarities between animal and human faces such as those shown in Figure 1.6, and similar comparisons appeared in the nineteenth-century caricatures of Daumier. The nineteenth-century novelist Balzac also drew renowned animal analogies. One character is described as "malicious as an old monkey," another as "ignorant as a carp," and still another as "an eagle shut up in a cage." A scholar of Balzac noted that "these comparisons are often multiplied to heighten the reader's appreciation of an individual's character."[62] Further evidence for the propensity to compare humans and animals is provided by Chinese folklore, which categorizes people according to the animal year in which they were born, much as Western astrology categorizes them according to the star constellation under which they were born. Alternating in 12-year cycles are the year of the rat, ox, tiger, rabbit, dragon, snake, horse, sheep, monkey, cock, dog, and pig. Individuals born in the year of a particular animal are presumed to have traits similar to that animal: "Monkeys are intelligent and energetic. . . . What you don't want to be is one of the draft animals like the Cow or the Horse or an edible one like the Pig or the Sheep."[63] The Chinese people seem to take this belief quite seriously, increasing their fertility in propitious years. For example, in keeping with the preceding quotation, tradition says that children born in the Year of the Monkey, occurring in 1992, are clever and lucky, whereas those born in the Year of the Sheep, occurring in 1991, have bad luck. An official Associated Press news report from Beijing indicated that China experienced a baby boom in 1992, with pregnancies in one industrial city up 30 percent from the same time the previous year.

The penchant to draw analogies between the characteristics of animals and humans is not limited to ancient philosophers, physiognomists, and folklorists. It is deeply embedded in our everyday thinking as evidenced by trait adjectives such as sheepish, pigheaded, bully, birdbrained, lion-hearted, catty, bitchy, and foxy, as well as metaphors such as jackass, dove, hawk, bear, cow, pig, and wolf. It is interesting that similar terms are used in diverse languages. In Chinese, as in English, a fox is cunning, a sheep is submissive, and a wolf is cruel. The Chinese, like Americans, call a sharp man eagle-eyed and a seductive woman foxy.[64]

Although we usually apply epithets such as fox or leonine to people whose *behavior* resembles that of those animals, we may also see foxy or leonine behavior in people whose *faces* resemble those animals. The schematic human faces shown in Figure 3.3 were judged to have the same traits as the animals that they resemble. Foxes and fox-faced men were judged as shrewd, whereas lions and lion-faced men were seen as dominant and proud.[65]

The Emotion Overgeneralization Effect

People may be perceived to have traits that are associated with the emotional expressions that their features resemble, an overgeneralization that reflects the adaptive value of responsiveness to emotional expressions, such as avoiding an angry person and approaching a happy one. The person whose mouth naturally turns up at the corner may be perceived as happy, and the person with low-placed eyebrows may be perceived as angry. The former individual, who always looks happy, may then be perceived to have the more permanent traits of friendliness and a good sense of humor, whereas the latter individual, who always looks angry, may be perceived as aggressive and dominant.[66] Indeed, as mentioned earlier, faces with lowered brows are perceived as more dominant, at least in Western cultures.[67] Similarly, because fear drains blood from the face, producing a pallor, someone with a naturally pale complexion may be perceived as fearful and timid. Such overgeneralizations may sometimes be accurate. As noted previously, elderly people tend to have traits congruent with the emotional expression that their neutral face resembles.[68]

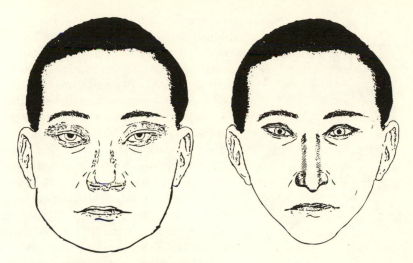

FIGURE 3.3   *Leonine and fox-like men.*

Sickness Similarities

People whose facial qualities resemble those observed in certain physical or mental disorders may be perceived to have traits that are associated with that disorder. This overgeneralization effect may reflect the adaptive value of responding to appearance indicators of fitness, such as avoiding those with communicable diseases and mating with those who are genetically fit. Those with a naturally pallid complexion may be perceived as physically weak, like someone who is anemic, and, by metaphorical association, as weak-willed as well. Those with a naturally florid complexion may be perceived as dissolute, like an alcoholic with dilated capillaries, because of the resemblance in complexion. People with sparse, fine hair or short necks may be perceived as low in intelligence, like those with Down syndrome, whose features these resemble. Someone with thick, dry skin or large or flabby ears may be perceived as low in intelligence like the cretin, whose features these resemble. Someone with a small head or a receding chin may be perceived as lacking intelligence like the microcephalic individual, whose features these resemble. Indeed, representations of "idiots," such as shown in Figure 3.4, depict a head in which the cranium is much smaller than that of an average head. Representations of people with other mental disorders, such as the "maniac" in this figure, show a standard ratio of cranium size to face size.

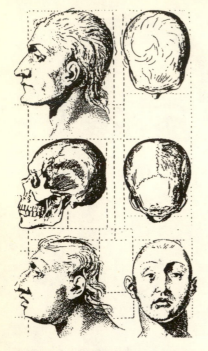

FIGURE 3.4　*A maniac (top) and an idiot (bottom). Phillipe Pinel (1801). Traité médico-philosophique sur l'aliénation mentale, ou la manie (Paris: Richard, Caille et Ravier, IX).*

Overgeneralization effects representing "sickness similarities" may occur not only when a person has facial features that resemble those occurring with a particular malady, but also when a person has features that signify a more general lack of fitness. As shown in Chapter 2, facial asymmetry and a facial structure that deviates markedly from the population average can indicate a lack of fitness in the intellectual, psychological, and physical realms. Consequently, people with more asymmetrical faces or more atypical faces may be perceived as lower in intelligence, psychological adjustment, and health.

The Attractiveness Halo Effect

People whose faces are judged to be attractive are perceived to have desirable traits and treated accordingly: External beauty is overgeneralized to internal assets. No definitive explanation has been provided for this much investigated attractiveness halo, which is discussed at greater length in Chapters 6 and 7. However, one possibility is that it reflects the sickness similarities overgeneralization effect, since facial attractiveness is enhanced by qualities that signify fitness, such as symmetry and average facial proportions. Another possible contributing factor is the positive feelings that beauty evokes in the beholder.

The Babyface Overgeneralization Effect

People whose facial qualities resemble those of infants may be perceived to have childlike traits and treated accordingly—an overgeneralization effect that reflects the adaptive value of responding to facial cues to maturity, such as nurturing the young and mating with the fertile. This principle is elaborated in Chapters 4, and 5, where it also is tied to sex stereotypes.

Summary

According to physiognomy as well as functionalist theories of perception, we may engage in face reading because a person's face is in fact an accurate indicator of his or her traits. There is considerable evidence that people can accurately judge dominance and extraversion from appearance, and some evidence for accuracy in judging conscientiousness, sexual availability, agreeableness, and honesty as well. However, only a small portion of this evidence demonstrates that facial qualities per se are sufficient to enable accurate judgments. There is even less evidence indicating what the diagnostic facial qualities are. Clearly, additional research is needed before any firm conclusions can be drawn regarding the extent and basis of accurate face reading. Nevertheless, the feasibility of accuracy is demonstrated by the existence of four possible routes to a true link between appearance and traits. The journey to accuracy on some of these routes is launched by expectations regarding links between appearance and traits that have several possible origins that are not mutually exclusive. These include direct instruction, direct experience with people who show particular face-trait correlations, an innate preparedness for particular face-trait correlations, and overgeneralized responses to facial cues that are valid indicators of adaptively significant qualities, such as fitness, identity, or age. Some of these overgeneralization effects are considered in more depth in the following chapters: the babyface overgeneralization effect, the attractiveness halo effect, and the related sickness similarities effect. In Chapter 4, I consider the foundation for the babyface overgeneralization effect: the disarming appearance of babies.

4

A Baby's Face
Is Disarming

We had been sternly ordered to keep our hands down and to refrain from speaking to the North Korean guards at the far side of the divided meeting room in Panmunjom, the border town straddling North and South Korea. The guards did look ominous, and the shootout that had recently occurred when a Russian attempted to escape through this room to South Korea made me take these instructions seriously. Suddenly, my son Loren waved his hand, and his high-pitched "hi" chimed across the room. I turned toward the nearest North Korean guard, expecting to see his automatic weapon trained on us. Instead, it was a large grin that was leveled at my son. The transformation in this "enemy" soldier's stony face brought tears to my eyes. He found my baby totally disarming.

The favorable response to a baby shown in this anecdote from my visit to Korea is universal. Moreover, our responses to babies engender the babyface overgeneralization effect that was identified in Chapter 3 as one basis for face reading: People whose facial qualities resemble those of infants may be perceived to have childlike traits. A careful consideration of exactly what responses a baby's face elicits as well as the appearance qualities that characterize a baby's face provide a necessary foundation for further discussion of this overgeneralization effect in later chapters.

Favorable Responses to Babies

Subsequent to my encounter with the North Korean guard in Panmunjom, I traveled through China with a group that included a 6-month-old baby. Crowds like the one shown in Figure 4.1 gathered around

Melanie wherever we stopped. The behavior exhibited toward the baby was very different from that shown toward adults. At home, the behavior that a baby elicits is so commonplace that it never drew my attention. But here, halfway round the world, I was struck by the fact that the Chinese showed the same stereotyped behavior toward a baby that Americans do. When Melanie looked at her Chinese admirers, they not only

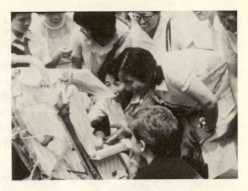

FIGURE 4.1 *The magnetism of a baby.*

smiled but also showed mock-surprise facial expressions, opening their eyes and mouth very wide, raising their eyebrows, and slightly raising and tilting up their heads like the people shown in Figure 4.2. Although this behavior seems quite natural when directed toward a baby, it would seem bizarre indeed if it were shown in adult-adult interactions. In fact, the facial expression directed toward babies is an exaggerated form of a universal facial greeting behavior documented by ethologists called the eyebrow flash. In adult-adult interactions, this facial expression is so fleeting that it can be seen only when single frames of films of people greeting one another are viewed in slow motion. But the same basic elements are there, as the greeting faces in Figure 4.3 reveal.

In addition to showing exaggerated facial expressions when interacting with Melanie, her admirers disregarded cultural rules that regulate eye contact between adults and stared at her shamelessly. It has been said that two adults do not gaze into each other's eyes without speech for over 10 seconds unless they are going to fight or make love. Yet adults engage in mutual gaze with an infant for 30 seconds or more.[1] They also show other "invasions" that would be unacceptable in social interactions with adults. Adults keep a certain "respectful" distance from one another, the exact span varying with their culture and sex and the nature of the relationship between the two people. However, when it comes to babies, complete strangers, regardless of culture, think nothing of coming eyeball-to-eyeball at the first encounter.

Melanie's entourage not only made funny looming faces but also emitted strange vocalizations like "ooooh" or "aaaah." Such utterances are an element of culturally universal baby talk.[2] When speaking to infants, adults from different continents speaking a diverse group of languages all use simple sentences, short utterances, and many nonsense sounds. They also show "cute" pronunciations, mimicking errors a child might make, such as

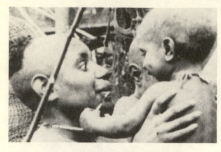

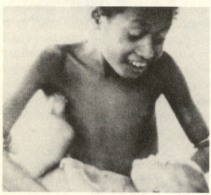

FIGURE 4.2   *Young Eipo woman (West New Guinea) addressing a baby with a smile and an eyebrow flash (top); eyebrow raising as an affectionate expression in the big brother–baby sister relationship (bottom). Reprinted with permission from I. Eibl-Eibesfeld.* Human ethology. *New York: Aldine de Gruyter. © 1989 Irenäus Eibl-Eibesfeldt.*

"pwitty wabbit" and "tummy." How people talk to infants is as distinctive as what they say. They use an affectionate and exaggerated singsong intonation, and the pitch of their voice is raised, often into the falsetto range. It seems almost physically impossible to speak to a baby in a deep voice.

A "candid camera" study of almost four thousand people walking down public streets in Germany and Italy revealed responses to a baby in those countries like those I had seen directed to Melanie. People who passed by a mother and baby were much more likely to smile than those who passed by the same woman without her baby. Many spoke baby talk to the baby or spoke about the baby to its mother, whereas no one spoke to the mother when the baby wasn't there.[3] Other studies have found that adults prefer pictures of babies to pictures of adults. When asked why, they say it's because the babies look so dependent, helpless, and vulnerable—most disarming attributes. Even children retain some of the disarming qualities of babies. The Masai of Africa and the Aboriginals of Australia take advantage of this fact by using young children to keep aggressors at bay. They approach outsiders with their hand on the shoulder of a child, who walks just in front of them.[4]

Geriatric patients with psychiatric disorders are also disarmed by babies, readily desisting from noisy, belligerent behavior when told "you'll wake the baby dolls."[5] Children, too, respond to babies. Indeed, infants as young as 4 months of age prefer looking at slides depicting infant faces to looking at those depicting faces of children or adults. By age one and a half, infants also show more smiling, gesturing, and vocalizing to the babies' faces.[6] When children can walk, they move toward babies. The pull of a baby's face is illustrated by the response of an 18-month-old to her grandmother's carefully chosen gift. The wonderful and expensive new musical toy was lifted from the box and placed next to Sonja. Ignoring the toy, Sonja made a beeline for the box, kissed the picture of the baby that it displayed, and exclaimed, "Baby! Baby!"

More systematic evidence for the magnetism an infant holds for a child is provided by observations of an infant's daily life among the !Kung bushmen of the Kalahari Desert. It has been found that children frequently run up to infants who are carried by their mothers in a hip sling and engage in some of the same stereotyped facial and vocal communications that adults express toward babies. Research in the United States has shown such behaviors by both boys and girls as early as 6 years of age. When interacting with an infant, children raise the pitch of their already high-pitched voices and they talk baby talk. They also raise their eyebrows, and they violate distance boundaries by nuzzling, patting, stroking, and kissing the baby. The behaviors elicited by an infant, therefore, are not limited to one age group or one sex. Learning from prior experience with infants seems to be unnecessary as does a biological or hormonal trigger. A sufficient condition for the elicitation of affectionate facial and vocal expressions is the presence of a disarming infant.[7]

A gaggle of people oohing and aahing over an infant generalizes not only across age groups and cultures but also across species. Field workers have reported that in many species of monkey and ape, the small infant acts as a so-

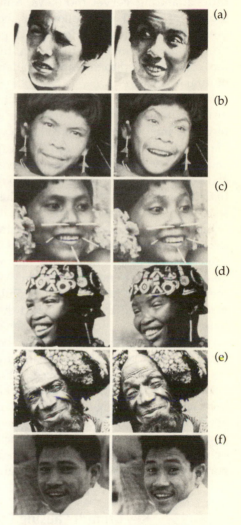

(a)
(b)
(c)
(d)
(e)
(f)

FIGURE 4.3   *Examples of the "eyebrow flash": (a) French woman; (b) Yanomami man; (c) Yanomami woman; (d) !Kung woman, central Kalahari; (e) Huli man, Papua, New Guinea; (f) Balinese man. Reprinted with permission from I. Eibl-Eibesfeld.* Human ethology. *New York: Aldine de Gruyter. © 1989 Irenäus Eibl-Eibesfeldt.*

cial magnet for other group members. The mother with her new infant forms the center of a cluster of interested group members, which may include juvenile and adolescent males and females as well as adult males. Indeed, among vervet monkeys, a new mother often acquires an entourage of animals that follow her about, waiting for an opportunity to touch the infant. Juvenile females, in particular, touch, cuddle, carry, and groom infants whenever they have the opportunity, a behavior pattern that can be likened to the human pattern of young girls playing with dolls or infant siblings.[8]

Monkeys show a preference for pictures of babies over those of adults, just as humans do. Rhesus monkeys who were reared in isolation from birth to 9 months of age were shown slides of monkeys and other scenes via a rear projection screen in their cages, and they could choose which slide to view again by pressing a lever. From 2 months of age on, they showed much more preference for looking at pictures of infant monkeys than adult monkeys.[9] The fact that this preference was shown in the absence of any experience suggests that it is innate.

Even among lower animals, where maternal behavior was long thought to be hormonally controlled, the infant is capable of eliciting nurturant and protective behaviors in the absence of hormonal support. Exposure to young pups was found to bring out maternal behavior from all manner of rats. Nonpregnant females, ovariectomized females, and castrated or intact males all retrieved the pups, licked them, began nest building, and even took the nursing stance, crouching over the pups as if they had milk to give.[10] Although hormones may not be crucial to the provision of nurturance to rodent pups, recent research indicates that there is genetic control over such behavior. Female mice lacking a gene called fosB fail to make nests for their newborn pups or to suckle them and keep them warm. Male mice and never-pregnant females who lack this gene also fail to nurture newborns. The mice who lack this gene have not lost sensory, cognitive, or hormonal functions that might be crucial to nurturing pups. The dysfunction brought on by lack of this gene has a specific effect, blocking a mouse's normal responses to the powerful stimulus of a newborn pup.[11]

Key Stimuli Causing Favorable Responses

Not content simply to document favorable responses to babies, ethologists have asked what exactly it is about a baby that can warm the coldest of hearts. This question has led to a search for what ethologists call *key stimuli*, which are specific components of an infant's appearance or behavior that can, by themselves, trigger a favorable response. Ethologists have provided many examples of simple stimuli that trigger caretaking responses from the adult and inhibit adult aggression.[12]

The cheeping of a baby chick releases protective behavior from the mother hen, whereas the chick's motor behavior does not: The hen won't attempt to rescue an unheard chick who can be seen struggling under a glass bell, whereas it will immediately come to the rescue of an unseen chick whose distress cries can be heard. Similarly, the female turkey recognizes her chick only by its calls, and she will kill her own young if she is deaf. In addition, she will brood a stuffed polecat, her natural enemy, if it utters the call of newborn turkeys (by means of a hidden loudspeaker). A quiet stuffed polecat, on the other hand, elicits a squawking, pecking, and clawing attack. The call of a mouse, rat, or hamster pup also elicits protective responses from the mother. These ultrasonic sounds cannot be heard by humans, who must use a "bat detector" to perceive them, but they are extremely salient to the animals. The sound of a pup is so effective in bringing mom to the rescue that female mice have been observed to chew the cover off a loudspeaker that is transmitting a tape recording of the pup's call.[13]

There are visual as well as auditory key stimuli. When the beaks of certain young birds reach a particular length, the mother birds push them from the nest.[14] If one paints the black bills of juvenile zebra finches red, like those of the adults, the adults do not feed these baby birds despite intense begging behavior. Although the gray feathers of the infant swan may make it an "ugly duckling," this coloration also provides beneficial protection from attack. Infant swans who, through some mutation, have the beautiful white color typical of adults are more apt to be attacked by the adults than their ugly brethren. Fur, like feathers, can serve as key stimuli. When mouse pups grow hair, they become vulnerable to attack, and a 14-day-old (adolescent) mouse will be attacked unless its hair has been shaved off, making it look like an infant.

Key stimuli persist even as we move up the phylogenetic scale, where one might expect them to be offset by experiential factors. Primate infants receive special treatment from adults during the time that they have infantile coloration and facial and body proportions, and differences between species in the length of time that mothers nurture their offspring are paralleled by differences in the length of time that the offspring retain their natal markings. For example, spider monkey mothers nurture their young longer than howler monkey mothers do, and infant spider monkeys keep their natal coats longer than the infant howlers. The langur infant is born with a dark brown natal coat that changes to the light gray adult color at 2 months. Only at this time does the mother entrust her infant to another female, who "baby-sits" for several infants at once. The power of the infant key stimuli to elicit protection is documented by reports that adults cuddle and groom infants who are unconscious or dead so long as they still have their natal coats.[15]

Field observations of baboons by primatologists provide a particularly dramatic example of the change in caretaking that occurs when the infant loses its natal coat, which turns from black to yellow at 12 weeks. Whereas the mother's attitude toward the infant is one of concern and protection while he wears the black natal coat, it becomes "sink or swim" when his appearance matures:

> Myrna approaches the stream with her twelve-week-old son Moley riding on her chest. She sits a few feet from the stream, which is six feet wide and running heavily. Moley moves off a few steps to pick at some leaves. Suddenly Myrna jumps across the stream, leaving Moley on the other side. Moley begins to scream as his mother stops on the other bank and looks back at him. After about 15 seconds, he jumps in and is immediately carried several feet downstream. Finally, he makes contact with the bottom and, his screams now gurgle, he struggles across to the opposite bank. As soon as he arrives, Myrna jumps back to the opposite bank again, landing a little farther downstream. Moley immediately jumps back in, still screaming, and is again carried several feet closer to the lake before making it to the other side. Moley climbs up the bank and charges after his mother who has disappeared into the bushes.[16]

The natal coat not only elicits maternal, nurturant behavior, it also gives the infant license to pester the most dominant males without incurring the aggressive reactions that an older primate would. For example, infant chimpanzees have white tail tufts, which tend to disappear at age 3, at which time they lose protection from the adult males. When chimps try to push the adult male off their mother at copulation, the male tolerates this behavior in infants with white tale tufts but hits out at juveniles.[17] Similarly, rhesus infants are exempt from attack so long as they show two head hair tufts and the natal fur, which typically disappear between 4 and 5 months of age.[18]

Do human infants also manifest key stimuli that automatically release adults' caretaking and inhibit their aggression? To answer this question, one must first identify critical physical differences between human infants and adults. Unlike other primates, human infants do not have fur that changes color as they mature. However, their hair color is lighter than that of adults, particularly in Caucasians, among whom babies are often blond and adults are typically brunette. Skin color is also lighter in infants, with human skin tending to darken from birth to puberty in various racial groups.[19]

The most obvious differences between infants and adults is their size: Babies are smaller than adults. If you look at early paintings of babies and adults, such as the one shown in Figure 4.4, you will see that a difference in size was all that the artist portrayed. Something is wrong with the baby in this figure; he doesn't look babyish, despite his small size. Ethologists have identified other differences that later artists also discovered. As Figure 4.5 reveals, a baby not only is smaller than an adult but also has a proportionately larger head and proportionately shorter and chubbier arms and legs. The ethologist Konrad Lorenz referred to these and other infant qualities as a Kindchenschema (baby-schema), proposing that they serve as key stimuli.[20] In fact, the visual features constituting the baby-schema are not fully developed at birth. The mother's protection at this time is elicited by many other signals, such as crying and eye contact. As interaction with non-family members increases, the baby-schema becomes full-blown, thereby protecting the infant from others' aggressive reactions.[21]

Other differences in the physical appearance of babies and adults that cannot be discerned in Figure 4.5 are readily apparent when we encounter a real baby. A baby's wide-eyed look is due to the fact that the eyes are proportionately larger in a baby than in an adult. The eyes grow very little from birth, whereas the face continues to grow, making the eyes of an adult smaller in relation to the face. The penetrating gaze of an infant reflects a relatively larger pupil size, which may compensate for the inefficiency of the immature retina at capturing light.[22] There is also a greater tendency for the iris and sclera to be blue in babies, at least in Caucasians. Soft, chubby cheeks are another hallmark of a baby's face. These cheeks may serve an adaptive function, facilitating sucking during feeding. Indeed, even starving, emaciated babies have "sucking pads" in their cheeks. Owing to sucking, babies' lips

FIGURE 4.4 *Giotto*, Madonna *(c. 1310). Ufizzi Gallery, Florence.*

FIGURE 4.5 *Masaccio*, Madonna *(1426). The National Gallery, London.*

may also be redder and proportionately larger than adults'. Babies have fine eyebrows, and it has been noted that high eyebrows are another sign of youth because children typically look up at adults, raising their eyebrows.[23] A baby also has a pug nose: a small, wide, and concave nose with a sunken bridge. It is only at puberty that longer, thicker brow hair develops and that noses become proportionately larger, narrower, and more convex, with a prominent bridge, particularly among boys. One never sees a baby with low bushy eyebrows or a "hook" nose.

Other aspects of the infant face are more subtle. A baby has a different head shape from an adult, whose cranium has been altered by maturation of the facial structure and the force of gravity. As shown in Figure 4.6, which depicts an infant's skull enlarged to the same size as an adult's, the baby's cranium is proportionately much larger and the face itself is proportionately smaller. An infant's face equals only one-eighth the bulk of the cranium; an adult's face equals one-half of the cranium. The profiles of an infant and an adult head shown in Figure 4.7 further reveal that the slope from the forehead to the chin is at a different angle in a baby and an adult. These age differences in craniofacial proportions reflect the fact that the brain, housed in the cranium, is well developed in the infant, whereas the jaw and nasal area are not. The jaw enlarges only as teeth develop, and the nasal area enlarges to accommodate adult lung capacity. The net effect of the differences between the head shapes of a baby and an adult is that the baby has a relatively larger, more vertically sloping forehead, relatively bigger and lower placed eyes, a relatively smaller nose and mouth, and a relatively smaller, more receding chin.[24]

Critical differences in the physical appearance of infants and adults have been identified; the question remains whether any of these human infantile features serve as key stimuli, releasing caretaking and inhibiting aggression. Research suggests that they do. Although infant-adult differences in head shape are subtle, we are highly sensitive to them. In the schematic profiles shown in Figure 4.8, it is readily apparent which is the more babyish. The profile on the left depicts a 3-month-old infant, and the profile on the right depicts the same child at 8.75 years of age. Similarly, a quick glance at the full-face drawings in Figure 4.9 reveals a clear difference, even though the only thing that varies is the shape of the facial outline, yielding the more babyish cranium and chin in the face on the right. Researchers have found that the shape of the head when seen in profile provides an accurate indication of who is older than whom. Changing the shape of the head by using a mathematical formula that has the same effect on the shape as actual growth does yields the series of profiles shown in Figure 4.10. People are able to identify the older of two profiles when

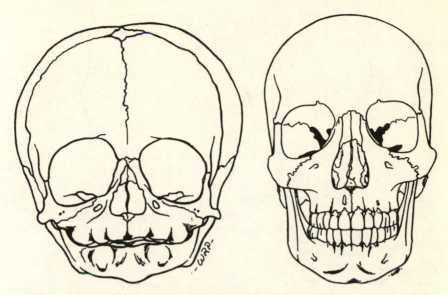

FIGURE 4.6 *A child's head enlarged to the same size as an adult's. D. H. Enlow (1982). Handbook of facial growth (Figure 1–10). Philadelphia: Saunders.*

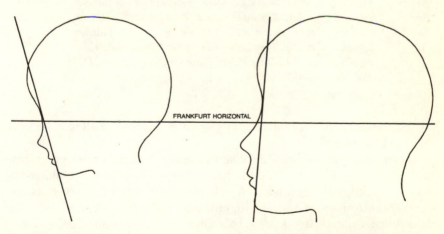

FRANKFURT HORIZONTAL

FIGURE 4.7 *Profiles of an infant and an adult. J. T. Todd, L. S. Mark, R. E. Shaw, & J. B. Pittenger (1980). The perception of human growth.* Scientific American, 242, *p. 139A. Copyright © by Scientific American Inc. All rights reserved.*

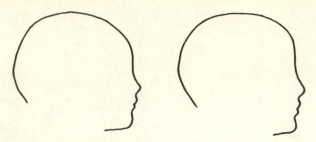

FIGURE 4.8   *Profiles of a 3-month-old infant (left) and an 8-year-old child (right). Reprinted from T. R. Alley (1983). Infant head shape as an eliciter of adult protection.* Merrill-Palmer Quarterly, 29, *No. 4, by permission of the Wayne State University Press.* © 1983 by Wayne State University Press, Detroit, Michigan, 48202.

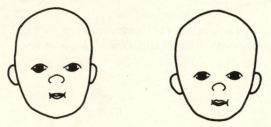

FIGURE 4.9   *Schematic faces with babyish and nonbabyish cranium and chin. Reprinted from T. R. Alley (1983). Infant head shape as an eliciter of adult protection,* Merrill-Palmer Quarterly, 29, *No. 4, by permission of the Wayne State University Press.* © 1983 by Wayne State University Press, Detroit, Michigan, 48202.

the difference in shape is only slightly greater than the smallest difference that can be detected.[25]

Not only can people readily discriminate a less from a more mature head shape, but also the infantile head shape stimulates caretaking impulses and inhibits aggression. A babyish head shape is viewed as less alert, less strong, and less intelligent, perceptions of dependency that should foster more caretaking. A babyish head shape is also seen as cuter, less threatening, and more lovable, perceptions of a disarming approachability that should not only foster caretaking but also inhibit aggression. There is one aspect of approachability that is lower for a babyish profile:

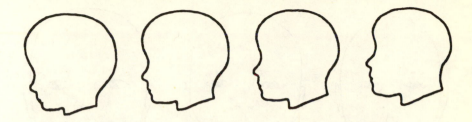

FIGURE 4.10 *Changes in craniofacial profile shape with increasing maturity. J. B. Pittenger & R. G. Shaw (1975). Aging faces as viscal-elastic events: Implications for a theory of nonrigid shape perceptions.* Journal of Experimental Psychology: Human Perception and Performance, 1, *p. 376.* © 1975 by the American Psychological Association. *Reprinted with permission.*

It is seen as less sexy than the mature one.[26] Like the other impressions of a babyish head shape, this perception is adaptive. The net effect of this key stimulus is to elicit behavior geared toward protecting and nurturing, but not sexually molesting, the young. Indeed, people do report a greater desire to protect more babyish profiles. When shown two profiles, such as those in Figure 4.8, and asked which they would feel more compelled to defend from a physical beating, they chose the more babyish of the pair.[27] Of course, it must be acknowledged that infants are sometimes physically or sexually abused, and infanticide is common in some parts of the world; however, reactions to babies who lack key infantile features indicate that a typical baby's appearance can have a protective effect.

What happens when the infant key stimuli are weak? According to observations of ethologists, a 2-month-old langur monkey infant with a precociously adultlike coat was badly neglected by its mother. An even worse fate befell a young turkey with noninfantile calls. The hen turkey killed it.[28] Is it possible that there are similar phenomena among humans?

Imagine a baby who has a small forehead, a long chin, small eyes, and a large nose. Would this child receive the same care and protection that a baby typically elicits? Although doting parents might say "he's so ugly that he's cute," the fact is that babies with such "nonbabyish" features are perceived as less cute than the "Gerber" types who have been blessed with a more prototypical babyface.[29] Worse yet, the phrase "she's so ugly, only a mother could love her" isn't quite true. Although parents do perceive their own infants as cuter than others do, the cuter infants are perceived to be by others, the more their own mothers smile at a photograph of them. Moreover, observations of face-to-face interactions between par-

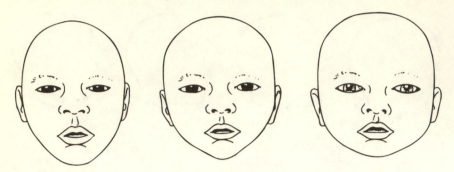

FIGURE 4.11   *Composite drawing of infants at conceptional ages 31–34 weeks (left), 35–37 weeks (middle), and 40 weeks (right). R. A. Maier, D. L. Holmes, F. L. Slaymaker, & J. N. Reich (1984). The perceived attractiveness of preterm infants.* Infant Behavior and Development, 7 *(Figures 2, 3, 4, p. 409).*

ents and their 3-month-old infants revealed that the cuter infants received more smiles and vocalizations from their fathers.[30] Thus, a baby who lacks the prototypical babyface may be treated less warmly by its own parents than one whose face manifests the key stimuli for eliciting nurturance.

The more positive reaction to greater babyishness in one's own infant is disheartening, given the ideal of unconditional mother love. Even more disillusioning is evidence of extremely negative reactions to infants who are very low in babyishness. Prematurely born infants lack the cute, babyish appearance of full-term babies—their eyes are less wide, their heads less round—and such infants are overrepresented among battered children. Whereas only 6–7 percent of newborns are premature, 20–30 percent of battered children were prematurely born. There are, of course, many contributing factors to child abuse, and a nonbabyish appearance does not necessarily lead to abuse. However, it has been suggested that infants who are less babyfaced are also less disarming: They do not as effectively release nurturing from adults, and they do not as effectively inhibit adults' aggression.[31] Consistent with this argument is the finding that parents who watched videotapes of premature or full-term infants showed higher physiological arousal in response to the premature infants, and they found these babies less pleasant. They also reported having less desire to interact with a premature baby even though they were unaware of its premature status. Although these negative reactions to premature babies were elicited in part by the distinctive sound of their crying, the visual appearance of the preemie was also unappealing. Other evidence for negative reactions to appearance per se is provided by judgments of composite drawings of premature and full-term infant faces shown in Figure 4.11. College students indicated less interest in taking care of and being close to the preemies, and they perceived them as less

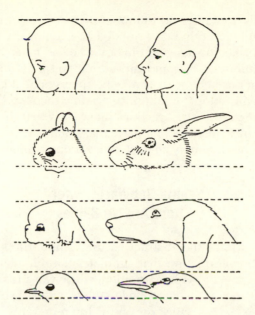

FIGURE 4.12 *Similarities across species in babyish versus mature facial qualities. K. Lorenz (1950). Ganzheit und Teil in der tierischen und menschlichen Gemeinschaft (Part and parcel in animal and human societies),* Studium Generale, *3(9). (Published by Springer-Verlag, Berlin.)*

likable and cute, more irritating, and less fun to be with. The more premature the infant depicted in the composite drawing, the more negative these responses were.

Not only do various species find their own infants disarming, but also there is evidence for such effects across species. As Figure 4.12 reveals, there are cross-species commonalities in the infantile facial qualities that can serve as key stimuli. Differences between infants and adults in head shape and feature placement are similar for a variety of mammals other than humans as well as for birds. These commonalities suggest that infants of one species may be capable of eliciting nurturant responses from members of other species as well as their own. Human affection for kittens and puppies reveals such a phenomenon. Some species, such as Pekinese dogs and Persian cats, are particularly endearing to humans even in their adult forms, owing to a neotenous appearance. Children, like adults, respond to infantile qualities in other species. Three-year-old children show the typical nurturant response to a kitten, euphorically tipping their heads, patting it, and talking pet names in a high-pitched voice.[32] Animals, too, respond to immature members of other species. A dramatic example recently was provided at a zoo near Chicago, where a female gorilla picked up a 3-year-old boy who had fallen down a concrete cliff into a pit full of gorillas and carried him to safety. Although legends of feral children raised by wolves may be apocryphal, it is a fact that a female hamster will "adopt" infant mice, feeding them and retrieving them if they leave the nest.[33] Such reactions make clear that the key stimuli are not the appearance qualities of a particular organism, but rather abstract infantile properties that may characterize various animals.

Seeing Babyfaces Where
There Are No Babies

Figure 4.13 illustrates the abstract nature of infantile key stimuli. The mathematical transformation that simulates the remodeling of the skull

FIGURE 4.13 *Babyish and mature craniofacial shapes represented in cars. J. B. Pittenger, R. E. Shaw, & L. S. Mark (1979). Perceptual information for the age level of faces as a higher order invariant of growth.* Journal of Experimental Psychology: Human Perception and Performance, 5, p. 486. © 1979 by the American Psychological Association. Reprinted with permission.

with maturation, which was discussed earlier, has been applied to the cars you see in this figure. The "cute" car on the top represents an early stage in this growth transformation; the one on the bottom represents a later, more "mature" stage. The film and toy industries have capitalized on the abstract nature of the key stimuli that elicit the positive responses to a baby. Many popular cartoon characters have babyish facial proportions, and a systematic study of the proportions of animals appearing in children's picture books revealed that illustrators draw animals so that those intended to appear as younger have relatively larger heads than those intended to appear as older. Moreover, there is a positive relationship between relative head size and how cute an animal is perceived to be.[34]

Figure 4.14 reveals that the disarming quality of Mickey Mouse has significantly increased over the last 50 years, as his creators increased the babyishness of his appearance to match the transformation of this character to his current lovable self. The relative size of Mickey's head and eyes increased over this time, as did the apparent protrusion of his cranium.[35] His limbs also became chubbier and shorter in proportion to his body. Similar changes have been documented for teddy bears during the time period between 1900

FIGURE 4.14   *The neotenization of Mickey Mouse. © Disney Enterprises, Inc.*

and 1985. The gradual changes in facial babyishness suggest that this increase reflected market forces: The more babyish teddy bears must have sold better, a testament to their appeal.[36]

The response to babyish key stimuli in entities other than babies seems to be culturally universal. By funicular and foot, I ascended the heights of Mount Sŏrak-san in the rural countryside of eastern Korea to observe Buddhist monks practicing their spiritual devotion far from the hustle and bustle of worldly endeavors. Near the summit, I found a strange icon indeed: a statue of E.T. nestled in a lovely park for visitors. The joyful squeals of Korean children on encountering E.T. and the facial expressions and utterances of their parents made it abundantly clear, even to one who understood little of the Korean language, that E.T.'s wide-eyed, chinless visage was as endearing to them as it was to me.

E.T. and Disney cartoon characters represent *supernormal key stimuli*, an exaggeration of the qualities of babyishness. For example, as seen at the top of Figure 4.15, the size of Huey, Louie, and Dewey Duck's heads in proportion to their bodies is much greater than it would be in a real baby. Similarly, E.T.'s eyes take up a much larger proportion of his face than do the eyes of a real baby. The film industry undoubtedly uses such supernormal configurations because they elicit stronger responses than those of a normal baby would. Consider which of the two heads in Figure 4.15 you find more appealing. The one preferred by most adults is the supernormal infantile head depicted on the right rather than a normal infantile head like the one on the left.[37]

A preference for supernormal infantile stimuli has been observed among lower animals as well as in humans. A certain type of egg elicits protective behaviors from the ringed plover, and abnormally large (artificial) versions of this egg are preferred by these birds even though they cannot sit on them.[38] Similar reactions to supernormal eggs are shown by the herring gull:

All birds which were given the large egg became very excited and made frantic attempts to cover it. In doing so, they invariably lost their balance, and their evolutions were, I must confess, most amusing to watch.[39]

FIGURE 4.15   *Supranormal Disney cartoon characters,
Huey, Louie, and Dewey (top).* © *Disney Enterprises,
Inc. A normal infant (bottom left) and a supernormal in-
fant (bottom right). Adapted from B. Huckstedt (1965).
Reprinted with permission from I. Eibl-Eibesfeld.
Human ethology. New York: Aldine de Gruyter.* ©
1989.

Supernormal infantile stimuli are also preferred by mice. Infant mice
who have been bred to have a short, round skull and a smaller than average size are preferred over their normal siblings by nursing females.[40] It
isn't only humans who prefer the babyish Mickey Mouse!

The abstract nature of the baby-schema can be seen not only in reactions
to certain cartoon characters and animals but also in the identification of
babyfaced adults. People show a moderate consensus in judging the babyfaceness of faces of various ages. Indeed, people show agreement when
judging the relative babyfaceness of 60-year-old men and women and even
when judging the relative babyfaceness of 6-month-old babies: Some babies are more babyfaced than others.[41] People also can see babyish facial
features in a racially unfamiliar person, which is consistent with the fact
that maturational changes in facial appearance are similar for all humans.[42]
Indeed, as noted previously, there are even similarities across species.

The ability to identify babyfaced individuals develops at an early age.
As mentioned in Chapter 2, infants can differentiate faces based on their

age. Not only can infants differentiate babies from older individuals, but also they can discriminate between babyfaced and mature-faced people of the same age. When 6-month-old infants were seated in an infant carrier between two television monitors, they tended to spend more time looking at the TV screen that showed a photograph of a babyfaced 18-year-old girl than at the screen that showed a mature-faced girl of the same age and attractiveness.[43] Young children, who can verbalize the basis on which they are differentiating two faces, reveal a keen sensitivity to variations in facial babyishness. As noted in Chapter 2, children as young as two and a half can accurately label which drawing of a craniofacial profile or frontal face is a baby, which is a boy, and which is a man.[44] Moreover, preschoolers are able to distinguish the babyfaceness of adults who do not vary in age. When shown two photographs of young adults—either both men or both women—and asked which one looks "most like a baby," children as young as 3 years old tended to choose the same face that college students judged as the more babyfaced of the two.[45]

Not only has it been found that babyfaced individuals are reliably identified, but also research has established the configuration of facial qualities that make someone look babyfaced. People are judged as more babyfaced than their peers if they have facial qualities that differentiate real babies from adults. More babyfaced individuals have rounder and less angular faces, larger and rounder eyes, higher eyebrows, smaller noses, and lower vertical placement of features, which creates a higher forehead and a shorter chin. These facial qualities contribute to a more babyfaced appearance for people ranging in age from 6 months to 60 years. A relatively round face and a small nose bridge strongly predicted babyface ratings of females from age 3 to 60, whereas a round face, large eyes, and thin eyebrows were strong predictors of babyface ratings for males across the same age range. Large eyes also strongly predicted babyface ratings of male infants, and a large cranium did so for female infants.[46]

Although the sex differences in features predicting babyfaceness may simply reflect the particular faces studied, it could also reflect average sex differences in facial appearance resulting from cultural practices or biology. Adult women in Western cultures often pluck their eyebrows and apply makeup to enlarge the appearance of their eyes. We may be so accustomed to seeing relatively large eyes and high, thin eyebrows in adult women that these features become less salient markers of babyfaceness than they are in men. On the other hand, nose bridge size may be a more salient marker of babyfaceness in adult women because, as discussed in Chapter 2, there is more variation in the shape of women's noses. Female noses tend to range from a straight to a somewhat concave profile, with a larger nose bridge in the former than the latter. On the other hand, anatomists have noted that the male nose usually ranges from a straight to a convex profile, with a fairly prominent nose bridge in all.[47] (See Figure 2.1.)

The features that make someone babyfaced show strong similarities across race, although there are also some differences just as there are across sex. The facial characteristics that predict how babyfaced white men are perceived to be are the same for perceivers of all races. More babyfaced white men have a rounder face, larger eyes, and thinner eyebrows, with each of these features showing strong, independent effects. The facial characteristics that predict the babyfaceness of black men are similar to those predicting babyfaceness of white men, as are the size of the effects. Like whites, blacks with rounder faces and larger eyes are seen as more babyfaced. However, rather than the thinner eyebrows of babyfaced white men, babyfaced black men have wider noses than their more mature-faced peers. Finally, a relatively round face and large eyes also predicted the babyfaceness of Korean men, with the effect of a round face being strong for perceivers of all races, and the effect of large eyes being moderate-to-strong. Thinner eyebrows and a wider nose were additional predictors, albeit not for all groups of perceivers.[48] In sum, it appears that a round face and large eyes are culturally universal features of babyfaced men, with thin eyebrows and wide noses also contributing to a babyface in some cases. As noted earlier, these distinguishing features of babyfaced adults are also key stimuli for identifying infants.[49]

Summary

Babies are disarming. They elicit warm, affectionate, and protective responses, and they deter aggression. Such reactions are seen not only in adults and children around the world but also in animals. These reactions seem to be elicited by key stimuli in the infant's appearance. In primates, the coloration of the infant serves as a disarming, key stimulus. In humans, a key feature is the infantile head shape, which is characterized by a large cranium with a perpendicular forehead and small lower face with a receding chin. Other possible key facial stimuli include the infant's large eyes and pupils; full cheeks; fine, high eyebrows; and pug nose. The human response to the key stimuli for babyishness is so strong that it extends to animals and cartoon characters and to adults in whom these stimuli appear. People of all ages and racial backgrounds see a baby's face in individuals who are not babies but merely resemble them. Even young infants can differentiate babyfaced from mature-faced adults. In the next chapter, I demonstrate that adults manifesting key babyish stimuli elicit very different social responses than do their more mature-faced peers.

5

The Boons and the Banes of a Babyface

Perpendicular foreheads . . . are certain signs of weakness, little understanding, little imagination. Retreating foreheads in general denote superiority of imagination and acuteness.[1]

This quotation from an eighteenth-century physiognomist attributes the infantile qualities of weakness and little understanding to adults with perpendicular foreheads. As shown in Figure 4.12, such foreheads are characteristic of an infant's face; therefore, this physiognomist is manifesting a babyface overgeneralization effect. That is, he is overgeneralizing his accurate perception of babies, attributing childlike personality traits to babyfaced adults. This babyface overgeneralization effect may derive from the adaptive value of responding to the valid age information that faces can provide. In particular, appropriate responses to age-related facial cues facilitate evolutionarily important behaviors such as mating with the fertile and nurturing the young. Indeed, Chapter 4 chronicled cross-cultural and cross-species evidence that certain key stimuli in an infant's appearance deter aggression and elicit warm, affectionate, and protective responses. The evolutionary necessity of quick, reliable, and appropriate responses to the needs of babies may have predisposed us to respond in a similar fashion to those whose appearance provides even a partial match to key infantile stimuli. This chapter illustrates the operation of the babyface overgeneralization effect in trait attributions of laypersons, physiognomists, and writers, as well as in social outcomes in the domains of relationships, social influence, occupations, and punishment.

The Babyface Stereotype

The babyface overgeneralization effect shown in the physiognomist's claims about perpendicular foreheads is also manifested in reactions to other facial features, with the more childlike traits of warmth, weakness, naivete, and ingenuousness attributed to adults with more babyish eyes, coloring, noses, mouths, and chins. Although this effect is most pronounced for adults who have an entire configuration of babyish features, it has also been shown in research that varied individual features.

Eyes

Compared with adults, babies have larger eyes relative to the rest of the face and fine, high eyebrows. Each of these eye characteristics produces the babyface overgeneralization effect in impressions of adult faces. Consider the two faces in Figure 5.1. Who looks more honest and less likely to cheat on an exam? Who looks more naive and more likely to believe a farfetched story? In response to these questions, college students gave higher ratings to the more babyfaced, large-eyed faces, such as the one on the bottom.[2] These judgments represent a babyface overgeneralization effect, and they echo physiognomists' claims such as the following: "Brilliant, wide-open eyes denote sincerity, honesty, trustworthiness, and frankness. If carried to the extreme, they denote credulous and trustworthy individuals."[3]

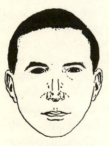

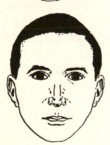

FIGURE   5.1 *Babyish large eyes (bottom) and nonbabyish small eyes (top).*

Students also rated the face on the bottom higher when asked the following questions: Who looks more cuddly and warm and less likely to turn a cold shoulder to your attempts at friendly conversation? Who looks physically weaker and less able to move several boxes of heavy books? Who looks more like the kind of person who would comply with all of his college roommate's wishes about furniture arrangement, quiet hours, radio stations, etc.?[4] These effects of eye size, which are all strong, also echo physiognomists' claims about the round-eyed: "When the under arch described by the upper eyelid is perfectly circular, it always denotes goodness and tenderness, but also . . . weakness . . . ."[5] The tendency to associate large eyes with goodness is shown not only by laypersons and physiognomists but also by novelists. The conspirators in Balzac's epic series of novels, *The Human Comedy*, typically

FIGURE 5.2 *Babyish high eyebrows (left) and nonbabyish low eyebrows (right). C. F. Keating & D. L. Bai (1986). Children's attribution of social dominance from facial cues.* Child Development, *57, p. 1271. © Society for Research in Child Development, Inc.*

have small eyes, and evil characters in Stendhal's *Le Rouge and le Noir* are described as having "evil little grey eyes" and "small dark eyes made to frighten the bravest of us."[6]

Consider the faces in Figure 5.2. Who looks more likely to tell other people what to do and to be respected? Who seldom submits to others? In response to these questions, people from Western cultures typically choose the men on the right, who differ from those on the left only in the lower position of their eyebrows.[7] This large effect of brow height is paralleled by physiognomists' assertions: "The nearer the eyebrows are to the eyes, the more earnest, deep, and firm, the character. The more remote from the eyes, the more volatile, easily moved and less enterprising."[8]

Coloring

Eye and hair color may also distinguish babies, at least among Caucasians, who are often blond and blue-eyed in infancy regardless of their adult coloring. The babyface overgeneralization effect is shown in the attribution of more childlike characteristics to adults with light-colored hair and eyes. Consider Veronica and Betty of Archie comic book fame. Blond, blue-eyed Betty is a warm, naive, and straightforward patsy, whereas raven-haired, dark-eyed Veronica is a cold, shrewd, and deceitful manipulator. The association of weakness, goodness, and naivete with blond hair also occurs in more serious literature. A study of physiognomy in the European novel concluded that strong characters are almost always dark-haired and dark-eyed, and a study of the heroines of the American novelists Melville and Hawthorne revealed that in addition to being portrayed as weaker than the dark-eyed, "the maiden with blue eyes and blonde hair is invariably 'innocent,' 'good,' and 'pure.'" For example, in his novel *Mardi*, Melville describes the golden-haired and blue-eyed heroine, Yillah, as a pure spirit who has seen nothing of the world. In his novel *Pierre*, the dark Isabel describes herself as follows:

> Say Pierre; doth not a funeralness invest me? Was ever a hearse so plumed?—Oh, God! that I had been born with blue eyes, and fair hair! Those make the livery of heaven! Heard ye ever yet of a good angel with dark eyes, Pierre?—no, no, no—all blue, blue, blue—heaven's own blue.[9]

The traits associated with light coloring are consistent with the naivete, warmth, and submissiveness of light-haired, blue-eyed babies, as well as with physiognomists' claims such as the following:

> Blue eyes are, generally, more significant of weakness, effeminacy, and yielding, than brown and black.[10]
> White, tender, clear, weak hair always denotes weak, delicate, irritable, or rather a timid and easily oppressed organization. The black and curly will never be found on the delicate, tender, medullary head . . . we shall seldom find white hair betokening dishonesty, but often dark brown or black.[11]

College students' impressions of blonds and brunettes are consistent with their portrayal in Archie comics and literature. When asked to rate blond and brunette females and males on a number of psychological traits, students judged blonds to be weaker and more delicate, dumber and more simple (particularly blond females), and more weak-willed. However, contrary to the images of Betty and Veronica, college students did not rate blonds as warmer or more sincere than brunettes. Differences in the psychological traits attributed to blonds and brunettes cannot be attributed to differences in their attractiveness, since the trait impressions hold true when they are adjusted for ratings of beauty.[12]

Nose and Mouth

As noted in Chapter 4, nursing babies' lips are redder and proportionately larger than those of adults, and a baby's nose is typically small, wide, and concave, with a sunken bridge, whereas adult noses, particularly men's, are proportionately larger and narrower and are convex with a prominent bridge.[13] The baby-face overgeneralization effect is shown in the attribution of more childlike characteristics to adults with childlike noses and mouths. Consider the people in Figure 5.3. Which one looks physically weaker and less able to move several boxes of heavy books? Who looks more like the kind of person who would comply with all of her college roommate's wishes? Who looks more naive and apt to believe a far-fetched story told on April Fools' Day? In response to these questions, college students gave higher ratings to more babyish, short-nosed faces, like the one on the top in this figure.[14] The perceptions of short-nosed people as weak, compliant, and gullible, which are medium-to-large effects, are consistent with physiognomists' assertions:

FIGURE 5.3   *Babyish short nose (top) and nonbabyish long nose (bottom).*

> Persons with small noses, and hollow in profile . . . their worth most consisted in suffering, listening, learning, and enjoying the beautiful influences of imagination . . . noses, on the contrary, which are arched near the forehead, are capable of command, can rule, act, overcome, destroy.[15]

The fact that the minor manipulation of nose size found in these schematic faces has a medium effect on trait impressions suggests that differences in real noses, like those shown in Figure 5.4, would yield even stronger effects.

Which of the people in Figure 5.5 looks more important, influential, and in charge of others? Who looks less easily influenced or controlled by others? In response to these questions, people gave higher ratings to the less babyish, thin-lipped face on the left.[16] Inasmuch as a thin lip tends to coincide with a straight upper lip area, the strong effect shown in these choices is consistent with the claim of a physiognomist that "the facial sign of firmness . . . is the perpendicular straightness or convexity and stiffness of the center of the upper lip."[17] The relationship between lip thickness and convexity of the upper lip can be seen in Figure 5.6. The babyface overgeneralization effect is shown not only in physiognomists' attributions of greater submissiveness to thick-lipped adults but also in their attributions of more goodness and warmth: "Well-defined, large, and proportionate lips . . . are never seen in a bad, mean, common, false,

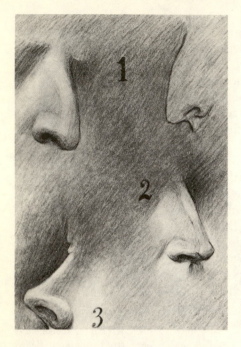

FIGURE 5.4 *Different types of noses. Reprinted by permission of the Putnam Publishing Group, from* Character Reading Through Analysis of the Features, *by Gerald E. Fosbroke. [Copyright] 1914 by Gerald E. Fosbroke; renewed © 1942 by Gerald E. Fosbroke.*

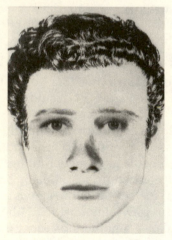

FIGURE 5.5 *Babyish full lips (right) and nonbabyish thin lips (left). Adapted from C. F. Keating (1985). Gender and the physiognomy of dominance and attractiveness.* Social Psychology Quarterly, 48, *Figure 1, p. 64. © by the American Sociological Association. Reprinted with permission.*

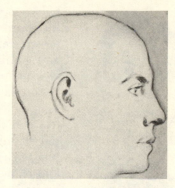

FIGURE 5.6   *Straight "stiff" upper lip with thin nonbabyish lips (left); curved "flexible" upper lip with thick babyish lips (right). Reprinted by permission of the Putnam Publishing Group, from* Character Reading Through Analysis of the Features, *by Gerald E. Fosbroke. [Copyright] 1914 by Gerald E. Fosbroke; renewed © 1942 by Gerald E. Fosbroke.*

crouching, vicious countenance. A lipless mouth, resembling a single line, denotes coldness, industry, a lover of order, precision."[18] These claims are echoed in literature. A study of conspirators and their targets in Balzac's *The Human Comedy* revealed that the active, and often immoral, conspirators are described as having tight, thin, or pinched lips, whereas the lips of their passive and honorable targets are described as thick, full, or fleshy.[19]

Face and Chin Shape

As described in Chapter 4, the shape of the face and chin also distinguishes babies from adults. The vertical placement of features is lower on the baby's face, yielding a relatively larger forehead and a shorter chin. The chin not only elongates with increasing age but also becomes more angular and prominent, jutting forward rather than receding. The baby also has fuller cheeks than the adult, and coupled with a small, round chin, this yields a rounder face. These distinguishing features of a babyface create impressions of childlike traits. Consider the two faces in Figure 5.7. Who looks more dominant? Who looks physically stronger? Who looks more shrewd? College students gave higher ratings to the face on the top with the larger chin and the smaller cranium. These large effects parallel the physiognomist claim that "a small deficient chin stands for weakness of will and physical endurance."[20]

The effects of face and chin shape can also be seen in impressions of schematic profiles, such as those depicted in Figure 5.8. Although the dif-

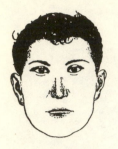

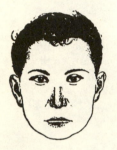

FIGURE 5.7   *Nonbabyish small forehead and large chin (top) and babyish large forehead and small chin (bottom).*

ferences between these two profiles are subtle, the more babyish profile on the top, with its larger cranium, more perpendicular forehead, and smaller, more receding chin, is seen as weaker, less alert, and less reliable than the profile on the bottom. The profile on the top is also seen as less threatening and more lovable but less sexy than the one on the bottom.[21] Differential impressions of people with varying face and chin shapes are not limited to schematic faces. Real people with rounder faces or smaller, rounder chins are judged as less intelligent, dominant, and shrewd than their equally attractive peers with more angular faces and chins.[22] These people are also judged as more warm and honest, echoing physiognomist claims: "The . . . 'let George do it' type is recognized by the round face . . . he is always good tempered, jolly, pleasant."[23] "The angular chin is seldom found but in well-disposed, firm men . . . flatness of chin speaks the cold and dry; smallness, fear; and roundness, with a dimple, benevolence."[24]

An Overall Babyface

Although a single babyish feature, like big eyes or full lips, can have a significant effect on trait impressions, a configuration of babyish features produces an even more marked effect. Consider, for example, the faces in Figure 5.9. The face on the top has larger eyes, a smaller nose, *and* a smaller chin than the one on the bottom. Differences in the perceived submissiveness, weakness, and naivete of these faces are much larger than the corresponding differences in perceptions of faces that differ only in eye size, nose length, or chin size, but not all

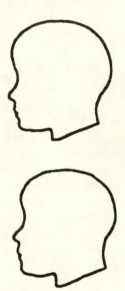

FIGURE 5.8   *Profiles of more babyish forehead and chin (top) and less babyish forehead and chin (bottom). J. B. Pittenger & R. G. Shaw (1975). Aging faces as viscal-elastic events: Implications for a theory of nonrigid shape perceptions. Journal of Experimental Psychology: Human Perception and Performance, 1, p. 376. © 1975 by the American Psychological Association. Reprinted with permission.*

three. Moreover, these large differences in trait impressions cannot be explained by differences in the faces' attractiveness or perceived age.[25]

Real faces typically have some babyish features and some mature features. Yet, as discussed in Chapter 4, such "mixed" faces can be reliably ordered according to their relative babyfaceness. Moreover, trait impressions of real faces also reveal a babyface overgeneralization effect.[26] The size of these effects remains very large for young adult men and medium for women, even when the faces do not differ in age or attractiveness. Thus, the impression that more babyfaced men and women are more dependent, submissive, naive, and weak cannot be attributed to a tendency to perceive them as younger than their more mature-faced peers. Also, the finding that babyfaced men and women are seen as more honest, warm, and affectionate cannot be explained by a tendency to attribute positive traits to more attractive people, a halo effect that is considered further in Chapter 7. These impressions simply reflect the babyface overgeneralization effect. Are they a boon or are they a bane? Being seen as naive and weak

FIGURE 5.9 *Babyish large eyes, short nose, large forehead, and small chin (top); nonbabyish small eyes, long nose, small forehead, and large chin (bottom).*

would be a bane for most adults, particularly men, whereas being seen as honest and warm would be a boon. The value placed on being seen as dependent and submissive may vary with culture, with more boon for those in Eastern cultures, where interdependence is valued, and more bane for those in Western cultures, where autonomy is valued.

Talking Faces

What happens to trait impressions when we can both see someone's face and hear his voice? Does the babyface stereotype persist when we know what the person sounds like? To answer this question, research has examined the impact of a babyface on impressions of videotaped people, all of whom were instructed to say the same thing so that vocal qualities, but not content, would influence impressions. The results revealed that physical measurements of men's babyfaceness predicted how warm and weak they appeared to raters who watched them in a videotape with sound track. Thus, natural variations in people's vocal qualities do not undermine the babyface stereotype, even though childlike traits also are attributed to those with a childlike voice.[27]

The Babyface Stereotype Across the Life Span

As noted earlier, perceivers can identify babyfaced individuals at every age that has been studied, ranging from 6 months to the 60s. Moreover, a strong babyface stereotype is found not only for impressions of young adults, as noted previously, but also for impressions of children and older adults, and it cannot be explained by differences in the attractiveness of babyish versus more mature-looking faces.[28] More babyfaced 6-month-olds are perceived as more dependent and more likely to cry when their parents leave the room than are mature-faced babies of the same age. More babyfaced infants are also perceived as more submissive and more likely to listen to parents when they say "don't touch." More babyfaced babies are also seen as more naive, more likely to be fooled into thinking a hidden toy has disappeared, and less likely to know that it is naughty to do certain things. All of these perceptions are large effects. Although all babies are relatively weak, there are also medium-to-large effects of baby-faceness on perceptions of strength. More babyfaced babies are seen as physically weaker than their mature-faced agemates and as less likely to be strong enough to take a toy away from a baby of the same age. Although all babies are cuddly, those who are more babyfaced are seen as more likely to enjoy being hugged, an effect that is large for girls and medium for boys.

The foregoing impressions of babyfaced babies are repeated in large effects of a babyface on impressions of preschoolers and children in elementary and junior high school. Babyfaced boys and girls at each of these ages are perceived as having less social autonomy: being more dependent and more likely to feel homesick at camp and more submissive and likely to give in to friends' wishes. The babyfaced children are also perceived as more naive: less likely to know right from wrong like an adult and less able to follow complicated instructions. Also, they are perceived as weaker and more affectionate than their mature-faced peers. The differential perceptions of babyfaced and mature-faced children of the same age suggest that more will be expected of mature-faced children and that babyfaced children may be overprotected, given more affection, and held less accountable for their mistakes. As we shall see in Chapter 8, such differential treatment of children who vary in facial maturity does in fact occur.

What about babyfaced older adults? Impressions of their traits are particularly interesting because at this stage of life, looking younger is associated with different traits than is looking babyish. To the extent that baby-faced people in this age group have a more youthful look than their mature-faced agemates, one might expect them to be less vulnerable to age stereotypes, which portray the elderly as weak, dependent, and mentally slow. The youthfulness of babyfaced older adults should make them appear stronger, shrewder, and less submissive than the mature-faced— just the opposite of the babyface stereotype. A babyface does indeed have a large effect on perceived age, with babyfaced people in their late 50s and early 60s looking younger than their more mature-faced peers. Although a babyface tends to make people look younger, it should be noted that being babyfaced and looking young are not exactly the same thing. For example, it is possible for a 60-year-old with babyish big eyes and a round face to look the same age or older than one with mature-looking small eyes and a prominent jaw if the babyfaced person has gray hair and wrinkles but the mature-faced person does not.

Imagine two men who are known to be 65 years old. One is very baby-faced and looks about 55. The other is mature-faced and looks his age. If looking young affects trait impressions more than looking babyfaced, the babyfaced 65-year-old, who looks 55, should be seen as physically stronger, more autonomous, and more astute than his mature-faced counterpart. On the other hand, if looking babyfaced has a greater effect on impressions, the babyfaced senior citizen, like babyfaced individuals of other ages, should be seen as physically weaker, less autonomous, and more naive than the mature-faced man. Research has supported the latter effect. Despite a more youthful appearance, more babyfaced older adults appear more dependent, more submissive, and more likely to give in to friends' wishes than their equally attractive, mature-faced peers. They are also perceived to be less astute: more naive and less able to follow complicated instructions. Whereas all of the foregoing effects of a babyface are strong, there is only a moderate tendency for babyfaced older people to look physically weaker than their mature-faced peers. This may reflect a tendency for a more youthful appearance to offset the babyface stereotype in the case of physical prowess.

The Babyface Stereotype Across Cultures

As noted previously, people clearly can recognize a babyface in someone of a different race. Moreover, the babyface stereotype is racially universal. Babyfaced men representing the three major racial groups are judged by perceivers of all races to be more submissive, naive, physically weak, honest, and warm than their more mature-looking peers. These effects are typically very large, and they all hold true when the men are equal in age and attractiveness.[29] The upshot of the racial universality of the babyface stereotype is that a Korean man who looks highly honest or dominant or strong to Korean perceivers also looks highly honest or dominant or strong to white and black perceivers. Likewise, the psychological traits of particular white or black men are perceived similarly by perceivers representing the three races. These findings suggest that in at least some interracial interactions, a person's facial structure may elicit the same preconceptions about his psychological traits to which he has become accustomed in interactions with people of his own race.

Development of the Babyface Stereotype

Differential responses to babyfaced people develop at an early age, and they may even be innate. As discussed in Chapter 4, infants and children can differentiate babyfaced and mature-faced adults of the same age. Moreover, children who can verbalize their impressions attribute different psychological traits to babyfaced and mature-faced adults. In one study, children between the ages of 4 and 7 were shown pairs of portrait photographs of adults, one of whom had high, babyfaced eyebrows and one of whom had low, mature-faced eyebrows, like those shown in Figure 5.2. Both sexes as well as various ethnic groups were included, although the two photographs in any one pair always depicted people of the same sex and race. After being shown a pair of faces, the children listened to a brief story that described a social interaction in which one person dominates another. For example, one story was as follows: "Look at these two people. They want to play a game together. Which person will say what the rules for the game are?" Children showed a strong tendency to choose the person with lower eyebrows as the dominant one, paralleling judgments of adults.[30] Another study examined children's perceptions of both the dominance and the warmth of babyfaced versus mature-faced adults. Rather than differing on one facial characteristic, such as eyebrow height, people in this study differed in overall babyfaceness, as determined by ratings of adults. Again, each child viewed a pair of faces and listened to a story about a social interaction in which one person either dominates another or is warm to another. A sample warmth story was as follows: "Look at these two people. One of them is very kind and likes to share things with his friends. Can you point to the kind person?" Children responding to these stories showed strong effects of babyfaceness, more often choosing the mature-faced man as the dominant one and the babyfaced man as the warm one, paralleling the babyface stereotype that is shown by adults.[31]

The Babyface Stereotype and Sex Stereotypes

I mentioned in Chapter 2 that the facial characteristics that differentiate babies from adults also tend to differentiate women from men. Indeed, a prominent anatomy textbook states that sex differences in facial features result from earlier cessation of maturation and growth in females and that "more of the morphological characteristics seen during pre-puberty years are retained in the skull of the adult female than in that of the adult male."[32] Women tend to have a smaller jaw and thinner, higher eyebrows, as well as a less prominent browridge and nose bridge, which gives their eyes a more prominent and larger appearance than men's. Women are also lighter skinned than men.

Although it would be simplistic to propose that stereotypes of women can be completely explained by a babyish appearance, it is possible that these sex differences in appearance make some contribution to sex stereotypes. Support for this possibility is provided by the finding that when a baby's sex is unknown to observers, more mature-faced babies are more likely to be perceived as males than are babyfaced babies.[33] The association of facial maturity with maleness, therefore, is shown in the judgments of lay perceivers as well as in anatomy textbooks. Furthermore, the psychological traits attributed to babyfaced adults of either sex parallel stereotypes of women, whereas the traits attributed to the mature-faced parallel stereotypes of men. Like a babyfaced person, the stereotypical female is perceived as warm, weak, submissive, and naive. Like a mature-faced person, the stereotypical male is perceived as cold, strong, dominant, and shrewd.

In one study investigating whether typical sex differences in facial maturity contribute to sex-role stereotypes, schematic male and female faces that varied in facial maturity were rated on sex-stereotypical traits. Typical sex stereotypes were obtained given typical facial maturity—males relatively mature-faced and females relatively babyfaced, as shown in the top half of Figure 5.10. Mature-faced men were seen as less warm than babyfaced women and also more powerful; these were very strong effects. However, when the natural association of sex and facial maturity was eliminated or reversed, as shown on the bottom of Figure 5.10, sex stereotypes were also weakened or reversed. Mature-faced women and babyfaced men were seen as equally warm, and mature-faced women were seen as more powerful than babyfaced men, a very strong effect.[34]

The photos of real people shown in Figure 5.11 reveal that the counter-stereotypical impressions created by a mature-faced woman and a babyfaced man are not limited to schematic faces. It should be noted that the contribution of sex differences in appearance to sex stereotypes is consistent with the cultural universality of these stereotypes.[35] Of course other explanations for sex stereotypes, such as the different social roles of men and women, are also consistent with universality.[36]

The Social Outcomes of a Babyface

A friend of mine from home has a babyface, big eyes, round face, the whole shebang; she always had a problem with people taking her seriously. At

FIGURE 5.10   *Typical and atypical male and female faces.*
Adapted from H. Friedman & L. A. Zebrowitz. The contribution
of facial maturity to sex-role stereotypes. Personality and Social
Psychology Bulletin, 18, *pp. 430–438.* © 1992 *by Heidi Fried-*
man. Reprinted by permission of Sage Publications.

meetings, she would have to have one of her male friends yell at people to
get them to pay attention when her voice kept getting lost in the chatting.
She also had a problem with her parents, who were very protective of her,
much more protective than they were of her older-faced, younger sister.[37]

[Former Harvard Business School Dean] McArthur's disarming demeanor
is a powerful tool that has put him atop two of the nation's most prestigious
institutions. . . . He's got that farm look . . . he looks like everything is going
past him. . . . His demeanor is disarming, but McArthur is one of the savviest
businessmen in the city.[38]

These divergent consequences of a babyface reflect the social interaction component of the babyface overgeneralization effect, and they can be
explained by a facial fit principle and a contrast effect. A facial fit effect
occurs when babyfaced people of either sex not only are expected to have

childlike traits but also are treated-like children, receiving social outcomes that match the warm, submissive, naive, and ingenuous traits that their faces lead others to expect. This effect is illustrated in the first of the preceding quotations, and it is the most common outcome of a babyface.[39] A contrast effect provides an important exception to the facial fit principle, since contrast effects can reverse the normal social outcomes of a babyface when people clearly disconfirm a trait expectation.[40] For example, if babyfaced people show very high competence, not only will they be treated in ways that do not fit the naivete they were expected to have, but they may be treated as if they are more capable than a mature-faced person who has shown the same competent behavior. This effect is illustrated in the second quotation. Similar contrast effects may occur when babyfaced people disconfirm a positive trait expectation. If they are clearly dishonest, not only will their social outcomes fail to "fit" the ingenuous disposition they were expected to manifest, but also their outcomes may be more negative than those of a mature-faced person

FIGURE 5.11 *A babyfaced man and a mature-faced woman. Courtesy of Nancy Carlston.*

who has shown the same dishonest behavior. These and other boons and banes of a babyface have been documented in psychological research in the domains of relationships, persuasion, occupations, and criminal justice decisions.

Making Friends and Influencing People

Do strangers smile at you on the street? Do they talk to you at bus stops? Are the people who are close to you physically affectionate? Do they share their feelings with you? The answer to these questions is more apt to be *yes* for those who are babyfaced. Since they look warmer and more trustworthy, one might expect people with babyfaces to be perceived as more apt to reciprocate a smile or a hug and less apt to rebuff a verbal overture or to violate a confidence. An investigation of over 5,000 social interactions described in diaries kept by 114 college students revealed that the interactions of more babyfaced men involved more self-disclosure and intimacy. Thus, men experience interpersonal outcomes that fit the traits that their faces lead others to expect.[41] Whether these moderate effects of a babyface on social interactions are boons or banes depends, of course, on how gregarious a person is. In either event, a babyface is likely to be helpful in the early stages of making friends and in the evocation of intimacy in established relationships. On the other hand, a babyface may be a liability in the pursuit of sexual intimacy. High school boys who look dominant, an appearance that is very highly correlated with looking mature-faced, were more likely to report having had coitus than those who look more submissive and thus more babyfaced. Moreover, this strong effect held true even when the mature- and babyish-looking boys were equal in attractiveness and in pubertal development, and it was as large or larger than the effects of attractiveness and development. Therefore, babyish-looking boys' relative lack of sexual experience is not caused by their being less attractive or less physically mature. However, it is consistent with the facial fit principle, since sexual activity does not fit the child-like qualities attributed to those who are babyfaced. Whether a babyface also delays girls' sexual experience remains to be determined.[42]

Do you have trouble persuading others to see things your way or to do what you want them to do? Do people fail to take you seriously? Do they expect you to follow their lead? These are likely social interaction patterns for those who are babyfaced. Because they look naive and submissive, the babyfaced are more apt than the mature-faced to be the recipients of social influence attempts. Indeed, highly assertive men and women, who tend to dominate others, prefer to date babyfaced rather than mature-faced people.[43] This large preference for the babyfaced is not shown by less assertive individuals. In addition to attracting domineering types, babyfaced individuals may be less apt than the mature-faced to succeed in their own efforts to influence others. For example, in the diary study described previously, babyfaced men reported moderately less influence and control in their social interactions. However, there are certain circumstances in which the babyfaced may be *more* influential than the mature-faced, thanks to their trustworthy appearance.

How persuasive a person is depends on how credible or believable that person is. Credibility, in turn, depends partly on how much expertise a person seems to have. This is where babyfaced people fall short. Compared with a mature-faced person of similar age and background, a babyfaced person is less likely to be viewed as knowing all the relevant facts about an issue. Credibility also depends on how trustworthy a person seems to be. Someone who is perceived as an expert who knows all the facts, but is not perceived as trustworthy enough to report those facts, is unlikely to be persuasive. It is on the dimension of trustworthiness that babyfaced people have an edge. Thanks to an honest face, they are more likely to be viewed as stating what they sincerely believe to be true.

Advertisers exploit the unique persuasive strengths of babyfaced versus mature-faced agents of persuasion by casting them in different types of television commercials. In a systematic investigation of such effects, college students read transcripts of 150 television commercials sampled from weekday broadcasts on three major networks, and they rated how much expertise and how much trustworthiness was revealed in the persuasive appeals contained in these commercials. Another group of students watched the same 150 commercials with no sound and they rated how babyfaced the spokespersons in each commercial were. The sound track was eliminated so that the content of the commercial message would not influence the facial ratings. It could then be determined whether the appeals given by babyfaced and mature-faced actors differed in expertise, trustworthiness, or both.[44]

Appeals were rated as "expert" when spokespersons appeared to have all the facts and to be knowledgeably communicating objective and valid information about a product by giving factual evidence on its behalf and by using aids such as statistics, scientific information, and doctors' reports. Appeals were rated as "trustworthy" when spokespersons appeared to be sincerely and honestly communicating product information that they believed by virtue of being a product user. These product users gave "testimonial" evidence on the product's behalf, emphasizing what they personally liked and believed rather than reporting objective facts.

It was found that in commercials that cast a babyfaced actor or actress as the product spokesperson, the persuasive appeals relied less on expertise and more on trustworthiness than in commercials featuring a mature-faced actor or actress. In a toothpaste commercial, "facts" are more likely to be spouted by mature-faced actors. Blowing smoke through a cloth, the mature-faced product spokesperson says:

> See this? That's how smoke stains your teeth. But Topol smoker's tooth polish can get your teeth brighter again. [Shows copy of a survey.] Of 250,000 Topol users surveyed, 94 percent said *yes,* they'd continue buying Topol. Use Topol and watch your teeth get whiter.

Babyfaced spokespersons, on the other hand, are more apt to give personal testimonials: "Topol really does the job. My teeth are whiter and brighter."

Those who produce commercials are evidently guided by the degree to which an actor's facial appearance fits the image of credibility in the commercial copy. They operate on the tacit or explicit assumption that mature-faced people "look right" delivering expert messages, whereas babyfaced people "fit the part" for trustworthy communications. This policy is consistent with evidence that an ad will be most effective when the message that is conveyed converges with the image of the endorser.[45] Since producers would be out of a job if their casting choices didn't yield persuasive commercials, it appears that babyfaced people not only are cast in different roles but also are more persuasive when the essence of the appeal is "trust me" and less persuasive when the appeal emphasizes expertise.

It is interesting to note that a persuader's age and sex have effects parallel to those of facial maturity. Like babyfaced people of either sex, women tend to be cast in commercials with appeals that are high in trustworthiness and low in expertise. Also like babyfaced people of all ages, younger persuasive agents tend to deliver appeals that require trustworthiness but not expertise. Moreover, the moderate effects of a babyface on the trustworthiness and expertise of appeals were comparable in magnitude to those of sex and age. Thus, the credibility of babyfaced individuals, regardless of age and sex, is similar to that of women or young people: they are seen as persuasive when emphasizing their trustworthiness. The credibility of mature-faced individuals, on the other hand, is similar to that of men and older people: They are seen as persuasive when relying on their expertise.[46]

When listening to some persuasive communication, one may have questions about the communicator's expertise or trustworthiness. Did Newt Gingrich really know what he was talking about when he argued for massive cuts in Medicare to save it from bankruptcy? Was Bill Clinton being totally candid during the 1992 presidential campaign when he recounted his draft status during the Vietnam War? The facial appearance of the communicator is likely to influence how we resolve our doubts. If the listener is skeptical about expertise, then a mature-faced communicator should have an edge, since his face will convey knowledgeability. If the listener is skeptical about trustworthiness, then a babyfaced communicator should have an edge, since his face will convey sincerity.

The foregoing conjectures concerning the impact of facial appearance on the fates of U.S. politicians are supported by a moderate effect of babyfaceness on students' reactions to candidates for a student position on the Tuition Advisory Board at a state college.[47] After viewing a videotaped speech by a candidate who was campaigning against tuition increases for out-of-state students, students indicated how persuaded they were by the arguments they had heard. When the voters had reason to suspect that the candidate's position might be tainted by self-interest—an out-of-state student arguing against a raise in tuition for out-of-staters—they were more persuaded by a babyfaced candidate than by a mature-faced candidate who gave the very same speech. The "honest face" of the babyfaced candidate compensated for the doubts raised by her apparent self-interest. A different pattern of persuasion was revealed when expertise rather than trustworthiness was in question—the candidate was a freshman with a "gut" major and no participation in university activities. In this case, they were more persuaded by a mature-faced than a babyfaced candidate giving the identical speech. The shrewd face of the mature-faced candidate compensated for the doubts raised by her uncertain expertise.

In addition to the bane of looking inexpert, another problem for the babyfaced is looking submissive. As noted earlier, babyfaced people report less control over their social interactions, and people who like to dominate others are drawn to the babyfaced because they expect it to be easy to manipulate them. Being babyfaced also has a strong negative effect on the likelihood that high school students will hold positions of leadership.[48] However, anecdotal evidence suggests that the contrast effect can provide a hidden boon to the perception that babyfaced people are not leaders. A very babyfaced colleague, who chaired a committee interviewing candidates for Dean of the Graduate School, recalled learning how one of the candidates had reacted to her. Noting that he had anticipated that the committee members would "eat her up alive," he marveled at her leadership during a politically tough meeting. Her ability to influence others stood in sharp contrast to his negative expectations and may have seemed more forceful than the same behavior by a mature-faced person. Therefore, when assertive behavior by the babyfaced is recognized, it may be more compelling. Similarly, when conciliatory behavior by the mature-faced is recognized, it may be more valued. It is possible that these hidden boons to looking submissive or dominant will turn sour if the behavior is too extreme. Very assertive behavior may seem so out of character for a babyfaced person that it is viewed as strident and tolerated less well than the same behavior by the mature-faced. Similarly, very conciliatory behavior may seem so out of character for a mature-faced person that it is viewed as "wimpy" and tolerated less well than the same behavior by the babyfaced. Like other parallels between the effects of facial maturity and those of sex that were mentioned earlier, it is interesting to note that very assertive behavior by women and very conciliatory behavior by men may have similar effects.[49]

Occupational Outcomes

The corporate jungle victor depicted in the cartoon in Figure 5.12 is mature-faced: narrow eyes, broad jaw, angular face. The vanquished head that is mounted on the wall is babyfaced: large eyes, small chin, round face. The fact that this cartoon would not be as humorous if the faces were reversed uncovers our assumptions about who looks like the boss.

Stereotyped images of executives have actually been codified into the Merton System of face reading, which was widely used by personnel directors from the 1920s to the late 1940s and may be practiced by some even today. This complex system involves rating several aspects of more

DUFFY®   by **BRUCE HAMMOND**

FIGURE 5.12   *Duffy. © 1990 Universal Press Syndicate. Reprinted with permission. All rights reserved.*

than one hundred specific locations on each side of the face. The results of these ratings are then synthesized to determine the match to various vocations. Although the vast majority of today's personnel officers would surely disavow the Merton System, the fact is that facial appearance continues to play a role in personnel decisions. Such effects can be explained by the facial fit principle.

The fact that babyfaced adults are perceived as weaker, warmer, and more naive, honest, and submissive than the mature-faced should affect the kinds of jobs for which they are seen as most suited, and research has shown this to be true. Business management students evaluated eight job applicants on the basis of brief resumes containing a black-and-white photograph of the applicant and some background information, including age, employment experience, high school and college class ranks, and college grade point average. The resumes depicted equal numbers of mature-faced and babyfaced males and females. All applicants were approximately the same age, and the babyfaced and mature-faced applicants were equally attractive. Finally, half of the applicants of each sex and facial maturity (e.g., one of the two babyfaced males) were high achievers, ranking in the top third of their high school and college graduating classes and achieving an A- grade point average in college. The other half were moderate achievers, ranking in the middle third of their high school and college classes and achieving a B grade point average in college. Students were given a one-page description of each of two job openings and asked to judge the suitability of all eight applicants for both jobs.[50]

Students evaluated applicants for two openings in a bank: the positions of loan counselor and loan officer. The loan counselor job description stressed attributes that are associated with babyfaced individuals, calling for submissiveness ("must yield to loan approval/disapproval decisions of the officers") and warmth ("must be a warm and encouraging person, who can understand and determine individuals' needs"). The loan officer job description called for dominance ("will be responsible for making decisions about the authorization of loans"), some degree of coldness ("must be willing to disapprove a loan request"), and shrewdness ("must be a shrewd financial administrator"). Babyfaced applicants were rated higher than the mature-faced for the loan counselor position, and mature-faced applicants were rated higher than the babyfaced for the loan officer position.

Two other applicant attributes—sex and achievement—influenced evaluations of suitability for the jobs in a manner that paralleled the effects of a babyface. Male applicants and high-achieving applicants were rated higher than females or low achievers for the position of bank loan officer. The moderate-to-large effects of applicant babyfaceness and sex were similar in magnitude. Thus, babyfaceness created as much of a handicap for men who aspired to the leadership position as gender did for women. Applicants' achievement, on the other hand, had a stronger effect on hiring recommendations than facial maturity. Further evidence for the connection between high achievement and facial maturity is provided in the finding that the high-achieving applicants were rated as more mature-faced than the moderate achievers despite the fact that they had the very same faces. (This was accomplished by systematically switching the photos attached to each resume so that a face that was attached to one level of achievement for half of the raters was attached to the other level for the remaining raters.) Thus, high achievement is perceived to "fit" a mature face. These results suggest that facial maturity may have consequences not only for hiring decisions but also for decisions concerning promotion and salary increments. Mature-faced employees may be erroneously perceived as higher achievers, and they may consequently receive an unfair share of promotions and remuneration.

The recommendation of babyfaced and mature-faced individuals for different jobs is a reliable effect,[51] and the general finding that people are favored for jobs that match the traits conveyed by their appearance has implications for a wide range of employment decisions. All other things being equal, the facial fit principle predicts that babyfaced people should be employed in jobs requiring a more submissive, warm, and honest nature and lower achievement than jobs held by mature-faced people: the "service" and "helping" professions, such as nursing, teaching, social work, and counseling. Research extending laboratory findings on personnel recommendations to the real world has tested this prediction by examining the effects of people's appearance on the jobs they actually occupy.

College students rated the babyfaceness of men and women in their 50s whose faces were depicted in black and white slides. Another group of raters judged the extent to which the jobs held by these individuals required the traits typically attributed to babyfaced people. These judges responded only to the occupational label and did not know the appearance of the person who held the job. There was high agreement among the judges regarding the extent to which the various jobs required babyfaced traits. It could then be determined whether babyfaced people actually had more "babyfaced" jobs. Compared with their mature-faced peers, babyfaced women did indeed have more babyfaced jobs, such as teacher and nursing aide. This moderate effect held true even when the babyfaced and mature-faced women were equated in attractiveness, educational attainment, and relevant personality traits. Indeed, the effect of babyfaceness on job type was comparable in magnitude to the independent effect of a submissive personality. These results suggest that babyfaced individuals are more likely to select or be selected for certain jobs quite apart from any unique qualifications for those jobs. It is interesting, however, that more babyfaced men did not have more babyfaced jobs. Rather, it was shorter men whose jobs were more babyfaced, and this moderate effect of a childlike bodily appearance was as large as the effect of an undependable personality.[52]

The astute reader may have observed that the jobs given to babyfaced people are all stereotyped as "women's work." This is in fact a meaningful connection. As noted previously, there are parallels between the kinds of jobs for which women are favored and those for which the babyfaced are favored, and there are also parallels between the facial appearance of women and the babyfaced. Just as typical sex differences in facial maturity contribute to sex-stereotyped trait attributions, so may they contribute to sex-stereotyped occupations. To investigate this possibility, people were asked to rate the suitability of schematic male and female faces for various occupational roles. In a typical facial maturity condition, in which males were relatively mature-faced and females relatively babyfaced, typical occupational stereotypes were obtained: Men were seen as less likely to take care of children than women but more likely to be financial providers. However, when the natural association of sex and facial maturity was eliminated or reversed, these moderate-sized stereotypes were weakened. Mature-faced women and babyfaced men, like those shown in Figure 5.10, were seen as equally likely to take care of children and as equally likely to be financial providers. It thus appears that typical sex differences in babyfaceness may contribute to sex-stereotypic occupational roles.[53]

Whereas babyfaced individuals are overrepresented in the helping professions, the facial fit principle suggests that they should be underrepresented in jobs requiring physical strength. As the cartoon in Figure 1.4 of Chapter 1 suggests, the round-faced, chinless babyfaced person is un-

likely to be seen as having the "muscle" or the "mettle" to be a police officer, athlete, or soldier. Among the mature-faced jobs that were less often
held by babyfaced than mature-faced women were those requiring physical strength, such as athlete. The babyfaced should also be underrepresented in jobs requiring leadership or shrewdness. Consistent with this
reasoning, babyfaced women were less likely to hold "mature-faced"
jobs, such as forewoman or law professor. Again, this effect was not
found for babyfaced men. Rather, it was short men who were less likely to
hold "mature-faced" jobs.

Investigations of the role of a babyface in men's military service also
have produced results concerning leadership jobs that are consistent with
the facial fit principle. More dominant-looking, mature-faced West Point
cadets achieved higher military ranks during their junior and senior years
than their more babyish-looking classmates. More dominant-looking men
were also more successful when a highly select group of soldiers com-
peted for the highest ranks of general near the end of their careers. The effect of appearance on rank was moderate-to-strong during the college
years but only weak at career's end. However, that weak effect is quite remarkable given that later rank was predicted from appearance during
college, more than 20 years earlier. At West Point as well as during com-
petition for the rank of general, promotions are made by members of a
board who personally know the candidates—and their appearance. On
the other hand, at mid career, when promotions are made by boards who
generally have no direct contact with the candidates, there is no relationship between appearance and military rank.[54]

Whereas a babyfaced appearance can be a bane when it comes to competing for promotions in the military, a contrast effect may make it a boon
if the babyfaced person is known to have performed heroically. A study of
men who served in the military during World War II and the Korean War
revealed a small-to-moderate tendency for more babyfaced soldiers to be
more likely to win a military award even when they had no more combat
experience than their mature-faced comrades. Although it is possible that
babyfaced men actually have traits quite opposite to the babyface stereotype, behaving even more heroically than the mature-faced, this unexpected finding is also consistent with the contrast effect. Inasmuch as
courageous actions violate the expectation that babyfaced individuals are
submissive, warm, and weak, such actions by babyfaced men may earn
more recognition because they are more striking than equivalent acts of
valor by the mature-faced.[55]

A babyfaced appearance may also have implications for achieving positions of political leadership. On the one hand, the apparent submissiveness and naivete of the babyfaced would seem to disadvantage them for
positions as political leaders. On the other hand, the apparent warmth

and trustworthiness of the babyfaced should be an asset in such positions. Indeed, the traits that Americans deem important in a president include not only leadership and competence but also trustworthiness, which includes integrity and empathy. Whereas the extremely mature-faced corporate executive shown in Figure 5.12 conveys leadership and competence, his face falls rather short on the trustworthy dimension. This attribute is conveyed by a babyface. It appears that the face that best fits Americans' image of a political leader would contain a mixture of babyish and mature features. It should be noted that this portrait of the ideal "presidential" face may be culturally variable. For example, Americans expect less authority and aggressive behavior from political leaders than the French do, and they respond less positively than the French to facial displays conveying anger and threat.[56] This suggests that Americans would respond more positively than the French to candidates with non-threatening, babyish features. Although research has not systematically examined the facial configurations of successful political candidates, evidence for the importance of appearance in selecting political leaders is provided by the commentary accompanying portraits of early U.S. politicians that are now hung in the National Portrait Gallery in Washington D.C. In the first half of the nineteenth century, when presidential aspirants generally did not campaign themselves, these portraits were important promotional devices, carried by supporters from one demonstration to another.

Recent trends in management may begin to redress the disadvantaged position of babyfaced would-be leaders. A recent article in the business section of *The Boston Globe* began with the following memo to top executives: "If you still have a picture of Gen. George Patton above your desk, you are in trouble. For a new model, try . . . Captain Kirk, Vaclav Havel, or the woman who rescued Girl Scouts of the USA, Inc."[57] Kirk, Havel, and Hesselbein (the Girl Scout leader) are more babyfaced and also less "macho" than General Patton. According to prominent business leaders, successful executives in the '90s have more of a warm, fuzzy, and democratic style than the "tough boss" types of the past. In a recent annual report of the General Electric company, the CEO stated that managers who insist on being "the autocrat, the big shot, the tyrant" will be losing their jobs to those who inspire "teamwork, trust and empowerment."

Mature-faced executives, who project an impression of the "tough boss," may lose their edge not only because of changes in the qualities of an ideal executive but also because there may be an advantage for those whose appearance belies their leadership skills. A quotation earlier in this chapter described the former dean of the Harvard Business School, dubbed "the disarming dean," whose effectiveness was attributed in part to his naive appearance. The perception of babyfaced McArthur as naive and trustworthy may have enabled him, by disarming others, to become a more effective leader than a mature-faced person whose directive efforts may meet more resistance. Greater efficacy of babyfaced leaders may derive not only from their ability to disarm the opposition but also from the aforementioned contrast effects in social influence and military awards, whereby bold behavior by a babyfaced person may be more compelling. On the other hand, as noted earlier, if the contrast with expectations is too extreme, it can elicit negative reactions that are detrimental to occupational success. The injustice of this reaction was recognized in a 1989 Supreme Court decision in favor of Ann Hopkins, whose promotion to partner in an accounting firm was denied because she was seen as too aggressive and unfeminine. The Court ruled that "an employer who objects to aggressiveness in women but whose positions require this trait places women in an intolerable Catch 22: out of a job if they behave aggressively and out of a job if they don't."[58] The same logic would apply to those who object to aggressiveness in babyfaced employees.

Violating Social Norms

The disarming quality of babyfaced people not only may facilitate their success as leaders but also may help them to violate social norms with impunity. This phenomenon has often been exploited in literature through characters who are not what they seem.

> As though nature concealed a trap, Cathy had from the first a face of innocence. Her hair was gold and lovely; wide-set hazel eyes. . . . Her nose was delicate and thin, and her cheekbones high and wide, sweeping down to a small chin so that her face was heart-shaped. Her mouth was . . . what used to be called a rosebud. Her ears were very little.[59]

Cathy Ames, prostitute and murderess in John Steinbeck's novel *East of Eden*, was not the innocent she appeared to be, and her deceptive, babyfaced appearance enhanced her ability to manipulate others. Babyfaced people in real life can also "get away with murder," if not literally then figuratively.

> [Billy] Crystal has a rare gift: People look at him and like him. He isn't threatening. He isn't demanding. You laugh because you want to, not because he insists on it. And he's clean . . . there is an air of wholesomeness that makes his double entendres seem singularly innocent.[60]

The American folk hero Babe Ruth is another prime example. In writing about Babe's life, Brendan Boyd noted that his "enormous head and broad face dominated every photograph he ever appeared in making him look like an extraterrestrial parade float." This babyfaced, "E.T." appear-

THE FAR SIDE   By GARY LARSON

And so I ask the jury . . . is that the face of a
mass murderer?

FIGURE 5.13   *The Far Side. Cartoon by Gary
Larson is reprinted by permission of Chronicle
Features, San Francisco, CA. All rights reserved.*

ance was clearly disarming. Boyd characterized Babe's belligerent behavior as a childish refusal to grow up. One can only speculate how the same behavior might have been viewed had it emanated from a man with a more ominous-looking face:

> He punched umpires, feuded with managers, baited commissioners, jumped teams, held out, was fined, suspended, missed curfews, trains, signals. It was a lifelong insurgency . . . nothing about it was bullying or rancorous. . . . Ruth's insubordination was only part of a larger childishness.[61]

The downside of Babe's childish appearance is that he was never allowed to become a manager, a disappointment that he took to mean that he was not taken seriously.

Most of us have known someone who, like Babe Ruth, was able to violate social norms with impunity, "getting away with murder." Gary Larson's cartoon in Figure 5.13 captures this effect. This cartoon echoes not only everyday observations about babyfaced people but also writings of the late nineteenth century school of "criminal anthropology." Influenced by evolutionary theory, these criminologists focused on the biology of criminals. Cesare Lombroso, the founding father of this scientific movement, argued that born criminals could be recognized by their morphological resemblance to apes. The "apelike" facial markers of the born criminal yield quite a different appearance from Larson's innocent defendant.

In his work, *The Female Offender*, Lombroso reported that, compared with normal women, female offenders are more apt to have receding foreheads, overjutting brows, large lower jaws, and prominent cheekbones.[62] Lombroso's female offenders clearly do not look like the babyfaced defendant in the Far Side cartoon. Indeed, their apelike features yield a much less babyfaced appearance than the average female, since human babies show less resemblance to our evolutionary ancestors than do human adults. An assumed link between facial maturity and criminality is also revealed in Lombroso's studies of hair color and eye color. He reported a higher incidence of dark-haired female offenders and a lower incidence of fair-haired offenders than in the general population. Dark eyes were also reputed to be more prevalent among female offenders than in the general population. Reported crime rates in geographical regions with varying numbers of dark- and fair-haired people revealed a similar pattern. Compared with regions of France and Italy in which light-haired people predominated, areas where dark hair was more prevalent reputedly had a higher incidence of "crimes of blood." Lombroso also reported a relationship between criminality and the babyishness of head shapes. Italian and French provinces marked by a predominance of dolichocephaly (long, narrow, mature-looking faces, as described in Chapter 2) showed an above-average incidence of crimes, whereas those marked by a predominance of brachycephaly (short, wide, juvenile-looking faces) showed a crime rate much below that for the country as a whole. These law-abiding brachycephalics would resemble Larson's babyfaced, innocent defendant. In sum, Lombroso's assertions about the physical markers of criminality can be viewed as a component of the babyface overgeneralization effect. People whose facial structure or coloring is least babyish are the ones whom Lombroso viewed as criminal.

The fact that we laugh at Larson's cartoon provides evidence for the persistence of Lombroso's assumptions about the recognizability of criminals. Additional evidence for such persistence is provided by research that showed a strong consensus in the general public as to who looks like a criminal.[63] Moreover, when students were asked to evaluate the guilt or innocence of photographed men, their verdicts depended on the defendants' appearance. For example, students delivered more guilty verdicts if a defendant charged with murder had been judged by others to look like a murderer.[64]

Facial stereotypes of criminals are held by law enforcement agents as well as the general public. In a book for new police officers, a veteran London police officer wrote the following:

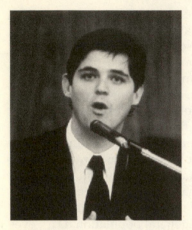

FIGURE 5.14 *William Kennedy Smith. AP/Wide World Photos.*

Several policemen talk about the ability to "feel" or "smell" a criminal, or to have a "sixth sense" about a person. What they are really talking about is the ability to see a criminal when they come across one. It is basically a question of being able to categorize or stereotype a person. ...The most skillful policeman will therefore not only be able to recognize a criminal when he sees one, but will often be able to state what type of previous conviction the particular criminal has.[65]

Anecdotal evidence, Larson's cartoon, and Lombroso's views about criminal faces suggest that babyish facial qualities may affect judicial decisions. The baby-faced appearance of William Kennedy Smith, shown in Figure 5.14, may have helped to undermine the credibility of the allegation that he committed rape. Reactions to Oliver North during the Iran-Contra scandal may be attributed at least in part to the fact that he does not fit our image of a man who would engage in treasonous activity.

During the "Irangate" hearings, Oliver North became almost a folk hero, receiving thousands of supportive telegrams and letters from around the country. At the same time that people were showing such strong sentiment for North, public opinion polls revealed that 72 percent of Americans rejected his cause—providing military aid to the Nicaraguan Contras. What then can account for North's widespread appeal? His boyish appearance may provide a clue. Oliver North looked the obedient innocent that he claimed to be when he told jurors that he felt like a pawn in a chess game played by giants and that he did not know that his actions were unlawful. In response to questioning by the chief counsel for the Senate committee investigating the Iran contra affair, North stated the following:

> This lieutenant colonel is not going to challenge a decision of the commander in chief, for whom I still work. I am proud to work for that commander in chief and if that commander in chief tells this lieutenant colonel to go stand in the corner and sit on his head, I will do so. ... If ... the activities were authorized by the commander in chief, the head of state, in his capacity to do, what would be wrong? You know, maybe I'm overly naive, but I don't see what would be wrong with that.[66]

As discussed in the last chapter, babyfaced people are seen as submissive and naive, just what North was claiming to be in the foregoing statements to the congressional investigating committees. Such people do not look like they are sufficiently shrewd or dishonest to have willfully broken the law, although they may be seen as negligent. Those judging North's case apparently agreed. He was ultimately acquitted of all charges and retained sufficient public regard to make a good showing in a 1994 congressional campaign.

Should the average person be concerned about how innocent he looks? Certainly few are ever involved in legal proceedings like those that faced Willy Smith or Ollie North. But most of us have some dealings with the law during our lifetime. A policeman once pulled me over as I tried to merge back into traffic after allowing a fire engine to pass. He walked up to my car shouting that I had cut him off. Then he looked at me, softened his tone, and told me that he'd let me go with a warning, since I looked like I didn't know what I was doing. Traffic violations, tax audits, and even civil suits are situations that confront the average citizen, and in all of these situations, a babyface can make a difference. This phenomenon has been demonstrated in the legal opinions offered by ordinary people as well as in the decisions of real judges in small claims courts.

One study investigated the effects of appearance on legal outcomes by eliciting college students' reactions to defendants whose cases were summarized in a pretrial intake report that is used by the Boston District Court System.[67] Although the cases were fictitious, the reports were filled out in an authentic manner, and affixed to each one was a picture of a babyfaced or a mature-faced male defendant. The photos of the baby-faced and mature-faced defendants were taken from a college yearbook; therefore, they were all of people who were about the same age. Preliminary ratings ensured that the people were also equal in attractiveness and that all of them had a serious facial expression. Therefore, if decisions favored babyfaced defendants, this couldn't be due to their greater attractiveness, younger age, or more pleasant facial expression.

The students judged defendants in one of four different cases. In two cases, the defendant was a waiter who was accused of underreporting tip income to the IRS. In one of these cases, students learned that the defendant was charged with the deliberate falsification of records, and in the other they learned that he was charged with the negligent maintenance of records. The other two cases were civil suits in which a plaintiff claimed that she had developed an allergic reaction to a home-cleaning product that the defendant had sold to her during his summer employment as a door-to-door salesman. The plaintiff claimed either that the defendant had actively misinformed her about the potential hazards of the product or that he had neglected to warn her about such hazards. In all four cases, the defendant had pled not guilty to the charges against him. After reading the pretrial intake report, which provided all of the information about only one of the four cases, the students were asked to decide whether they considered the defendant to be innocent or guilty of the offense with which he was charged.

Because babyfaced people are perceived to be more naive and more honest than their mature-faced peers, it was expected that babyfaced defendants would be less likely to be judged guilty of intentional offenses but more likely to be found guilty of those involving negligence. This is precisely what happened. Whether the offense was underreporting income to the IRS or failing to warn a customer about a product's hazards, if the action was alleged to be intentional, babyfaced defendants were less likely to be found guilty. Although this effect was weak, it suggests that babyfaced people look less likely to commit intentional wrongs, a conclusion supported by other research, discussed later in this chapter. On the other hand, when the very same action was alleged to be negligent, babyfaced defendants were *more* likely to be found guilty. This large effect indicated that they looked naive enough to have unwittingly screwed up. These results are consistent with the facial fit principle: Verdicts depend on the match between alleged crimes and traits suggested by an individual's facial appearance.

There was an interesting twist to these findings when the pretrial intake reports were changed to indicate that the defendant had pled guilty to the charges rather than not guilty. Since the defendant was admittedly guilty, students who read these reports were not asked to render a verdict. Rather, they were asked to indicate how severe a sentence they felt was appropriate for the described offense: Should it be close to the minimum sentence or close to the maximum? The recommended sentences revealed a small contrast effect. More specifically, men who admitted negligent misconduct received more severe punishment for their offense if they were mature-faced. Thus, negligent behavior by the mature-faced produces a contrast effect: They are punished more harshly for negative behavior that fails to fit expectations. The contrast effect was also shown when men admitted intentional misconduct. In this case, it was the babyfaced defendants who tended to receive more severe punishment. We may be more horrified and angered when we believe that an intentional or heinous crime has been committed by someone who looks harmless, perhaps because this threatens faith in our ability to steer clear of dangerous people. We would somehow feel safer if Jeffrey Dahmer, the Milwaukee murderer and necrophiliac, looked as evil as his deeds.

An investigation of over five hundred cases heard in small claims courts by 25 judges in the greater Boston area demonstrated that babyfaced and mature-faced people experience different fates in the hands of actual judges.[68] In each of these cases, two observers rated the babyfaceness and attractiveness of both the plaintiff and the defendant as they approached the judge's bench to give their testimony. Whereas the study with student judges examined reactions to individuals who were either extremely babyfaced or extremely mature-faced, a wide range of babyfaceness was represented among the litigants in this study. Observers also rated the attractiveness of the litigants. After making these appearance ratings, they listened to the testimony and determined whether the plaintiff was accusing the defendant of intentional or negligent actions, how much monetary damage the plaintiff claimed, whether the defendant admitted or denied responsibility, and what kind of support for their case the defendant and plaintiff provided, such as a lawyer, a witness, photographs, or other material evidence to document damages. Finally, the observers obtained information about the judge's decision from the Clerk of Court's records department on a date subsequent to the proceedings.

Babyfaceness had a dramatic impact on the outcomes for defendants who denied responsibility for claims involving intentional actions. Indeed, the effect of the defendants' babyfaceness was comparable in magnitude to the effect of evidence to support their case. A typical case was that of the defendant who did not pay for a car battery installed by the plaintiff. The defendant was accused of doing something intentionally: requesting a battery and then refusing to pay for it. The defendant denied this wrongdoing, arguing that he had not authorized the installation. In cases such as this one, 92 percent of the most mature-faced defendants were found at fault, whereas only 45 percent of the most babyfaced defendants received this judgment. Even experienced courtroom judges are vulnerable to the perception that babyfaced people are too honest and naive to have a high probability of committing a premeditated offense. The effect of babyfaceness on judicial outcomes was not limited to defendants falling at the two extremes of appearance. Rather, small increments in defendants' babyfaceness were accompanied by consistent declines in judgments against them. Not only were babyfaced defendants less likely than the mature-faced to be found at fault for claims involving intentional actions, but also highly babyfaced defendants were more likely to be found at fault for negligent than intentional actions, whereas the reverse was true for the highly mature-faced defendants.

It should be noted that the impact of the defendant's babyfaceness on the judgments was robust. The effect held true regardless of the litigants' age, attractiveness, and degree of support for their case. The foregoing consequences of a defendant's babyfaceness also held true regardless of the plaintiff's appearance. However, this was not the case when defendants admitted fault for the claim against them. In these instances, the size of award ordered by the judge to compensate the plaintiff for damages depended on the babyfaceness of both the plaintiff and the defendant. As defendants became more mature-faced, they had to pay larger awards to plaintiffs but only when the plaintiffs were relatively babyfaced. Babyfaced plaintiffs seem to be protected from admittedly guilty, mature-faced defendants by the judgment of large awards, whereas average-faced or mature-faced plaintiffs do not receive this protective treatment. Consider, for example, the case in which the defendant, as maid of honor, admitted to accidentally ironing a huge hole in the middle of the bride's wedding gown just before the ceremony. Both the bride and the maid of honor were relatively mature-faced, and the bride was not awarded all of the damages she sought. Had the bride been very babyfaced and the maid of honor mature-faced, the bride may have successfully exacted the award she requested: payment for the dress and the wedding pictures.

In any particular encounter with the legal system, there are many factors to consider when deciding how to proceed, and the insights to be gained from the research on babyface effects are no substitute for a good lawyer. Still, this research does provide some useful information. Babyfaced people who wish to enter a not guilty plea may be better off pleading not guilty to a charge of intentional misconduct than to a charge of negligence, assuming that the charge can be negotiated. However, this is a calculated risk. Although babyfaced people are less likely to be found guilty of the intentional offense, the penalty is likely to be higher for that offense if they are found guilty. For this reason, babyfaced people who have decided to admit fault may be much better off if they can plea-bargain the allegation down to a negligent offense. They will be less harshly penalized for such an offense than for an intentional one. Finally, it should be noted that facial appearance can affect the criminal justice process well before a person goes to trial. Indeed, lower bail was set for attractive defendants appearing before Texas judges than for their less attractive counterparts.[69] Protective impulses toward the babyfaced may provide them with a comparable advantage. Similarly, facial appearance may determine whether someone is given a speeding ticket or a warning, whether someone is arrested, and whether or not someone is identified by an eyewitness. The innocent appearance of those who are babyfaced may allow them to elude the ticket or arrest, although their highly distinctive appearance may make them more readily identified in a lineup.

Summary

Physiognomists, novelists, and ordinary people-watchers show a babyface overgeneralization effect that may derive from the evolutionarily adaptive value of responding to the veridical age information that appearance can provide. This effect is revealed in stereotyped impressions of babyfaced people: the attribution of childlike traits like weakness and warmth to people with babyish facial qualities, regardless of their sex, age, or race. It is also revealed in the social outcomes of babyfaced people. Many of these outcomes are consistent with the facial fit principle: Baby-faced people are more likely to acquire influence, jobs, and judicial convictions when the influence techniques, job descriptions, or alleged crimes fit the traits they are expected to have. There are interesting parallels between the effects of facial maturity on impressions and social outcomes and the effects of sex, which are produced in part by the more babyish appearance of women. Although the facial fit principle can account for much of the data reported in this chapter, people may be able to harness the babyface stereotype to reverse some of its undesirable social outcomes through contrast effects. For example, babyfaced soldiers who show valor are more likely than mature-faced soldiers to be decorated, perhaps because their bravery is so unexpected. Further implications of the interplay between appearance-based expectations, social outcomes, and confirming or disconfirming behaviors are discussed in Chapter 8. First, however, I consider another facial quality: attractiveness.

6

Analyzing Attractiveness

The indispensable element of all beautiful things is the smooth serpentine line . . . the soft flowing contour such as we see in . . . the gentle curve from the brow to the tip of her nose . . . the wavy line of beauty.

—William Hogarth

Beauty is not a quality in things themselves; it exists merely in the mind which contemplates them; and each mind perceives a different beauty.

—David Hume

Whereas we know what makes someone babyfaced, these two observations by philosophers reveal less clarity in what makes a person attractive. Are there indeed some indispensable ingredients in beauty? Or is beauty in the eye of the beholder? The fact is that there is some truth to both assertions. Beauty does show some relativity from culture to culture, perceiver to perceiver. At the same time, there are universal elements.

Cultural and Historical Variations in Standards of Beauty

Exotic images from primitive cultures support the adage "beauty is in the eye of the beholder." Westerners certainly would not agree with the attractiveness judgments of members of South American and African tribes, who view artificially enlarged lips like those shown in Figure 6.1 as a sign of beauty. Nor would they find attractive the intricate facial scarification practiced by dark-skinned peoples of Africa and South America, as shown in Figure 6.2. The elaborate facial tattooing shown in Figure 6.3, which is practiced by lighter skinned peoples from many regions of the world, is equally alien to modern Western standards of beauty. Western readers of this book would most certainly disagree with the attractiveness judgments of some East Malaysian tribes, who value the toothless appearance of women with teeth blackened by betel leaf chewing. The beauty of teeth filed to small points, as depicted in Figure 6.4, although admired in other cultures is equally alien to Westerners.

FIGURE 6.1   *Lip enlargement. Courtesy of Musee de l'Homme, Paris.*

Also odd to modern Western sensibilities is the elongated head that results from applying pressure to babies' soft skulls, an ancient practice that still exists in some areas of the world today. The beautiful Egyptian Queen Nefertiti would seem less attractive were she to remove her headdress to reveal a deformed skull like that shown in Figure 6.5. Historical fashions within Western cultures have also yielded changing markers of beauty. In the Middle Ages, the English fashion was for women to shave their eyebrows and the hair at the front of their heads, giving them a very high forehead. Whitened faces were found among English women in the time of Queen Elizabeth I, as well as among the Japanese geishas.[1]

Cultural and historical variations in the elaboration of beauty have many origins. Some derived from puberty rituals, others were viewed as safeguarding health. Still others were markers of clan membership and status. Whatever their origin, however, it

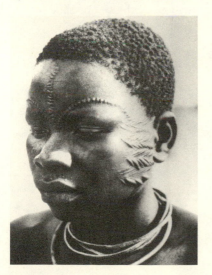

FIGURE 6.2   *Facial scarification. Courtesy of Musee de l'Homme, Paris.*

FIGURE 6.3   *Maori tattooing, New Zealand. Courtesy Peabody Museum, Harvard University.*

is unlikely that the form these elaborations took is purely arbitrary. Rather, as discussed later, many can be linked to more universal aesthetic standards that may reflect evolutionarily adaptive preferences.

Shared Standards of Beauty

Within a culture, people show strong agreement when they are asked to judge the attractiveness of photographed faces.[2] Moderate agreement is found even when the faces being judged have been selected to be representative of the general population rather than to include particularly attractive individuals, such as beauty contestants.[3] Moreover, only a brief glance at a face is necessary for agreement in attractiveness judgments to occur. When people rated the attractiveness of faces they had seen for less than a quarter of a second, their judgments showed strong agreement with those made by others whose viewing time was not constrained.[4] The consensus on attractiveness holds true regardless of the sex or race or age of those being judged. People show agreement on which face is more attractive whether they are judging males or females, people from their own or a different racial background, infants, children, teenagers, young adults, or old adults.[5] Although there is agreement regarding the attractiveness of a variety of faces, it is stronger for faces that are the same race as the perceiver and stronger for female than male faces. People also make more distinctions regarding the attractiveness of female than male faces, and they give more extreme ratings to female faces. This tendency to be more responsive to variations in attractiveness among women is particularly marked when the judges are men.[6]

FIGURE 6.4   *Teeth filing. Courtesy of Musee de L'Homme, Paris.*

FIGURE 6.5   *Queen Nefertiti, c. 1360 B.C. (left). Courtesy, Agyptisches Museum, Berlin. North American Indian of the nineteenth century with head deformation (right). Courtesy Peabody Museum, Harvard University.*

Heterogeneity among perceivers, like variations among targets, does not eliminate the consensus on attractiveness. Although average agreement among judges of the same race is higher than between-race agreement, Koreans and white and black Americans have been found to agree with each other regarding the relative attractiveness of various faces.[7] Contrary to the popular belief that men and women have different standards for judging a woman's attractiveness, men and women agree with each other in their ratings of women's faces.[8] Similarly, contrary to men's claim that they cannot evaluate the attractiveness of other men, they not only show moderate agreement among themselves when rating a group of male faces, but also their ratings agree with those made by women.[9] In addition, homosexual men and women agree among themselves regarding the attractiveness of men and women, and homosexuals and heterosexuals agree with one another, albeit to a lesser extent than they agree with individuals of their own sexual orientation.[10]

Judgments of attractiveness also show constancy across perceiver age. Young adults in their 20s and 30s agree with older adults in their 60s and 70s regarding the attractiveness of older adult faces.[11] Preschoolers make judgments of other children and adults that agree with the attractiveness ratings of adults.[12] Even 6-month-old babies seem to agree with adults as to who is more attractive than whom: They show a preference for looking at slides of faces that are rated by adults as attractive over those rated as unattractive. This effect holds true whether the faces are infant or adult, black or white, and male or female, although, as is true for adult perceivers, the responsiveness of babies to attractiveness seems to be stronger for female than for male faces.[13] It should be noted that infants' preference for attractive over unattractive faces cannot be explained by differences in their babyfaceness, which also can command the attention of babies. Six-month-old infants prefer to look at an attractive female face over an unattractive one even when the two are equal in babyfaceness.

What Makes a Face Attractive and Why?

Although agreement on attractiveness judgments is not perfect, the moderate-to-strong consensus clearly shows that beauty is not totally in the eye of the beholder. These findings imply that we should be able to identify the facial characteristics that make a person attractive. However, this has proved to be a difficult task despite abundant literary observations on the subject, such as the following:

> She was a fine and handsome girl . . . her mobile peony mouth and large innocent eyes added eloquence to colour and shape.[14]
>
> Alyosha was at this time a well-grown, red-cheeked, clear-eyed lad of nineteen, radiant with health. He was very handsome . . . with a regular, rather long, oval-shaped face, and wide-set dark gray, shining eyes.[15]

These and other literary depictions of the attractive face are rich and evocative, but it is difficult to draw from them any clear generalizations regarding what makes a face attractive. One reason is that useful hypotheses must go beyond individual features, like a "peony mouth" or "dark gray, shining eyes," since attractiveness is a configural quality, as Pope declared:

> *Tis not a lip, or eye, we beauty call,*
> *But the joint force and full result of all.*[16]

Hypotheses about the configural properties that make a face attractive can be found in folklore, ancient philosophy, and psychology. In these writings, one finds the suggestion that straightness, symmetry, youthfulness, and the typicality of facial structure are keys to attractiveness as well as the notion that inner qualities are what beautify the face. It is interesting that each of these qualities may communicate a person's biological fitness, and some modern evolutionary theorists argue that this is why we find them attractive. Darwin, on the other hand, argued that aesthetic preferences in selecting a mate can be quite independent of the

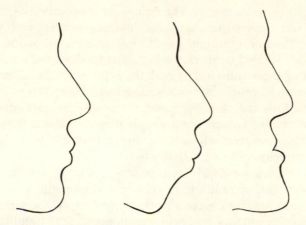

FIGURE 6.6   *Straight profile (left), convex profile (middle), and concave profile (right). N. Powell & B. Humphreys (1984).* Proportions of the aesthetic face *(p. 10). New York: Thieme-Stratton. Reprinted with permission.*

processes that promote survival of the fittest. The truth may be somewhere in between. At least some aesthetic preferences may reflect overgeneralized responses to facial qualities that can communicate a lack of fitness when they are extreme (e.g., an extremely atypical face) but not necessarily when they are in the middle range, where they still influence attractiveness. Although such overgeneralizations could derive from personal experience with unfit individuals, the rarity of extreme facial qualities makes an evolutionary basis more likely.[17]

Straight Profiles

The straight face is considered the handsomest. . . . The profile falls vertical down the brow and again from upper lip to point of chin.[18]

This maxim is consistent with principles that guide cosmetic and orthodontic surgery, in which attention is focused primarily on a side view of the face with a straight facial profile as the aesthetic goal. As shown in Figure 6.6, a straight profile is one in which the jaw is in relatively vertical alignment with the forehead rather than rotated forward or backward to create a concave or convex profile. Even young children respond to this marker of attractiveness. Indeed, a study that examined numerous facial measurements found that profile straightness was the only measure to have a reliable, strong effect on children's judgments of peers depicted in frontal and profile photographs. The straighter the profile, the more likely the children were to say that there was "nothing wrong" with the face.[19] The attractiveness of a straight profile has also been documented in a study of beauty contest winners, professional models, and actors and actresses.[20] All of these individuals had the type of molar alignment that produces a straight profile, although their teeth tended to be positioned slightly more forward than the ideal. Of course, factors other than a straight profile could account for the high attractiveness of these individuals. However, other researchers have shown that profile straightness in and of itself contributes to attractiveness.

In one study, adolescent girls were photographed with their jaws positioned into straight, protruding, or receding alignments. Orthodontists, artists, and lay judges all agreed in their ranking of the girls' faces as more "pleasing" when they had been positioned into a straight jaw alignment than into a protruding or receding one.[21] Another study systematically varied profile straightness in schematic drawings that were based on the faces of real women. Ratings of the attractiveness of the women's profiles revealed a moderate effect of profile straightness, with the same basic face judged more attractive when the jaw was aligned with the forehead than when it was rotated forward or backward to create a concave or convex face.[22]

Why is a straight profile preferred? It may be that it signals genetic fitness, since there is a functional aspect to such a profile. It results from a normal relationship between the molars, which contributes to a positive prognosis for keeping one's teeth, something that may have had evolutionary survival value. Indeed, research has shown that the best predictor of profile attractiveness is the extent to which the profile approximates the functionally ideal one that develops with normal growth and guarantees efficient chewing. It should be noted that the functionally ideal profile depends on a person's facial shape, and it therefore does not look identical from one individual to another. Universal aesthetic principles do not necessarily mean that we all have to look the same in order to be beautiful.[23]

Although people with extremely convex or concave jaw alignments would be less fit than those with a straight profile, it is unlikely that fitness is related to smaller variations in profile straightness. Thus, the demonstrated relationship of attractiveness to such variations may reflect the overgeneralization of an adaptive aversion to faces with truly unfit profiles. Finally, it should be noted that although a straight profile is attractive, this facial quality cannot readily account for the consensus in attractiveness judgments in psychological research, which has used frontal facial photographs. Indeed, even orthodontists have trouble making reliable judgments of facial attractiveness on the basis of profile straightness when it is varied in frontal photographs.[24]

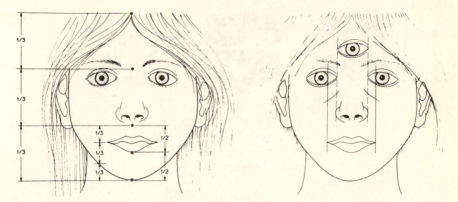

FIGURE 6.7 *"Golden" vertical facial proportions (left); "golden" horizontal facial proportions (right). Reprinted with permission from G. W. Lucker, K. A. Ribbens, & J. A. McNamara, Jr. (Eds.). (1981).* Psychological aspects of facial form *(Figures 1, 2, pp. 50–51). Ann Arbor: Center for Human Growth and Development, University of Michigan.*

Orderly Proportion and Symmetry

The chief forms of beauty are order and symmetry and definiteness.

This quotation of Aristotle shows that he, like other ancient Greeks, viewed orderly facial proportion and symmetry as primary determinants of beauty. This view is retained by modern-day cosmetic surgeons, who draw on Plato's "golden proportion" standards of facial beauty.[25] The ratio of the size of one segment of the face to another is the key element in these standards. On the basis of this general principle, it has been proposed that three vertical segments of the face should be approximately equal in height, as shown in Figure 6.7 (left). One of the three equal segments extends from the hairline to the browridge, another from the browridge to just under the nose, and a third from just under the nose to the tip of the chin. The distance between the top of the face and the tip of the nose is said to be "golden" if it is approximately two-thirds of the total length. Following the golden proportion principle, further subdivisions in the lower third of the face should also yield three equal segments: one from just under the nose to the point at which the upper and lower lips meet, another from the meeting point of the lips to the depression below the lower lip, and a third between that depression and the tip of the chin. Finally, the distance from just under the nose to just under the lips should equal the distance from just under the lips to the tip of the chin.

Horizontally, the ideal face should be approximately two-thirds of its length, another golden proportion. As shown in Figure 6.7 (right), ideal horizontal dimensions are marked by a mouth width equal to the dis-

FIGURE 6.8   *Symmetry around a vertical axis (left); symmetry around a horizontal axis (middle); asymmetry (right). M. H. Bornstein, K. Ferdinandsen, & C. G. Gross (1981). Perception of symmetry in infancy.* Developmental Psychology, *17, p. 84, Figure 1.* © *1981 by the American Psychological Association. Reprinted with permission.*

tance between the inner borders of the iris, a nose width equal to the distance between the eyes, and eye separation distance equal to the width of an eye. These horizontal distances should also yield golden proportions. For example, the width of the nose should be approximately two-thirds the width of the mouth.

There has been little systematic investigation of the Greek assertions regarding aesthetically pleasing proportions. However, some support is provided by research demonstrating "golden proportions" in vertical segments of the facial profiles and frontal views of beautiful women. Also, adolescent girls are judged less attractive when the lower half of their face is lengthened in proportion to the upper half.[26] Golden proportions in the width of features has also been shown for beautiful women.[27] What is lacking in this research is a systematic comparison of the facial proportions of attractive and unattractive people to determine whether the former are significantly more "golden."

Related to the golden proportion is symmetry in the size, form, and arrangement of the facial features. Evidence for the attractiveness of symmetrical horizontal segments—segments that are symmetrical on either side of a vertical axis—is provided by the preference for such symmetry in art and architecture. Indeed, even young children draw houses with a door in the middle flanked by equal numbers of windows on both sides. Young babies also show a particular sensitivity to symmetrical patterns of this type. When one of the abstract patterns shown in Figure 6.8 is presented repeatedly to 4-month-old babies, the babies are quicker to show bored inattention to the one on the left, which is symmetrical around a vertical axis, indicating that it is more familiar to them. When two of these patterns are shown simultaneously to 12-month-old babies, the babies prefer to look at the symmetrical pattern on the left over the asymmetrical pattern on the right and over the middle pattern, which is symmetrical around a horizontal rather than a vertical axis.[28]

The general preference for symmetry is consistent with the negative impact of crooked teeth on the attractiveness of children and young adults.[29] Evidence for the attractiveness of symmetry is also provided by the finding that more symmetrical male and female faces are judged as more attractive than less symmetrical ones. This effect is medium-to-large for judgments of people between the ages of 10 and 15 and small-to-medium for judgments of the same people when they are aged 18 to the late 50s.[30] Although the age-related change in the importance of symmetry is small, it could reflect the fact that facial asymmetry shows marked increases during the years of maturation and then levels off. Therefore, asymmetry may be a more salient determinant of attractiveness in younger faces because it is rarer.[31] The association of symmetry with youth may also explain its greater influence on the attractiveness of female than male faces, since there is a greater preference for youthfulness in females, as discussed later in this chapter.[32] Finally, it should be noted that although natural variations in symmetry are positively related to attractiveness, perfectly symmetrical faces that are created by making chimeras—two right or two left halves—may not be highly attractive. On the other hand, the more natural-looking perfect symmetry that results from blending mirror images of faces does appear to be highly attractive.[33]

Why is symmetry preferred? Modern evolutionary theorists have argued that symmetry is a marker of good genes and resistance to disease that can cause asymmetrical development.[34] Mate preferences among lower organisms are consistent with this argument. Birds and insects favor symmetry in their choice of mates.[35] Female swallows prefer male swallows with tails that are both long and symmetrical. Female zebra finches prefer males wearing symmetrical colored leg bands. Japanese scorpionflies prefer the scent of a male with a symmetrical body that is hidden from their view. The mating value of symmetry may lie behind the human beautification practices of facial scarification and tattooing. As shown in Figures 6.2 and 6.3, the resultant facial patterns are highly symmetrical, and the attractiveness of these designs can be appreciated by Westerners even though they are unaccustomed to seeing such patterns on the face. Although research has not yet linked human facial symmetry to mating value, measures of bodily asymmetries predict copulatory behavior. Men and women with more symmetrical bodies report more sexual partners and a younger age at first intercourse, even when they are equated in facial attractiveness to those with less symmetrical bodies.[36] Since facial attractiveness is correlated with men's body symmetry as well as with their facial symmetry, there is reason to expect that men with symmetrical faces will also be more sexually successful.

It is important to note that even if symmetry does enhance sexual success, this does not necessarily imply that it is a marker of good genes. As noted previously, Darwin argued that sexual attraction to individuals with certain appearance qualities may reflect aesthetic preferences that are quite independent of the processes that promote survival of the fittest.[37] However, there is some more direct evidence of links between symmetry of facial features and genetic fitness. As mentioned in Chapter 2, people with a variety of chromosomal and other congenital abnormalities have more asymmetrical faces. They may also have more crooked teeth. Also, those who are genetically related to people with cleft palates show more asymmetrical teeth than others, even though they themselves have normal palates. Facial asymmetry also is higher in schizophrenics. It thus appears that asymmetrical faces or teeth may advertise lack of intellectual, physical, or psychological fitness.[38]

Facial asymmetry has also been correlated with relatively mundane variations in physical fitness among college students. However, there was no consistent tendency for asymmetry to be positively related to students' self-reports of some common ailments, such as headaches, nausea, muscle aches, sore throat, backaches, and feeling jittery, in two samples of men and women.[39] Because self-reports of health may be subject to various biases, research using more objective indicators of physical health is needed to determine clearly whether facial symmetry does indeed mark good genes and resistance to illness in normal populations without any gross genetic defects. The only pertinent evidence has examined the relationship between facial attractiveness and health.[40] Since attractiveness is correlated with symmetry, the results may be pertinent to the effects of facial symmetry as well. Facial attractiveness of adolescent males and females was unrelated to health as assessed from ages 11 through 18 by means of clinical examinations and detailed histories. Adolescent facial attractiveness also failed to "honestly advertise" later health in the 30s and 50s, when genetic susceptibility to chronic rather than infectious conditions becomes a significant factor. It is interesting, however, that attractiveness was positively related to *perceived* health in this and other studies, a strong effect that held true for perceptions of men as well as women.[41] Moreover, the relationship between people's actual health and their perceived health becomes stronger when they are equated in attractiveness. People's judgments of others' health are, therefore, "blinded by beauty." It is possible that they are also "shrouded by symmetry": The preference for symmetry in a normal population of faces may be the overgeneralization of an adaptive aversion to more extreme asymmetry in individuals with genetic anomalies.

Regardless of whether facial symmetry is a marker of good genes, there are other reasons we may have evolved to prefer it. In particular, this preference may be a by-product of the need to recognize objects no matter how they are positioned.[42] Symmetry also may be preferred because symmetrical faces (or tails or bodies) are closer to the population average, which is another determinant of attractiveness that is discussed later.[43] However, even if the preference for symmetrical faces evolved for one of these reasons, it could have contributed to the evolution of a relationship between such faces and good genes insofar as people with symmetrical faces had an advantage in the mating game. As noted previously, whether people with more symmetrical faces are more genetically fit is a question to be answered by further research. Judging from animal work, the answer may not be simple. Male lions with a more symmetrical pattern of spots on their faces have been found to live longer than those with lopsided faces, but the reverse was true for the females.[44]

Youthfulness

> *What I have in mind are faces made*
> *attractive by youth, coloring, and complexion.*"[45]

Although faces may indeed be made attractive by coloring and complexion, these attributes cannot easily account for the consensus in attractiveness judgments in psychological research, which has typically used black and white photographs. Youthfulness, on the other hand, does provide a possible explanation for the greater attractiveness of some faces than others in this research. If younger looking people are more attractive, babyfaceness should enhance attractiveness. Although observed relationships between attractiveness and babyfaceness have been variable, this may reflect idiosyncrasies of the faces selected for study. The most appropriate test of the relationship is to examine a representative sample of the population. One study that did so found a moderate-to-strong positive relationship between the attractiveness and babyfaceness of men and women in their 30s and late 50s. Attractiveness and babyfaceness of the same individuals were unrelated in late childhood, at puberty, and in late adolescence.[46] Not only are attractiveness and babyfaceness positively related in adulthood, but also specific "babyish" features have been linked to attractiveness. Among these are large eyes, large pupils, and a small nose. Eyes are particularly influential, typically showing moderate-to-large effects on attractiveness, although these effects are more reliable for judgments of female than male faces.[47]

Although an overall babyfaced appearance as well as specific babyish facial qualities enhance attractiveness, the relationship between babyfaceness and attractiveness is far from perfect. There are babyfaced people who are unattractive, and there are attractive people who are not babyfaced.[48] Of course, babyfaceness does not capture the entire range of appearance qualities that make someone look youthful. Indeed, as noted in Chapter 5, even older adults can be babyfaced. The multifaceted nature of youthfulness is captured in the multiple fitness model of attractiveness, which assumes that attractive features include a combination of qualities, many of which signal mating potential. A preference for fertile individuals will lead perceivers to view faces as attractive when they lack aging features, such as graying, thinning hair and wrinkles, and when they display sexual maturity features, which may differ for men and women. A preference for receptive individuals will lead perceivers to view faces as attractive when they look nonthreatening and approachable either by virtue of expressive features, such as a large smile, or by virtue of babyish features, such as large eyes.[49] The multiple determinants of attractiveness suggest that it may come in many forms. An attractive man may be "rugged" like Clint Eastwood or a "pretty boy" like Paul McCartney. Similarly, an attractive woman may be "sexy" like Sophia Loren, "cute and wholesome" like Sally Field, or "elegant and sophisticated" like Grace Kelly.[50]

Consistent with the hypothesis that a receptive appearance increases attractiveness, a smile has this effect.[51] The greater attractiveness of faces with dilated pupils, noted previously, also may reflect a preference for receptive individuals, since large pupils not only are an infantile quality but also an indication of interest and attention. Some studies have shown that certain sexual maturity features also increase attractiveness, and these effects have been documented for many different groups of perceivers, including Taiwanese, Hispanics, and black and white Americans.[52] However, other studies have failed to replicate some of the sexual maturity effects, perhaps because of an insufficient range of attractiveness among the rated faces; most of the confirming studies of female faces included beauty contestants. Sexual maturity features are not all equal in their influence on attractiveness. A woman is attractive if she has mature, high cheekbones but not if she has a mature, large nose. A man with a mature, rugged jaw is attractive, but one with mature, small eyes is not. The particular maturity features that increase attractiveness are discussed further in the section on gender prototypicality.

The hypothesis that a fertile appearance increases attractiveness is consistent with the views of evolutionary theorists who argue that we are programmed to perceive the "fertile" and "healthy" face as attractive because such preferences have promoted species survival. Because younger adults are generally more fertile and healthy than older ones, this programming should lead to a preference for youthful faces. It is consistent with this hypothesis that both men and women decline in attractiveness with increasing age, and this strong effect holds true whether they are judged by children, adolescents, or young adults.[53]

Another prediction of the evolutionary hypothesis is that the decline in attractiveness should occur at an earlier age for women owing to their earlier loss of fertility. However, one study found that the decrease in women's attractiveness was only moderate from age 30 to the late 50s, when fertility would decline the most, whereas the decrease in attractiveness was very large from age 18 to the early 30s, when there would be smaller declines in fertility.[54] Moreover, these age-related decreases in attractiveness were equivalent for men and women, a further indication that they are not caused by age-related declines in fertility. It should be noted that these results were based on a comparison of the attractiveness of the same individuals across the life span. Other research that has found evidence of a "double standard of aging," with more detrimental effects for women, has compared attractiveness ratings of younger faces with ratings of faces of different people at an older age.[55] What appeared to be a greater detrimental effect of age on women's attractiveness in that research could merely reflect the selection of particularly unattractive older women. Although there is no convincing evidence to support the hypothesis that attractiveness declines at an earlier age for women, equal declines in attractiveness may have more adverse social consequences for women than men.

The evolutionary hypothesis predicts not only an earlier decline in attractiveness for women but also that men will find youthfulness of the opposite sex more attractive than women do. This is because males' reproductive success depends on age of partner more than females' does. A study of sex differences in human mate preferences in 27 countries from all parts of the globe revealed a large and universal tendency for men to prefer younger mates than women do.[56] Although this sex difference in human mate preferences is consistent with the evolutionary hypothesis that men will find youthfulness more attractive than women do, it does not implicate perceived fertility as the most important determinant of attractiveness. If it were, one would expect the men to prefer women younger than the 25 years of age that was seen as ideal, since peak fertility in women occurs in the early rather than the mid 20s. Further evidence that fertility may not be central is provided by an analysis of personal ads. Men in their 50s preferred women in their 30s or 40s, not women in their 20s, which suggests a preference for qualities other than fertility.[57] However, it is also possible that personal ads do not reflect people's ideal mates; rather, they may reflect people's more realistic aspirations, which could raise the age of women preferred by men in their 40s and 50s. Even if men really do prefer younger women, this alone does not establish perceived fertility as the causal factor, nor does it prove that variations in physical attractiveness are crucial. For example, men might prefer younger women because the age difference fosters greater power for men in the relationship.

In addition to suggesting that youthfulness is attractive because it is related to perceived fertility, the evolutionary hypothesis also suggests that youthfulness is attractive because it advertises health. Certainly, more youthful-looking people are likely to be healthier when a broad age range is considered, but it is less clear whether this would be true if the people judged were all the same age. However, as noted in Chapter 2, younger looking people are in fact healthier than older looking people of the same age: Men who looked young for their age proved to be physiologically younger on examination by a physician. Young-looking men also lived longer, particularly those who were between the ages of 45 and 75. This finding indicates that some signs of youthfulness may be attractive because they do indeed signal fitness, consistent with evolutionary arguments. Exactly what those signs are remains to be determined.

Averageness

Attractive faces are only average.[58]

There are at least two reasons why an average facial configuration may be attractive. First, average faces may be more attractive because their averageness makes them more familiar, and there is considerable evidence that people prefer familiar things. For example, American men and women show an aversion to red hair, which is statistically rare.[59] The preference for the familiar is consistent with Kant's notion that beautiful things are those that are easy to know and to comprehend. A second reason for the attractiveness of an average face is that evolutionary pressures should yield a preference for individuals who have characteristics close to the population average, since such individuals would be less likely to carry harmful genetic mutations. Although people whose faces are far from the population average may be genetically unfit, it is unlikely that fitness is related to averageness in a normal range of faces. Thus, the relationship of attractiveness to averageness within a normal range may reflect the overgeneralization of an adaptive aversion to faces that are far from the population average.

Supporting the hypothesis that average faces are attractive is the finding that composite faces, created by "averaging" computer images of many individual faces, tend to be judged as more attractive than any one of the individual faces. The more faces that have been "averaged," the more attractive the resulting composite.[60] This large effect can be seen in the faces shown in Figure 6.9. Composite faces are in fact perceived as more average in appearance. In particular, they are perceived as more difficult to pick out of a crowd at a busy railway station than individual faces. Additional evidence that averageness is attractive is provided by a moderate, positive relationship between how attractive normal, noncomposite faces are and how difficult they are to pick out of a crowd. Finally, as shown in Figure 6.10, faces decrease in attractiveness when they are

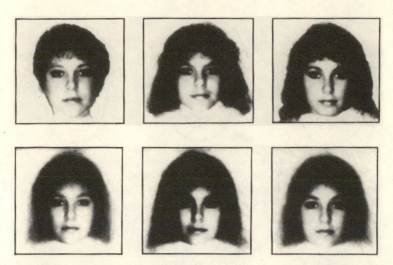

FIGURE 6.9 *Four-face composite (top) and 32-face composite (bottom). Adapted from J. H. Langlois, & L. A. Roggman (1990). Attractive faces are only average.* Psychological Science, 1, 115–121. © *1990 by the American Psychological Society. Reprinted with the permission of Cambridge University Press.*

made highly distinctive through a caricature computer program, and they increase in attractiveness when made less distinctive—more average—through an anticaricature program.[61]

The principle stating that faces close to the population average are more attractive raises the question of what are the distinguishing characteristics of the average face. Although it is possible that composites and anticaricatures are more attractive simply because they are closer to the population average and thus look more familiar and normal, there are other possible explanations for their appeal. If we cannot describe the physical qualities that make averaged faces more attractive than individual ones, the puzzle of attractiveness is only partially solved. Perhaps average faces have the "golden proportions" that Plato idealized, although this has not been investigated. Other distinguishing characteristics of these faces that may contribute to their greater attractiveness include symmetry, roundness, lack of blemishes, and youthfulness.

The greater attractiveness of averaged faces and anticaricatures may be due in part to their greater symmetry since, as noted previously, symmetry is attractive.[62] At the same time, there is evidence to suggest that symmetry is attractive because it is closer to the population average.[63] To the extent that symmetry and averageness are inextricably linked, it may not make sense to view them as competing causes of attractiveness. Averag-

FIGURE 6.10   *Faces that are less average (caricature) and more average (anticaricature). G. Rhodes & T. Tremewan (1996). Averageness, exaggeration, and facial attractiveness.* Psychological Science, *7, 106. © 1996 American Psychological Society. Reprinted with the permission of Cambridge University Press.*

ing more faces not only creates more symmetry but also creates a more rounded and less angular appearance. Consistent with Hogarth's claim that "the indispensable element of all beautiful things is the smooth serpentine line," research has shown more favorable reactions to rounded, curvilinear forms than to angular ones, which are viewed as threatening.[64] These strong effects suggest that roundness rather than typicality per se could be what make the averaged faces attractive. The process of averaging faces to create a composite also eliminates any blemishes that might appear on the individual faces. The resultant appearance of greater healthiness could contribute to the attractiveness of the averaged faces.[65] Finally, there is a strong tendency for averaged faces to be more youthful looking than the individual faces that have been combined to create them.[66] As discussed previously, youthfulness has been linked to attractiveness, which suggests that this aspect of average faces may contribute to their greater attractiveness.

A complete answer to the question of what characteristics of averaged faces make them more attractive may depend in part on what faces have been averaged, since the average face for the world's population will be different from the average face for a particular nation or racial or ethnic group. Moreover, to the extent that average faces are preferred because they are more familiar, the attractiveness of an average face should depend on the similarity between the racial or ethnic background of perceivers and the faces that are averaged. Although research has not directly tested this hypothesis, some evidence of racial differences in standards of beauty can be construed as reflecting differences in population averages.

When Asian-American and Caucasian women were asked to rate the facial features that they find most attractive in men and women, their responses showed a large preference for features typical of their own race. Compared with Caucasians, Asian Americans rated straight hair and black hair as more attractive and frizzy hair and a roman nose as less attractive.[67] Other evidence for a preference for features more typical in one's own population is provided by the finding that the relationship between black women's attractiveness and the "whiteness" of their features is weaker when the judges are African blacks than when they are American blacks or whites, both of whom showed an equivalent preference for "white" features.[68]

Although average faces such as those generated in computerized composites and anticaricatures may be more attractive than a random single face, this effect is by no means the whole story of attractiveness. There are numerous examples of highly attractive faces that are anything but average in their features or "golden" in their proportions. Consider the eyes of Sophia Loren and the chin of Kirk Douglas. Loren's eyes are much larger than average, and their shape is anything but typical. Similarly, Douglas's chin is considerably larger than average, and its unusual cleft is a hallmark of his appeal. Explicit comparisons of the attractiveness of average and exceptional features in a large group of more ordinary faces has shown that large chins are indeed more attractive in men than average-sized chins. Moreover, a female composite face that exaggerates the differences between a composite based on highly attractive faces and a composite based on moderately attractive faces is the most attractive of the three.

The exaggerated composite deviates from an average female face in the following ways: higher cheekbones, narrower lower jaw, larger eyes, and shorter distances between nose and mouth and mouth and chin. These markers of feminine beauty were found not only for British judges of British faces but also for British and Japanese judges of Japanese faces.[69] These findings give credence to the observation of Sir Francis Bacon that "there is no excellent beauty that hath not some strangeness in the proportion."[70] Like the beauty of a peacock's exaggerated feathers, the faces of people that exaggerate ordinary attractive features have the greatest appeal.[71]

Gender-Prototypicality

> *Elements that contribute to the beauty of a woman*
> *would be marks of effeminacy in a man.[72]*

This maxim suggests that attractive features are those that are prototypical for the person's sex. Evolutionary pressures could account for this if people with faces atypical for their sex are less genetically fit than those with more gender-prototypical faces. However, it seems unlikely that fitness and gender-prototypicality are related in a normal range of faces. Thus, any relationship of attractiveness to gender-prototypicality within that range may reflect the overgeneralization of an adaptive aversion to faces that are very sex-atypical.

As discussed in Chapter 2, the prototypical adult female face—the model, archetypal example—differs from that of the prototypical adult male, with a smaller jaw, a smaller nose, and larger looking eyes and cheekbones in the female face, differences that may result from the differential effects of male and female hormones at puberty as well as the earlier cessation of facial growth in women. It is interesting that the exaggerated composite of female faces described previously as highly attractive has characteristics that exaggerate the differences between male and female faces. Therefore, the exaggerated composite may be perceived as most attractive because it is the most feminine.

Differences between the adult male and female faces may also account for evidence that the sexual maturity features that contribute to attractiveness differ for men and women.[73] The fact that a large chin increases the attractiveness of a man but not a woman is consistent with the fact that the mature male jaw is typically more prominent than the female jaw. The fact that mature, high cheekbones more reliably augment the attractiveness of a woman than a man is consistent with the fact that the cheekbones of women typically appear more prominent than those of men owing to the protrusiveness of the male forehead and nose. Therefore, the particular mature features that are attractive are those that differentiate the two sexes, and exaggerated versions of these features are more attractive than those that are merely average. Oddly, however, the large nose that distinguishes the adult male face does not seem to augment attractiveness.

Since the adult female face retains more infantile characteristics than does the adult male face, the gender-prototypicality principle also suggests that infantile features make a more positive contribution to the attractiveness of women than men, for whom mature features should be more attractive. This phenomenon is illustrated in Figure 6.11. Although the man and woman are both highly attractive, they differ in facial maturity. The woman is babyfaced with large eyes, a round face, and full lips, whereas the man is mature-faced with smaller eyes; an angular, large-jawed face; and thin lips. Consistent with these examples of female and male attractiveness, people show a large preference for babyfaced women and mature-faced men when asked to rate the facial features that they find most attractive. Small-chinned, heart-shaped faces with pug noses, full lips, and fair skin were deemed most attractive in women, whereas square-shaped faces with roman noses and tan skin tone were judged to

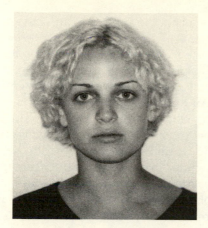

FIGURE 6.11   *A babyfaced woman and a mature-faced man. Courtesy of Nancy Carlston.*

be most attractive in men.[74] A videotaped interview with an !Kung bush-woman shown at the Peabody Museum of Archaeology and Ethnography at Harvard University underscores the diversity of cultures that favor a babyish facial structure in females. This woman, who played the wife in the movie *The Gods Must Be Crazy*, said she got the part because she is beautiful. Boasting, she said, "Look at my face . . . they call me short face, squirrel face . . . my sister said, 'Give me your face, mine is too long.'"

Research in which people were shown various faces and asked to make attractiveness ratings rather than simply report what they think is attractive also has revealed large effects that confirm the greater attractiveness of a babyface in women than in men. Referring back to Figure 5.10 reveals that a female face with the babyish features of large eyes, high eyebrows, and a small chin is more attractive than one with mature versions of these features. On the other hand, a male face with mature features is more attractive than one that is babyfaced.[75] Judgments of profiles of real people show effects paralleling those found for schematic faces. Whereas a straight profile is most attractive for both sexes, the effects of different types of malocclusions varies by sex. Both children and adults show a strong tendency to judge female targets more negatively when they have an exceedingly mature jaw that is too prominent than when they have a babyish, receding jaw. Male targets, on the other hand, are judged slightly more negatively when their jaw is receding than when it is too promi-nent.[76] A woman with the convex profile shown in Figure 6.6 would be more attractive than a woman with the concave profile, whereas a man with the convex profile would be less attractive than one with the concave profile. Jay Leno's protrusive jaw is not the liability to attractiveness that it would be in a Jane Leno.

Another babyish quality that makes a more positive contribution to female than male attractiveness is light skin, which, as noted in Chapter 4, characterizes infants in various racial groups. This element of female beauty is often captured by poets. An analysis of female beauty in medieval French and Spanish poems concluded that the hair and skin are preferably light, as revealed in the metaphors "hair of gold" and "ivory." The relatively large forehead is white, at times compared to a lily. Teeth are white, like "pearls." The ears are white "like sheep's milk."[77] The preference for light-skinned women does not seem attributable to the domination of Western, white standards of beauty, since it holds true in a variety of cultures, many of which are relatively isolated from Western influence. Specifically, an examination of preferences for lighter versus darker skin color among 51 diverse cultures studied by anthropologists revealed that people in 92 percent of these cultures preferred lighter skin, primarily in females. The cultures showing this preference included 12 sub-Saharan African ones, and it has been documented in cultural artifacts that predate contact with white Europeans.[78] Other research has shown that lightness of skin among black American women is strongly related to how babyfaced they are judged to be as well as to how attractive they appear to both black and white judges.[79]

Whereas the greater attractiveness of lighter skinned women cannot be attributed to Western standards of beauty, it is consistent with the greater typicality of light skin for women than for men. The "fair sex" is in fact more fair-skinned, and this sex difference in pigmentation has been documented in a wide variety of cultural groups representing every major inhabited area of the world. Light skin may be more attractive in women not only because it is more prototypical but also because it is a sign of fertility. It is with the onset of fertility at puberty that boys become darker skinned than girls. Moreover, women's skin darkens during periods of infertility such as pregnancy, ingestion of oral contraceptives, and the infertile phases of the menstrual cycle. In the words of a Hopi, "I preferred a light complexion, for we say that a woman with a dark skin may be half man."[80]

The use of cosmetics highlights women's search for beauty in babyfaceness. The appearance of the eyes is enlarged with eyeliner. The eyebrows are plucked to make them appear thinner and higher. Lipstick is applied to redden the lips and make them more prominent, like those of a nursing baby. Rouge recaptures a childlike, rosy-cheeked appearance, and powder recreates the fair-skinned appearance of childhood. Some of the more extreme measures to enhance appearance also can be construed as efforts to appear more babyfaced. The fashion during the Middle Ages for English women to shave their eyebrows and the hair at the front of their head can be construed as efforts to attain the very high forehead of a baby. One might even speculate that the elongated "cone" head produced by deformation practices resembles the head of the neonate, fresh from the womb, as does the toothless or baby-toothed appearance produced by blackening with betel juice or teeth filing. The ancient practice of using belladonna to enlarge the pupils also can be construed as increasing babyfaceness, since infants have larger pupils than adults. The whitened faces found among Englishwomen in the time of Queen Elizabeth I, as well as among the Japanese geishas, can be viewed as an exaggeration of the infantile quality of light skin. In modern times, the bleached blond hair that has often been popular among white women may serve to recapture the towhead appearance of infancy. Modern women also have their nose and jaw reduced in size, yielding a more childlike appearance, and in old age, they have their sagging eyelids repaired to recapture the large-eyed appearance of a child. Men may also repair their sagging eyelids, which is consistent with the finding that large eyes may enhance the attractiveness of both sexes.[81] On the other hand, men are more apt to have their jaws augmented than reduced, and men are not apt to have their nose "bobbed."[82]

Familiarity

I've grown accustomed to her face.

The sentiments expressed in the song "I've Grown Accustomed to her Face" from the musical *My Fair Lady* suggest that we find most appealing those faces that are familiar to us. Contrary to the old proverb "familiarity breeds contempt," considerable research supports the songwriter's suggestion that we like familiar stimuli, including faces.[83] Indeed, people even like their own face better when they view it in a familiar way—the way it looks in a mirror—than when they view it the way it looks in a photograph. On the other hand, their close friends prefer nonmirror, photographic images of these people's faces, the likeness that is familiar to the friends.[84] The appeal of familiar faces may contribute to ethnic and racial differences in standards of beauty, inasmuch as own-group faces are apt to be more familiar. Familiarity appears to affect us at a gut level; experiments have shown that frequent exposure leads to greater liking even when the exposure is so brief that people aren't even aware of it.[85] People therefore prefer objects that they have been familiarized with at a subliminal level even when they cannot consciously recognize those objects as familiar. The appeal of average faces that was discussed earlier may be accounted for at least in part by their greater familiarity. Both the effect of averageness and the effect of familiarity may reflect an adaptive tendency to be wary of unfamiliar things until we learn that they are not dangerous.

Pretty Is as Pretty Does

Who is good will soon be beautiful.[86]

The account of attractiveness most in keeping with democratic ideals is that it is produced by inner beauty. Certainly we have all had the experience of finding someone more attractive as we grew to know him. This could be a consequence of mere exposure to the person's face, since as just noted, people prefer more familiar faces. However, "pretty" behavior can also influence people's attractiveness. This sentiment is reflected in George Orwell's adage, "At 50, everyone has the face he deserves." It is also found in the above quotation from the Greek poet Sappho. Consistent with these maxims is the finding that 70 percent of college students judged an instructor's physical appearance as appealing when he behaved in a warm and friendly manner, whereas only 30 percent judged the same instructor to have an appealing appearance when he was more cold and distant.[87] Students also rated as most attractive those classmates whom they perceived to be high in academic or athletic ability,[88] and they rated a woman as more physically attractive when they had received a favorable description of her personality.[89] Indeed, the large effect of personality on ratings of attractiveness was sometimes strong enough to outweigh the large effect of attractiveness as judged by those who had no personality information. Consequently, unattractive women with a favorable personality were judged equal in attractiveness to average-looking women with an unfavorable or neutral personality, and average-looking women with a favorable personality were judged as more attractive than attractive women with an unfavorable personality.

The tendency to find people more attractive when we know and like them may contribute to the widespread belief that "beauty is in the eye of the beholder." However, this tendency differs from Sappho's claim that good behavior influences actual attractiveness and it cannot account for the consensus in attractiveness judgments made by strangers. Perhaps, a person's inner beauty can be detected even by strangers, as suggested by their consensus in strangers' judging of positive traits like extraversion and conscientiousness that was described in Chapter 3. That is, the positive traits that a person's appearance communicates may be what makes her attractive. However, there is a chicken-egg problem here. As discussed in Chapter 7, it is equally likely that the attractiveness of a person's appearance is what makes her appear to have good traits.

Summary

There clearly are some objective qualities in a facial configuration that increase attractiveness. These include facial and dental symmetry, "golden" facial proportions, youthfulness, and certain sexual maturity indicators, with the result that a mixture of babyish and mature features may be more attractive than only youthful ones. Faces that are average, as opposed to idiosyncratic, are also attractive, although faces that deviate from average in ways that are prototypical for the person's sex are even more attractive than average ones. Some evolutionary theorists argue that the facial qualities that augment attractiveness do so because they advertise health and fertility. However, there is no definitive evidence that individuals with a more youthful appearance or more prominent sexual maturity features are in fact healthier or more fertile when age does not vary. There is also no definitive evidence that people with more average or symmetrical faces are in fact more fit when those with serious genetic anomalies are excluded. The preference for faces with these qualities may reflect the overgeneralization of an evolutionarily adaptive rejection of mates whose faces are extreme on these dimensions: very old, totally lacking in sexual maturity features, very asymmetrical and discrepant from the population average, and very atypical for their sex. There is also some evidence that "beauty is in the eye of the beholder." Familiarity with a face may increase its appeal, and an appearance that is average for one's own racial or ethnic group may be more attractive than one that is average for another group, perhaps because the former is more familiar. These effects of familiarity may reinforce the view that beauty is in the eye of the beholder. Culturally unique beautification practices may do the same, although these may exaggerate one or more of the universal elements of beauty, such as symmetry or youthfulness. Finally, knowledge of someone's inner beauty may add luster to that person's face. As discussed in Chapter 7, however, the attractiveness of a person's face also augments perceptions of inner beauty.

7

The Advantages of Attractiveness

What is your fortune, my pretty maid?
My face is my fortune, sir, she said.

There may be considerable truth to this old English nursery rhyme. Physically attractive people elicit more favorable evaluations from others, and these positive trait impressions have significant social advantages. As discussed later, this attractiveness "halo effect" may derive from the adaptive value of responding to the valid fitness information that faces can provide: an instance of the sickness similarities overgeneralization effect. The positive affect that beauty evokes in the beholder provides another possible explanation for the attractiveness halo. A face that elicits positive feelings not only may create positive trait impressions but also may foster the advantageous outcomes that have been found in interpersonal relationships, occupations, criminal justice decisions, and health care.[1]

The Attractiveness Halo: What Is Beautiful Is Good

In fairy tales, the heroes and heroines are attractive, and the villains are ugly. This pattern is repeated in literature throughout the ages. Balzac, for example, gives his murderers crooked teeth, which we have seen are recognized as unattractive even by young children and which follows the physiognomist Lavater's assertion that decayed, ugly, or unequal teeth indicate moral imperfection.[2] In *The Brothers Karamazov*, Dostoyevsky's portrayal of the evil Fyodor also includes bad teeth:

140

His countenance at this time bore traces of something that testified unmistakably to the life he had led. Besides the long fleshy bags under his little, always insolent, suspicious, and ironical eyes . . . add to that a long rapacious mouth with full lips, between which could be seen little stumps of black decayed teeth.[3]

Stevenson's evil Mr. Hyde is unattractive: "Pale and dwarfish, he gave an impression of deformity without any nameable malformation, he had a displeasing smile." The good Dr. Jekyll, on the other hand, is attractive: "A large, well-made, smooth-faced man . . . the moon shone on his face . . . it seemed to breathe such an innocent and old-world kindness of disposition."[4]

The association of beauty with goodness in literature is echoed in people's impressions of men and women depicted in facial photographs. Those who are more attractive are seen as warmer, kinder, stronger, more sensitive, sexually responsive, interesting, poised, modest, sociable, and outgoing.[5] This halo effect is tempered by some negative impressions of attractive people. In particular, more attractive women are rated as more vain, egotistical, materialistic, and snobbish.[6] However, the large effects are in the domain of good social skills and sexual warmth, and there are only weak effects in the area of vanity. Attractiveness also has moderate effects on the attribution of other good traits, including adjustment, dominance, and sociability, and it has small-to-medium effects on the attribution of intellectual competence.[7] Recent research, elaborating the domain of dominance, has revealed that more attractive individuals are seen as having more social influence, more persuasive ability, more ability to get others to comply with a request, and a greater likelihood of being followed or imitated.[8] Although a negligible halo has been found in the arena of integrity and concern for others, this effect shows considerable variability across studies, and research has often found higher honesty ratings for attractive individuals.[9]

The magnitude of the attractiveness halo effect varies not only across traits but also with the type of attractiveness. Attractive women who are highly babyfaced—the cute types—are perceived as more honest, sincere, warm, and sociable than those who are not cute. On the other hand, attractive women who are not babyfaced, such as the sexy types, are rated as no more sincere, warm, or sociable than less sexy women, and female raters perceive them as less honest.[10] This may account for the negligible halo in judgments of integrity for the entire range of attractive people. It is only the babyfaced, cute types who look more honest.

The epithet "ugly as sin" and countless folktales filled with wicked ugly witches suggest that people believe not only that "what is beautiful is good" but also that "what is ugly is bad." To determine whether these images are reflected in everyday views of unattractive people, it is necessary to compare impressions of faces that are average in attractiveness to impressions of those that are either very attractive or very unattractive. Although most research on the halo effect has merely compared impressions of attractive faces to those of unattractive faces without ascertaining which differ from a neutral face, some studies have made the latter comparisons. The results reveal both a positive halo for attractive faces and a negative halo for unattractive faces.

Sex Differences in the Halo Effect

It is widely believed that good looks are more valued in women than men, which suggests that the attractiveness halo effect may be more pronounced for women. However, comparisons of the magnitude of the halo effect for men and women across many studies have revealed a significant difference only for one impression: sexual warmth.[11] The tendency for attractive people to be perceived as sexually warmer than less attractive people is large for impressions of women but only moderate for impressions of men. One study also found that the tendency for attractive individuals to be seen as having more social influence is stronger for men than for women.[12] In addition, as men increase in attractiveness, they are rated higher in masculinity but not in femininity, whereas the reverse is true for women.[13] The traits on which the strength of the halo effect differs for men and women may account for sex differences in some of the social consequences of attractiveness that are discussed in this chapter.

The Halo Effect Across the Life Span

More favorable impressions of attractive faces obtain for faces of all ages.[14] More attractive babies ranging in age from 3 to 9 months are perceived as more healthy, affectionate, attached to mother, cheerful, responsive, likable, and smart, as well as causing fewer problems. More attractive elementary school children are perceived by teachers as more popular and having better character as well as more intelligent and more likely to get advanced degrees. Attractiveness creates a more favorable impression even in old age. Attractive people between the ages of 60 and 95 are perceived to have more socially desirable personality characteristics than their less attractive peers. The attractive elderly are also judged to have had more favorable life experiences, such as being a good parent, being an understanding spouse, and leading an interesting, eventful life. In addition, they are judged to have achieved higher occupational status, such as being a physician rather than a janitor. These halo effects are shown not only by young adult judges but also by judges of the same age as those being rated.

Development of the Halo Effect

More favorable reactions to attractive people develop within the first year of life. As mentioned earlier, young infants prefer to look at attractive rather than unattractive faces.[15] Moreover, infants behave very differently toward an attractive than an unattractive stranger. If 12-month-olds are spoken to and played with by a stranger who is wearing an unattractive lifelike latex mask—narrow, close-set eyes; a long nose; and lowered eyebrows—they are less likely to show positive affect, such as smiling and laughter, than if the stranger wears an attractive mask. The infants are also less likely to show involvement in play with the unattractive stranger, such as accepting toys from her, and they are more likely to show resistance to the unattractive stranger, such as pushing her away. These effects are clearly precipitated by the stranger's face and not her behavior. Not only did the stranger follow a well-learned script when interacting with the infants, but also the same woman wore the attractive mask sometimes and the unattractive one other times, and she never knew which mask she had on. Therefore, she could not have inadvertently behaved differently toward the infants when wearing one mask versus the other. A study of infants' reactions to attractive and unattractive inanimate dolls reinforces the conclusion that they are reacting to the face per se. When seated within reach of two dolls, infants spent more time touching the one with an attractive face (traced from a photograph of a real infant that had been judged by adults as highly attractive) than the one with an unattractive face. Finally, it does not appear that infants' differential reactions to unattractive and attractive faces reflect greater familiarity of the attractive face rather than its greater attractiveness per se. Infants show more favorable reactions to attractive faces even when the face that is most familiar to them—their own mother's face—is relatively unattractive.[16] The early development of positive affective reactions to attractive adults may be rudiments of the full-blown attractiveness stereotype. By the time children are old enough to give verbal indicators of the attractiveness halo, it is present.[17]

The Halo Effect Across Cultures

Although the attractiveness halo effect holds true across various ethnic and racial groups, some variations have been observed. On the one hand, there is an attractiveness halo in ratings of black, white, and Hispanic infants and children by black, white, and Hispanic judges. Moreover, the physical attractiveness of infants and children has a bigger impact on how positively judges evaluate them than does their ethnicity.[18] Similarly, cross-race judgments of adult men by whites, blacks, and Koreans show higher honesty attributed to more attractive men of all races. On the other hand, the attribution of more warmth to more attractive men was not consistent across these three groups.[19] These findings suggest that although the attractiveness halo effect is racially universal, the particular traits on which the halo effect shows up may depend on cultural values or expectations.

Consistent with the suggestion that cultural values may influence the traits that show a halo effect is the fact that impressions of intelligence show a stronger attractiveness halo for Chinese than for Americans, whereas the reverse is true for impressions of sociability.[20] Evidence that this reflects differences in cultural values is provided by the finding that Chinese students cite "good at school work" as one of the most important traits for choosing friends. This trait is not high on the list for American students, who, unlike the Chinese, cite "sociable" as an important basis for choosing friends.[21] Differences in cultural values can also explain differences in the halo effect for Koreans and Americans. Attractiveness has a stronger effect on Koreans' impressions of moral integrity and worth than on their impressions of dominance, which is consistent with the value placed on traits that facilitate harmonious relationships in collectivist cultures like Korea. The reverse pattern is found for Americans, who show a moderate halo effect for impressions of dominance and a small or null effect for impressions of integrity and concern for others, consistent with the traits of self-assertion that are valued in individualistic cultures like the United States. Traits that are equally consistent with collectivist and individualistic values—social competence, adjustment, and sexual warmth—show strong halo effects in both cultures.[22]

Origin of the Attractiveness Halo

The question remains as to why an attractive face creates a positive halo effect. Although the answer has not been clearly established, a number of possibilities may be entertained.

Accuracy

One explanation for the halo is that it is accurate, deriving from direct observations of attractive and unattractive people. This explanation can account for the fact that the attractiveness halo is strongest for judgments of social skills and popularity, which are readily observed, and weaker for judgments of adjustment and intellectual competence, traits that are less visible. The accuracy explanation has been put to the test in a systematic assessment of the correspondences between the attractiveness halo and people's actual traits as assessed by self-reports, personality and ability test scores, and behavioral observations.[23] Although this assessment concluded that "good-looking people are not what we think," there is evidence for a small kernel of truth to the halo effect, which will be discussed at greater length in Chapter 8.

Although there is a kernel of truth to the attractiveness halo, the real differences between attractive and unattractive people are inadequate to account for the halo's magnitude. Moreover, the question remains as to where the real differences come from. One possibility is that they derive from self-fulfilling prophecy effects. To the extent that attractive individuals elicit more positive expectations, they will be treated differently, and they may consequently develop more positive traits. This possibility is discussed at greater length in the next chapter; however, it does not answer the question of why attractive individuals elicit more positive expectations in the first place.

Cultural Stereotypes

Another explanation for the attractiveness halo is that it derives from exposure to cultural representations of attractive and unattractive people. This contribution to the halo effect is discussed more in Chapter 9. As noted previously, Western culture, and probably others as well, associates beauty with good things and ugliness with bad things. However, this explanation begs the question of why these cultural tendencies exist.

Sickness Similarities

The attractiveness halo may derive from the adaptive value of responding to the valid fitness information that faces can provide. As I discussed in Chapters 2 and 6, facial qualities such as symmetry and average facial proportions are markers of intellectual, psychological, and physical fitness, and these qualities also make a face attractive. Thus, the attribution of higher intellectual competence to more attractive people may reflect an overgeneralization of the accurate perception of lower competence in mentally retarded people who have various facial anomalies. Similarly, the attribution of greater social competence to more attractive people may reflect an overgeneralization of the accurate perception of lower competence in emotionally disturbed people who have various facial anomalies.[24]

The sickness similarities overgeneralization effect not only provides a plausible explanation for the attractiveness halo but also may explain some variations in the halo that have been observed. For example, the finding that the halo is more reliably shown for impressions of attractive women who are highly babyfaced can be explained if the facial indicators of fitness, such as symmetry and averageness, are more marked for baby-faced attractive women than for the sophisticated or sexy types. A sickness similarities effect has some difficulty accounting for other variations in the halo, requiring an additional mechanism to explain why there are cultural differences in the traits for which it is most pronounced. Such a mechanism may be provided by affective associations to attractive faces.

Affective Associations

The evolutionary selection pressures that may produce a sickness similarities overgeneralization effect, causing people to attribute more positive psychological traits to more attractive people, may also produce more positive affective responses to more attractive people. Such responses not only could foster social interactions that would promote survival of the fittest, but also could contribute to the attractiveness halo. In particular, if a face elicits a positive feeling in perceivers, this feeling may make them more likely to think of positive traits.[25] Evidence that our feelings can affect our thoughts is provided by the finding that people tend to view others more positively when they are feeling good than when they are in a neutral mood, and they tend to view others more negatively when they are feeling bad than when they are in a neutral mood, regardless of the cause of the mood.[26] Positive feelings produced by an attractive face not only may contribute to the attractiveness halo but also may account for variations in the halo across cultures and traits. In particular, it makes sense that the good feelings evoked by an attractive face would influence impressions of those traits that are most culturally valued.

More direct evidence that the positive affect produced by attractive faces may contribute to the halo effect is provided by research that capitalized on the fact that dilated pupils elicit more positive affect than constricted ones. People shown in photographs with dilated pupils induced more positive feelings as well as more positive trait impressions than the same people shown in photographs that were retouched to show constricted pupils.[27] Similarly, line drawings of faces that are "pleasant" to look at elicited the full-blown attractiveness halo, even though these drawings are too fragmentary to be viewed as representing real people.[28] To the extent that attractive people, like dilated pupils and the foregoing line drawings, elicit positive feelings whereas unattractive people elicit negative feelings, these affective reactions would create divergent trait impressions to yield the attractiveness halo effect. People do in fact report more positive moods after viewing attractive faces than average ones, albeit only for faces of the opposite sex, a result that may be due to countervailing negative affect that can be produced by comparing oneself to very attractive faces of one's own sex.[29]

Social Outcomes of the Attractiveness Halo

The positive responses to attractive faces extend beyond trait impressions to provide significant social advantages. Like the social outcomes of a babyface, many of these advantages can be explained by the facial fit principle. A facial fit effect occurs when attractive people not only are expected to have positive traits but also receive social outcomes that match the traits that their faces lead others to expect. Such outcomes have been documented in a variety of domains, including interpersonal relationships, occupational success, criminal justice decisions, and health care.[30]

Dating and Mating

In a classic study of the advantages of attractiveness in dating situations, college freshmen were matched with blind dates for a big dance. A great deal was known about these freshmen, including their scores on IQ tests and various personality tests. However, the only thing that predicted whether or not partners wanted to see their dates again was observers' ratings of the date's physical attractiveness; the date's IQ and social skills made no difference. Other studies have shown similar results. After a brief interaction or after one blind date, more attractive individuals, particularly women, were liked better than those who were less attractive.[31] When men and women were asked to select a potential date from photographs coupled with brief personality descriptions, attractive individuals were highly preferred, whereas those with positive personality traits were only slightly preferred to their less favorable counterparts.[32]

The importance of attractiveness in dating choices is seen not only in psychology experiments but also in everyday life. Analyses of "lonely hearts" personal ads have revealed that both sexes, but particularly men, seek the attribute of attractiveness in a prospective date and that both sexes, but particularly women, offer attractiveness. People not only say they want attractiveness but also choose it.[33] When the most frequently chosen members of a videodating organization were compared to the least chosen, the only difference found between them was their physical attractiveness, even though their written profiles provided information regarding warmth, humor, and occupation.[34] Finally, self-reports of attractive and unattractive individuals corroborate these preferences for attractive individuals. Attractive men and women are more popular and date more often. This moderate effect is somewhat stronger for women, an outcome that may reflect the stronger tendency to attribute sexual warmth to attractive women than to attractive men.[35] The preferences shown for attractive dates could derive from the influence of attractiveness on impressions of a person's other attributes. People in the blind date study may have preferred attractive dates not simply because they were attractive but because the halo effect made them appear to be more fitting companions: more socially skilled, sexually warm, well-adjusted, and intellectually competent.

The high value placed on attractiveness extends from choosing a date to choosing a mate. When samples of people from 33 different countries from around the globe were asked to rank order the desirability of 13 characteristics in a potential mate, physical attractiveness was ranked fifth by men and seventh by women.[36] This sex difference in the importance of physical attractiveness held true across age and racial groups in a representative sample of unmarried U.S. residents, although it was stronger for whites than for blacks.[37] The higher valuation of attractiveness by men than women is found even among homosexuals.[38] Although attractiveness is highly ranked in mate selection, it is reassuring to find that the attributes of kindness, intelligence, an exciting personality, and health receive higher ranks than good looks from both men and women. (Women also place the characteristics "easygoing" and "creative" above attractiveness.) Less important than attractiveness to both sexes are the attributes "wants children," "good earning capacity," "college graduate," "good housekeeper," "good heredity," and "religious." [39]

Men's high valuation of attractiveness in a mate is corroborated by actual marriage patterns. Attractive women are chosen more often, or at least more quickly. A study from the 1930s found that approximately 30 percent of attractive women had married within a few years of graduation from the University of California, compared with only 14 percent of unattractive women.[40] The advantage of attractiveness in the marriage market extends as long as 15 years after high school graduation, when one study found that the most beautiful women were 10 times more likely to have married than the homely ones. This attractiveness advantage may not accrue to men; some researchers have found that they are equally likely to be married whether handsome or ugly.[41] This difference may reflect cultural norms that give men an advantage in mate selection as well as the lesser importance of attractiveness to women's mate preferences. Although attractiveness may signal intellectual, psychological, and physical fitness to women just as it does to men, evolutionary psychologists have argued that attractiveness may have less impact on women's mate selection because it has been adaptive for them to respond most positively to potential mates who will be good providers, an attribute that may be conveyed by attributes other than attractiveness.[42] The cogency of this argument is reinforced by evidence regarding the type of men whom beautiful women marry. One study found that girls who were very attractive as early adolescents were more apt than their plainer peers to "marry up," raising their social status through marriage.[43] Other research has also shown that husbands of attractive women have higher incomes than those married to the less attractive.[44] The flip side of this pattern is that an attractive wife may make a positive contribution to her husband's social status, since men thought to be involved with attractive women are seen as more confident and likable.[45]

Whereas the foregoing studies have revealed a preference for more attractive romantic partners, this result is at variance with everyday observations of couples who, more often than not, seem to match one another in attractiveness. Beauty and the beast are not a common pair. Rather, systematic studies of the attractiveness of real-world couples provide moderate-to-strong support for a matching effect: People appear to prefer those who are similar to themselves in attractiveness.[46] Couples who met through a videodating service and progressed beyond two dates were more similar to each other in attractiveness than those who had not progressed so far even though they were no more similar in age or occupation. Ratings of the facial attractiveness of newlyweds and other married couples also show similarity between husband and wife. Attractiveness matching is so striking that people can do much better than chance at picking out who is married to whom, and the degree to which couples are matched in attractiveness is exceeded only by their similarity in educational attainment and heterosexuality.[47] The pull of attractiveness matching can have comical effects, as in the formation of the International Diastema Club, which brings together people who have a gap of at least 2 millimeters between their two front teeth and who vow not to seek orthodontic correction! [48]

How can attractiveness matching in ongoing relationships be reconciled with the preferences for highly attractive people shown in the date-seeking studies? It has been proposed that matches in attractiveness could derive from everyone actually preferring the most attractive people: The most attractive men and women pair up, followed by the pairing of the most attractive remaining men and women, and so on. However, attractiveness within couples is even more similar than this hypothesis would predict. It appears that there may be at least two forces operating: pure attractiveness seeking moderated to some degree by similarity seeking. The latter may reflect a decision to "settle" rather than be rejected by a highly desirable attractive individual.[49] Consistent with this possibility is research that has shown that men are likely to ask out the most attractive woman in a group when they have been told she would be willing to date them but may select a less attractive woman when they are uncertain about who will accept.[50]

Influencing People

Not only are attractive individuals viewed as more influential than their less attractive peers, but this perception is accurate.[51] Advertising is a case in point. Endorsements of a disposable razor by more attractive celebrities produced more positive attitudes and intentions to try the product than endorsements by less attractive celebrities. Moreover, experimental investigations using unknown endorsers have shown that attractiveness per se makes a difference. College students reacted more positively to an advertisement for a new pain reliever when the ad depicted an attractive communicator than an unattractive one, and magazine subscribers were actually more likely to buy something advocated by an attractive woman. Men also reported that they would be more likely to seek out or try a cologne when it was advertised by an attractive women than when it was advertised by an unattractive one. These effects can be accounted for by the positive feelings that attractive communicators elicit in the audience, feelings that can spread to the product being endorsed. Evidence consistent with this explanation is provided by the fact that communicators' attractiveness affects persuasion without influencing their perceived expertise or trustworthiness. Rather, it appears to be positive feelings toward attractive communicators that account for their success, since the tendency for attractive communicators to be more persuasive is diminished when the likability of attractive and unattractive communicators is equated. Moreover, the relationship between communicator attractiveness and persuasion may be reduced when attention is focused on message content, thereby reducing the more superficial effects of positive affective reactions to the communicator.[52] Although the existence of more positive feelings toward attractive communicators appears to account for the greater influence of these people, there is some evidence that a facial fit effect may also play a role. Indeed, fashion editors agreed that they would cast different types of beauties in advertisements for different merchandise.[53]

Occupational Success

> By the school's "merit system" she was tops in her medical school class. Her advisor wrote "Her past record is the best in the school. Her examination scores are at the very top of the school. She has functioned at a high level and has had no problems with a patient at any time." Yet, she was dismissed by the dean on the verge of graduation. The grounds the dean gave for dismissal were tardiness, bad grooming, and an abrasive personal style.[54]

This anecdote concerns Charlotte Horowitz, whose dismissal from a Missouri medical school was brought before the Supreme Court. All parties to the case agreed that she was brilliant. They also agreed that she was unattractive, overweight, and unkempt. Had she been more attractive, her "abrasive personal style" might have been overlooked. Indeed, her appearance may have contributed to the dean's perception of her character via a negative halo effect.

Although discrimination against a brilliant medical student on the basis of her appearance may seem farfetched, such employment discrimination is taken seriously by legal scholars. A note in the 1987 *Harvard Law Review* argued that the Rehabilitation Act of 1973 "should be construed to protect people against employment discrimination on the basis of largely immutable aspects of bodily and facial appearance."[55] The Equal Employment Opportunity Commission (EEOC) has fought unjustified height and weight job requirements. However, Charlotte Horowitz's case was not tried on the grounds of discrimination based on facial appearance. Rather, it was tried on the narrower grounds of whether she was given proper notice and a fair hearing. Indeed, one EEOC official was quoted as stating that a campaign to eliminate job bias on the basis of attractiveness would "make a farce out of our whole effort to fight discrimination because of race, national origin, or sex." Whether or not that is true, the fact is that appearance-based employment discrimination does exist and it is not trivial to those who experience it. More recent complaints may motivate the EEOC to challenge discrimination based on facial appearance. For example, a woman recently filed a federal sex discrimination complaint, alleging that her facial hair—a mustache—is the reason she was fired from her job as an audiovisual technician.[56]

Most investigations of employment discrimination against the unattractive have been simulation studies like those described in Chapter 5 investigating babyfaceness. Photos of attractive or unattractive job applicants are affixed to identical resumes that are then evaluated. Such studies have shown that applicants with attractive faces are ranked higher for a variety of jobs than their unattractive counterparts with equal scholastic standing. Not only are attractive applicants perceived as more qualified, but also they receive higher starting salary recommendations— as much as 8 to 20 percent more. These effects are equally strong whether the evaluators are college students or professionals, males or females. Moreover, they are far from trivial. Indeed, an applicant's attractiveness can make more of a difference in expectations of achievement and the likelihood of being recommended for the job than an applicant's sex.[57]

More real-life demonstrations of the employment benefits of attractiveness were provided by "candid camera" scenarios staged for an ABC 20/20 television program.[58] Two men were sent to apply for one job opening, and two women were sent to apply for another. The clothing worn by each pair of applicants was the same, but one person in each pair was highly attractive, and the other was plainer, although by no means ugly. A male interviewer offered the job to the more attractive woman right on the spot and gave her a salary at the top of the range that had been mentioned to the plainer woman, who didn't even get a phone call to inform her that she hadn't gotten the job. A similar outcome accrued to the more attractive of the two men, even though the interviewer was again a male. When debriefed about this little experiment, the interviewers expressed surprise at the influence attractiveness had shown. One interviewer attributed his choice of the more attractive woman to her vocal qualities; ironically, the less attractive woman had her own radio show, suggesting that her voice was just fine.

The effects of attractiveness in hiring simulation studies may result both from the positive affect that attractiveness elicits and from the influence of attractiveness on trait impressions. As such, these decisions can be explained at least in part by the facial fit principle: They reflect the match between the job requirements and the traits that attractive faces lead others to expect. For example, an oncologist once confessed that he gave preference to attractive women when selecting interns. His justification for this was that he thought they'd be more socially skilled in dealing with cancer patients, owing to being happier. This physician would reject Charlotte Horowitz, the Missouri medical student, because of the traits that he associates with her unattractive appearance. Similarly, since attractive individuals appear more popular and more socially competent, they may also appear better suited to managerial positions, which are perceived as requiring a likable personality and good interpersonal skills. The appearance of intellectual competence and dominance may be crucial to the attractiveness advantage in other jobs. The interviewer who selected the more attractive male applicant in the 20/20 show claimed that applicant was more able to make him feel confident of his abilities and that he "looked like a stockbroker."

Even children show the facial fit effect in selecting teachers. In one segment of the 20/20 television show, an attractive and an unattractive teacher each read a book to a first grade class. In some classes the unattractive teacher went first, and in others the attractive teacher went first, and each teacher read each story in half of the classrooms. After hearing both stories, the children were asked which of the two teachers they would prefer as a substitute. The more attractive teacher received an overwhelmingly stronger endorsement for the job. Moreover, many of the children acknowledged that they preferred her because she was prettier. When the children were asked why they like a pretty teacher, a typical response was, "If they're pretty, then they're smarter."

Studies of discrimination against unattractive individuals in real organizations lend more systematic support the facial fit principle. Facially unattractive men and women working as business administrators earn lower salaries than their more attractive peers 5 years after receiving the

MBA degree, whereas unattractive male accountants do not receive lower pay. This is consistent with the fact that the positive social traits ascribed to attractive individuals "fit" the work of business administrators but are less relevant to the work of accountants. Other research has provided additional support for the facial fit principle. Whereas attractive job applicants are favored when a job involves face-to-face contact with others and thus requires the positive interpersonal characteristics stereotypically associated with attractiveness, favoritism toward attractive individuals is eliminated in the case of jobs that involve little interpersonal contact. Similarly, attractive women are more likely to be employed in jobs that are judged to require traits stereotypically ascribed to attractive individuals.[59]

The facial fit principle suggests that the advantages of attractiveness in the workplace should depend not only on the type of job but also on the sex of the employee. Sex differences may occur because the attribution of more social influence to attractive people is stronger for men than women. Also, to the extent that attractive women look very feminine, they may be perceived to fit different jobs than attractive men, who look very masculine.[60] Indeed, unattractive women may be perceived suited to the same jobs as attractive men. Consistent with this reasoning is research that has found that attractive women are evaluated less favorably than unattractive women for typically masculine jobs that are high in prestige and power: managerial positions. On the other hand, women experience the usual favoritism toward attractive individuals when evaluated for typically feminine jobs in the lower ranks of an organizational hierarchy: clerical positions. Attractive men are evaluated more favorably for both types of jobs. It seems that the traits attributed to attractive women make them seem unfit for "masculine" jobs, whereas those attributed to attractive men do not disqualify them for "feminine" jobs. It would be interesting to see whether the detrimental effects of attractiveness for women seeking high-level jobs varies with the type of attractiveness. Perhaps sophisticated-looking attractive women would not be disadvantaged.

The facial fit principle has implications for political success as well as for success in other occupations. Research on political choices indicates that candidates will be more effective to the extent that they make us feel good and we view them as competent and trustworthy. Insofar as attractive people fit this bill, attractiveness should foster political success. Consistent with this reasoning, fictitious attractive male candidates for the U.S. Congress were evaluated more favorably than less attractive candidates. This effect was particularly strong when both candidates also had favorable personality descriptions, which suggests that the political benefits of attractiveness are not solely to create favorable personality impressions. The positive affect that attractiveness elicits may also be important, and it may account for the tendency for people to perceive an attractive candidate's position on the issues to be more similar to their own, even though issue positions were in fact unrelated to the candidates' attractiveness.[61]

The beneficial effects of attractiveness to political candidates has been demonstrated not only in the laboratory but also in real elections. Attractive males received more votes than unattractive ones in a Canadian parliamentary election during the 1970s.[62] However, the meaning of this result is unclear, since the more attractive candidates represented more popular political parties. Of course, that in itself is an interesting phenomenon. The Canadian electorate is not alone in favoring more attractive politicians. One study found that more attractive representatives in the U.S. House of Representatives were perceived as more competent.[63] Although this relationship held true for both male and female representatives, there is some evidence to indicate that attractiveness is more apt to be a political asset for men. In a mock election, attractive men received more votes than unattractive men, whereas attractiveness had no effect for women.[64] Sex differences in the advantages of attractiveness for political success may be explained by the facial fit principle. Whereas certain types of male attractiveness are positively associated with impressions of dominance and power, the strong component of youthfulness in female attractiveness does not fit these impressions, and the association of high social influence with attractiveness is stronger for men than women.

Although attractiveness may not be a great asset to female politicians, unattractiveness may still be a liability, and it is exploited in political campaigns. In the 1994 Illinois gubernatorial race, campaign posters not only accused the Democratic candidate, Dawn Clark Netsch, of being a tax cheat but also stated that "the truth is as ugly as she is." Netsch responded with a new campaign slogan: "More than a pretty face." Ad hominem attacks on unattractive candidates are not restricted to women. The Illinois Senator Paul Simon came to Netsch's defense, recalling that when he ran for president in 1988, a Dallas newspaper had stated that he had "a face made for radio." Simon also reported President Lincoln's retort to the criticism that he was too ugly to be president: "At least I'm not two-faced. Otherwise I wouldn't be wearing the one I'm wearing right now."[65]

Eluding Condemnation

Attractive people who break the law get a break all the way from the scene of the crime to the courtroom.[66] First, they may be less likely to be noticed or reported when committing a crime. Shoplifters with attractive clothing and facial appearance are less likely to be reported by other customers even when their actions are clearly observed. Even if reported, attractive individuals may be advantaged in the courtroom, where the fundamental right to a fair trial that is guaranteed by the Fourteenth Amendment to the U.S. Constitution can be compromised by the litigant's facial appearance. Simulated criminal trials using mock juries and fictitious litigants have shown that physically attractive defendants are less likely than unattractive ones to be convicted. Moreover, if they are convicted, attractive defendants receive more lenient sentences. Favoritism toward attractive individuals is found in actual court decisions as well as simulated ones. Although the defendants' attractiveness did not influence whether they were found guilty, it was found to influence sentencing of those who were convicted in Pennsylvania criminal trials. Attractive defendants received shorter sentences than less attractive ones who had been convicted of equally serious crimes.[67]

A compelling example of the ability of attractive individuals to elude condemnation was provided in mock trials staged for the 20/20 television program mentioned earlier. The defendant, who was charged with robbery, was either very attractive or ordinary looking. Although each defendant just sat there during the testimony and never was called to the stand to testify, the attractive defendant was less likely to be found guilty by the mock jurors. When interviewed, the jurors reported that the attractive defendant seemed like a reasonable, honest, intelligent "nice guy." Attractive defendants may even be favored in real murder trials. Arguing for judicial reform, a New York City judge recalled the following:

> It was an overwhelming case of clear guilt. Yet there was a hung jury. One juror was convinced that the defendant was not guilty. How did she know? Well, as she explained it, "Someone that good-looking could not commit such a crime."[68]

The ability of attractive individuals to elude condemnation may be explained by the facial fit effect and the positive feelings these people evoke. The favorable outcomes accruing to attractive individuals in the criminal justice system fit the positive traits that they are assumed to have, and they also follow from the tendency for people who are feeling good to be less punitive than those who have been exposed to some unpleasant stimulus.[69]

Whereas most evidence has revealed a general positive effect for defendant attractiveness, there also is some indication that the effects of attractiveness may vary with the nature of the alleged transgression. For example, attractive women defendants in simulated criminal cases were given stiffer sentences than less attractive women when their actions produced very serious consequences, such as a fatality in an auto accident, or when their actions exploited their attractiveness, for example, conning a middle-aged bachelor. A contrast effect may explain these findings. When attractive people show negative behavior that clearly disconfirms perceivers' positive expectations, it may seem even worse than the same behavior by an unattractive person, with the result that the attractive person is punished more severely.

The attractiveness of the plaintiff can also influence judicial outcomes. Attractive people who are victimized are more likely to be vindicated. In simulated rape trials, jurors are more likely to give guilty verdicts and to recommend longer sentences when the victim is attractive, although these effects are not always found. Similarly, the defendant in a simulated trial is more likely to be found guilty of an automobile theft when a female plaintiff, who had taken precautions against the theft, is attractive than when she is unattractive. A bias in favor of attractive plaintiffs has been reported for civil as well as criminal cases. Mock jurors are more apt to find in favor of an attractive plaintiff in a civil suit resulting from an automobile accident and to award significantly higher financial damages to the attractive plaintiff. The benefits of attractiveness accrue to plaintiffs in real courtroom decisions as well as in simulated ones: More attractive plaintiffs were favored in the decisions rendered in cases brought before Massachusetts small claims courts.[70] Like the benefits of attractiveness that accrue to defendants in the courtroom, those that accrue to the plaintiff may be explained by the perception that attractive people are honest and by the positive feelings that their appearance evokes, since good moods have been shown to increase altruistic behavior in other settings.[71]

Procuring Aid

The more favorable response to attractive plaintiffs suggests that there may be a general tendency to provide more aid to people in need if they are attractive.[72] Investigations of bystander reactions to emergency situations have confirmed this prediction. An experiment on a moderately traveled suburban road north of Baltimore, Maryland, revealed that male motorists who had only a brief glimpse of a woman in a stalled car were more likely to stop and offer help when the woman was made up to look attractive than when she appeared less attractive. Although one might attribute this effect to romantic rather than altruistic motives, an experiment in the New York City subway system showed that altruistic motives alone will benefit attractive people in need. More people of both sexes and all ages came to the aid of an attractive man who fell down in a subway car than a similarly indisposed unattractive man. People also were more likely to come to the aid of an attractive than an unattractive person who lost an urgent letter containing a graduate school application form with an attached photograph. The letter with the attractive photograph was more apt to be mailed by a stranger who found it in a public phone booth in a large airport. Direct appeals for help have shown similarly advantageous outcomes for attractive individuals, although there is some indication that attractive people receive more help only when the need is great.

Even professional helpers may be more apt to aid attractive individuals. Unattractive individuals are less often accepted for therapy and, if accepted, more often placed into group therapy, where treatment may be less intense. The greater help offered to attractive individuals stands in contrast to evaluations of their mental health. Professional counselors give more favorable diagnoses and prognoses to physically attractive patients than to those who are lower in attractiveness, assessments that are consistent with the facial fit principle: The role of patient better suits those with an unattractive face, who tend to look less healthy owing to the sickness similarities overgeneralization effect.[73] Consistent with their more favorable prognosis is the fact that more attractive mental patients are hospitalized for shorter periods of time than unattractive ones, even when the two groups are equated in levels of adjustment. While in the hospital, more attractive patients are visited more frequently.[74] One explanation for some of the foregoing results is that attractive faces look happier and healthier than unattractive ones. However, another explanation must be invoked to explain the fact that unattractive individuals are visited less often when hospitalized, less often accepted for therapy, and if accepted, more often placed in group therapy where treatment may be less intense. Although unattractive people may look more in need of help, people shun them. Such avoidance is consistent with the argument that unattractive faces evoke negative affect as well as with the negative traits attributed to unattractive people.

Whereas one might argue that more favorable prognoses for attractive individuals will have positive effects on their treatment outcomes in the domain of mental health, this is less certain in the domain of physical health. Consider the following experience of a young woman who was in the hospital recovering from minor surgery following an automobile accident. A physician who came by to check on her cheerily observed, "You're a fine-looking healthy young woman, and that will heal right up." She was indeed a fine-looking, even healthy-looking, woman. But the doctor was so misled by her appearance that he neglected to read her chart. When he did so (at the patient's request), he discovered that she suffered from a chronic illness that would make the healing process problematic and slow.

Consistent with the foregoing anecdote is research that has shown that attractive individuals do indeed receive more positive diagnoses when their physical health is being evaluated. Medical residents evaluated photographs of simulated women patients as if they had just met them and were treating them for the first time. Both attractive and unattractive photographs of each patient were created by variations in hairstyle and cosmetics. Of course, any one doctor saw only one photograph of each woman. Accompanying each photograph was a description of the patient's symptoms, such as the following:

Nancy is a 22 year old woman currently attending the University of Saskatchewan. She is suffering from back pain that was caused by lifting a heavy object. She complains of pain when engaged in any activity that requires her to bend, lift, or carry.

The doctors' evaluations revealed that they took the attractive women's symptoms less seriously, perceiving these patients as experiencing less pain, distress, and negative affective experiences than the unattractive women. It was not surprising, given these differential assessments, that the doctors also indicated greater concern and sympathy for as well as desire to help unattractive patients, whom they perceived as less healthy than attractive ones.[75] Fortunately for unattractive individuals, these results indicate that doctors can overcome the tendency to be more helpful to those whose appearance evokes more positive feelings and trait attributions. On the other hand, the healthy appearance of attractive people may lead doctors to provide less treatment than their condition warrants.

Whether attractive patients receive less treatment may vary with the credibility of the patient's complaint. The origin of the patient's complaint in the foregoing case was lifting a heavy object, which is a moderately credible cause of back pain. However, when nurses were informed that routine tests had revealed either no cause for this symptom or a highly credible cause—a kidney stone—the attractiveness of the patient had no effect on their evaluation of the patient's pain.[76] Thus, moderately credible complaints of attractive patients are taken less seriously, whereas this is not true for complaints that have high or low credibility.

Although medical professionals may underrate the pain of attractive patients, they also interact more positively with them. Physicians who were watched through a one-way mirror while interacting with patients were observed to give more nonverbal attention and courtesy to the more attractive patients. Although such behaviors may have a salutary effect on health, it is not clear, on balance, whether attractive or unattractive patients will be advantaged in the medical care they receive. To the extent that placebo effects are strong, and they often are, positive expectations will benefit attractive patients. To the extent that more appropriate treatment derives from viewing the patient's condition as more serious, unattractive patients will benefit.

Summary

Attractive people of both sexes and all ages are perceived to have more positive traits. This halo effect is shown in early infancy and in diverse cultures, although the particular traits ascribed to more attractive people may be influenced by cultural values. The halo effect also produces advantageous social outcomes that are consistent with the facial fit principle: Attractive people receive outcomes that match the traits that their faces lead others to expect. They are preferred as dates and mates; they have more social influence and better job prospects, particularly when the job requirements match their expected traits; they receive more help from strangers; and they get more favorable treatment both in the criminal justice system and from mental health professionals. Attractiveness is not without disadvantages. One disadvantage is that the physical ills of attractive people may be taken less seriously by physicians, probably because these patients look healthier than those who are less attractive. Although additional research is needed to elucidate the origins of the attractiveness halo effect, it may derive both from a sickness similarities overgeneralization effect that yields the attribution of greater intellectual, social, and physical fitness to more attractive people and from the positive affect that attractiveness evokes in the beholder. Cultural representations also contribute to the development of the halo effect, and so may actual differences between attractive and unattractive individuals, a possibility that is considered in more depth in Chapter 8.

8

Formative Faces and Pulchritudinous Personalities

I called him the "little professor"—my bespectacled preschooler. He seemed self-sufficient and wise beyond his years. Now Caleb has grown into an intellectual, responsible young man, who seems sometimes more my parent than my son. Our friends called their fat-cheeked son Bobby the "little lover." We thought him affectionate, dependent, and ingenuous. Perhaps Bobby, with whom we've lost touch, has grown into an affectionate, naive young man, who needs to be cared for by others. Evidence of different traits in bespectacled, mature-looking Caleb and fat-cheeked, babyfaced Bobby would suggest that the social consequences of facial appearance that have been documented in the preceding chapters may reflect something more than biased perceptions. Individuals who differ in babyfaceness or attractiveness not only may be perceived to have different traits but also might actually have different traits.

Chapter 3 described several causal routes to a connection between facial appearance and psychological traits. One possibility is that both may be influenced by the same biological factors: The gene responsible for Bobby's fat cheeks may also contribute to his dependent disposition. A second possibility is that appearance and personality may both be influenced by the same environmental factors: Parents who are watchful enough to detect a preschooler's need for glasses may socialize a conscientious child. In this chapter, we consider evidence for the remaining causal routes: an influence of early appearance on later traits and an influ-

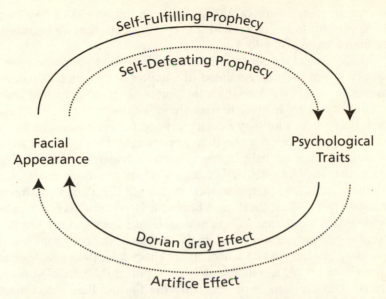

FIGURE 8.1 *Four possible developmental relationships between facial appearance and psychological traits: (a) self-fulfilling prophecy: people develop the traits that their appearance leads others to expect; (b) self-defeating prophecy: people develop traits opposite to those expected; (c) Dorian Gray effect: people develop an appearance that matches their traits; and (d) artifice effect: people develop an appearance that camouflages their traits.*

ence of early traits on later appearance. These pathways are illustrated in Figure 8.1.

A *self-fulfilling prophecy effect* occurs when the expectations that appearance creates are realized. Chubby cheeks or eyeglasses may lead to social interactions that elicit affectionate and conscientious behavior, respectively. The elicited behavior can then influence an individual's skills and self-conceptions such that similar behaviors are shown even in the absence of specific social expectations. In this manner, people may acquire the psychological traits that their facial appearance led others to expect. A *self-defeating prophecy effect* occurs when the expectations that appearance creates produce environmental effects that elicit behavior just the opposite of what is expected. There are two ways that this can happen. One is that the target of the expectancies defeats them because the social interactions produced by the expectancies are negative. For example, the chubby-cheeked boy who is expected to be cuddly and affectionate may reject this childlike image and compensate by becoming hostile. A second mechanism is that the person holding the expectancies engages in social interactions that themselves defeat the prophecy. For example, people may explain things very carefully to the chubby-cheeked boy because they expect him to be naive, with the consequence that he becomes less naive than a more savvy-looking child.

A *Dorian Gray effect* occurs when variations in traits cause *congruent* variations in appearance. As noted in Chapter 3, this effect is named for the novel by Oscar Wilde in which the portrait of the protagonist changed over time, matching his face to his behavior. Similarly, the conscientious student who reads a lot may develop a need for eyeglasses, or the naive individual may develop a childlike appearance through facial mannerisms that can increase babyfaceness, such as widened eyes, smiling, or raised eyebrows.[1] An *artifice effect* occurs when variations in traits cause *incongruent* variations in appearance. Although this path is not revealed in the anecdotes about Caleb and Bobby, it is possible that a dependent individual would attempt to look more self-sufficient and mature than he really is to achieve certain social goals. Similarly, the conscientious intellectual may choose contact lenses in an effort to appear less "bookish." Evidence that people can deliberately manipulate their facial appearance to convey certain traits is provided by the finding that individuals are perceived as more powerful when they are attempting to look dominant than when they are attempting to look submissive even when they keep a neutral emotional expression.[2]

This chapter considers the causal links between appearance and psychological traits found in research on attractiveness and babyfaceness. The first section of the chapter examines the path from early appearance to later traits, and it considers (a) early environmental effects of appearance, (b) conditions conducive to self-fulfilling and self-defeating prophecy effects, and (c) evidence for a causal influence of early appearance on later traits. The second section of the chapter examines the path from early traits to later appearance, and it considers (a) early environmental effects of traits, (b) conditions conducive to Dorian Gray and artifice effects, and (c) evidence for a causal influence of early traits on later appearance. The final section examines the evidence for appearance-related differences in traits, that is, the accuracy of the attractiveness and babyface stereotypes.

The Path from Early Appearance to Later Traits

Early Effects of Appearance on Environmental Warmth

The positive feelings evoked by an attractive face and the nurturant responses evoked by a babyface should produce a warmer social environment for those with these appearance qualities. Indeed, attractive individuals are treated more warmly than unattractive ones from an early age, and as documented in Chapter 7, this pattern continues into adulthood.[3] Less attractive infants receive less kissing, cooing, smiling, eye contact, and close cuddling from their mothers than those who are more attractive. Mothers of less attractive infants also tend to ignore them, interacting more with others while feeding or playing with them, whereas attractive infants are more apt to receive their mothers' undivided attention.[4] Fathers as well as mothers respond more warmly to their more attractive offspring, and other adults may also treat attractive infants more warmly. Indeed, adults show a strong tendency to perceive attractive 3- to 9-month-old black, white, and Hispanic babies as more likable and as causing their parents fewer problems than babies who are less attractive. This bias holds true for adults of all three ethnic groups, and as noted in Chapter 7, an infant's attractiveness is a stronger predictor of adults' reactions than the infant's ethnicity.[5] Since attractiveness and babyfaceness are highly correlated in infancy, the evidence for greater warmth toward more attractive children in the first months of life also represents greater warmth toward more babyfaced children. As discussed in Chapter 4, infants with "non-babyish" features, such as a small forehead, a long chin, small eyes, or a large nose, are perceived as less cute than the "Gerber" types. Moreover, there is a small-to-moderate tendency for infants who lack the prototypical babyface to be treated less warmly by their own parents.

In childhood, as in infancy, more attractive individuals are likely to elicit greater warmth. Parents of less attractive daughters express more disappointment in their child, and more attractive children receive more positive trait ratings from their parents and their teachers.[6] Attractiveness also has medium-to-large effects on the responses children receive from their peers. According to the reports of children about their classmates, attractiveness increases the likelihood of being wanted as a friend and having many friends, being liked by others, and being picked as a leader.[7] More attractive boys between the ages of 9 and 14 also are more highly accepted by their peers at summer camp.[8] Attractiveness not only is a strong predictor of actual popularity but also is a stronger predictor of popularity than academic performance among students between grades 5 and 11.[9] More attractive children have fewer negative peer relations as well as more positive ones. In particular, they are less likely to be teased, to be left out of games, or to be the target of aggression.[10] Indeed, some research has shown that children who are consistently bullied are significantly less attractive than nonbullied classmates of the same sex.[11] Children with craniofacial handicaps may be particularly at risk for peer rejection.[12]

There is some indication that more babyfaced children, like more attractive children, encounter warmer social environments, although the evidence gathered to date is limited to the way people talk to these children. One study had college students teach some games to children over the telephone. The student teachers were told that the child was 4 years old, and they were shown a picture that ostensibly depicted the child with whom they were interacting, although in reality it was a picture of a different 4-year-old who had been judged previously to be mature-faced or babyfaced. When instructing children who were perceived as babyfaced, student teachers showed a moderate tendency to use more of the affectionate "baby talk" speech style that adults typically use when talking to real babies: higher pitch and more changing intonation.[13]

Interactions between second grade teachers and their students provide additional evidence of more affectionate speech directed at younger looking children. Teacher and student were videotaped while discussing a book that the student had recently read. Ratings of the student's appearance were made by judges who saw a soundless videotape depicting only the child's face, and ratings of the teacher's pitch and intonation were made by another group of judges from audiotapes of the interaction. Although the children's overall attractiveness and babyfaceness did not predict the teacher's use of baby talk in this study, the specific feature of "baby teeth" did. Teachers used higher pitch and more changing intonation when conversing with second graders who still had their baby teeth than with those who had grown their mature, secondary teeth.[14]

The greater warmth shown to more attractive and more babyfaced children extends to reactions to their misbehavior. Consider the following evaluation of a 7-year-old child who was reported to have hurt someone:

> She appears to be a perfectly charming little girl; well-mannered, basically unselfish. It seems that she can adapt well among children her age and makes a good impression . . . she plays well with everyone, but like anyone else, a bad day can occur. Her cruelty need not be taken too seriously. [15]

This evaluation, which discounted the child's bad behavior, was typical of college students' reactions to an attractive child.[16] When the same misdeed was reported in a teacher's daily activity report about an unattractive child, students saw the child very differently:

> I think the child would be quite bratty and would be a problem to teachers . . . she would probably try to pick a fight with other children her own age . . . she would be a brat at home . . . all in all, she would be a real problem.[17]

The more punitive reaction to an unattractive child may reflect the negative feelings that unattractiveness creates in the beholder as well as its influence on impressions of the child's other attributes. Since a negative halo effect makes the infraction fit the assumed traits of an unattractive child, people show a strong tendency to believe that it will recur, which can yield harsher punishment. It seems that misbehavior by an unattractive child tends to be seen as reflecting a stable, antisocial tendency, whereas misbehavior by an attractive child is written off as a fluke. Although the college students in the foregoing study were reluctant to recommend severe punishment for any of the children, large effects of attractiveness on punishment severity have been shown in performance situations in which some punishment was socially sanctioned. College women, who were playing the role of mother to a 10-year-old child, administered more severe punishments—which consisted of louder noises—to unattractive children when they made a mistake in a learning task.[18] College women also took away more pennies from unattractive than attractive boys as punishment for mistakes, although they did not show this effect for girls.[19] As is discussed later, a tendency for the effects of appearance on punitive behavior to be more pronounced in cross-sex interactions has also been found in other studies.

It is not only college students participating in psychology experiments who treat unattractive children more harshly. Even the children's own parents may do so. A study of parenting behavior during the Great Depression showed that a girl's unattractiveness was a risk factor for maltreatment by a stressed father. With increasing economic hardship, fathers showed moderately more rejection and less emotional support of their unattractive daughters, whereas hardship had no such effect on the treatment of attractive daughters. There was no parallel effect for unattractive sons, another indication that the effects of appearance on punitive behavior may be more pronounced in cross-sex interactions.[20]

Experienced female teachers also treat unattractive children more punitively. In one study, teachers were given a written description of a child falling down the stairs at school and asked to evaluate the culpability of one of the children at the top of the stairs who was grinning slightly after the incident. A photograph of the suspect child was attached to the description. When an unattractive boy was the suspect, he was more likely to be blamed for the incident than an attractive suspect. Although a boy's attractiveness had only a small effect on teachers' belief that he was guilty of the misdeed, it had a medium effect on the severity of punishment recommended when teachers were asked to assume that the child had indeed committed the misbehavior, with stronger punishment recommended for unattractive boys. It is interesting that attractiveness had no significant effect on the punishment recommended for girls.[21] Since the teachers were all women, this could once again reflect stronger effects of appearance on reactions to the opposite sex.

Like the misbehavior of attractive children, the transgressions of baby-faced children tend to be punished less severely than the same behaviors by their equally attractive, more mature-faced peers. This effect may re-

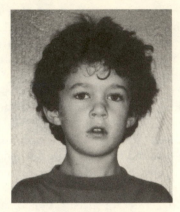

FIGURE 8.2   *A more babyfaced child (left) and a more mature-faced child (right). Courtesy of Nancy Carlston.*

flect warmer feelings toward babyfaced children, but it is also consistent with a tendency for babyfaced children to be judged less likely to know right from wrong. When parents read descriptions of misbehaviors by various children whose pictures and ages were shown, the actions of more mature-faced children, like the preschooler on the right in Figure 8.2, were perceived as more intentional than the very same acts by more babyfaced children of the same age, like the preschooler on the left. It is interesting that this large effect held true only for mothers' judgments about boys and fathers' judgments about girls, which suggests that adults are more sensitive to the facial maturity of children of the opposite sex, just as they are more sensitive to their attractiveness. However, after they judged a misbehavior as intentional, mothers and fathers responded similarly. They recommended more severe punishments when actions, such as kicking another child in the stomach during a soccer game or failing to complete various chores, were perceived as intentional than when they were perceived as accidental.[22] Since the misdeeds of mature-faced children are more likely to be perceived as intentional, these children are more likely to be the recipients of harsh punishment.

The tendency to perceive the misbehaviors of mature-faced children as more intentional could set the stage for abuse. There are, of course, many contributing factors to child abuse, and a "mature" facial appearance is not by itself a sufficient condition. Nevertheless, differences in perceptions of the capabilities and intentions of mature- versus babyfaced children may be one contributing factor. Indeed, a study of physically abused children between the ages of 2 and 15 found that they had more mature craniofacial proportions than nonabused children, and this large effect held true even when the two groups were matched for age, sex, and ethnic background.[23]

The contrast principle that was discussed in Chapters 5 and 7 can account for some interesting reversals of the tendency to react more punitively to the transgressions of unattractive or mature-faced children. For example, when experienced teachers evaluated the classroom behavior of an attractive versus an unattractive 10-year-old boy who either threw a tantrum or stole lunch money, they showed moderately less tolerance of the *attractive* boy's misbehavior.[24] It may be that such actions are so unexpected for an attractive child that the positive feelings evoked by his attractiveness are offset by teachers' negative reaction to having their favorable expectations disconfirmed. When a transgression is just too bad to fit into the "beautiful is good" stereotype and cannot be explained away as a mistake or a fluke, the attractive child may be punished more severely. The contrast with the facial stereotype may make the action seem even worse than it would if performed by an unattractive child. Similarly, when misbehavior cannot be assimilated to the stereotype of babyfaced children as naive and vulnerable, then it may be punished more harshly. In one study, parents showed a strong tendency to recommend harsher punishment for babyfaced than mature-faced children when the misbehavior was severe and unexpected for a child of that age.[25] This pattern parallels effects of facial maturity on judicial decisions, as discussed in Chapter 5. Although the majority of children's misbehaviors may be sufficiently harmless to be assimilated to facial stereotypes, with the result that misbehavior by attractive and babyfaced children is seen as more innocuous and treated less harshly, more extreme misbehavior—as in the case of delinquents—may elicit harsher punishment if the culprit is attractive or babyfaced.

Early Effects of Appearance on the Intellectual Environment

Teachers have higher expectations for the performance of attractive children, as revealed in the following observation made by a first grade teacher:

> John is such a pretty boy with big old brown eyes, and he smiles all the time, even his eyes smile. Wants to please, well behaved. Really joins in with any activity that is going on, and his work has been nice. I'm expecting him to be one of the better boys.[26]

Although this comment was made on the third day of school, such biased judgments can persist even when the teachers know the children's grades, attitudes toward school, and work habits. In one study, hundreds of teachers were asked to help evaluate the informativeness of report cards by estimating from them children's IQs and the amount of education they would ultimately receive. The report cards included a photograph of the child as well as information more diagnostic of intelligence and achievement potential: grades in reading, arithmetic, and several other subjects and school attendance records. There was a medium effect of attractiveness on judgments of IQ and a large effect on estimates of likely educational attainment, with more attractive children rated higher on both dimensions. Other studies have revealed similar effects, with teachers predicting more creative and intellectual ability for attractive children.[27]

Teachers' higher expectancies for the academic performance of attractive children may be accompanied by more favorable evaluations of their written work. The same essays are rated higher if they are attributed to attractive authors than if they are attributed to unattractive authors, an effect that is most reliable for female students.[28] The effects of student attractiveness on teacher evaluations is not confined to students whom the teachers do not know. Research has revealed that attractiveness can have medium-to-large effects on the appraisals of academic potential that students receive from their own teachers.[29]

Although there is abundant evidence that teachers expect better performance from attractive children, the evidence that they treat these students differently is less consistent, and further research is needed before any definitive conclusions can be drawn.[30] However, there is pertinent evidence from research examining treatment of individuals from whom high performance is expected for other reasons. An integration of over 100 studies has revealed that the following teacher behaviors both characterize interactions with students for whom they have positive expectancies and have a positive influence on the students' performance: more interaction with the student, presentation of more material or more difficult material, more praise of the student, more smiling and eye contact, staying closer to the student, and providing more encouragement.[31] Many of these helpful teacher behaviors involve showing greater warmth; as such, one would expect attractive students to receive more of them.

The effects of babyfaceness on children's intellectual environment has received much less attention than the effects of attractiveness. Moreover, it is less clear what effects should be expected. On the one hand, facial babyishness should elicit the warm behaviors, such as smiling and eye contact, that teachers usually show when they have high performance expectations. On the other hand, facial maturity should elicit higher performance expectations and may consequently elicit warm behaviors as well as more challenging tasks.

There is some evidence to suggest that parents and teachers do expect more from mature-faced children. Parents judged older looking 6-month-old infants, whom they did not know, to have higher communication skills, such as responding to their own name; more advanced motor abilities, such as sitting; higher cognitive abilities, such as uncovering a hidden toy; and higher self-help skills, such as feeding themselves with fingers. Parents not only showed a moderate-to-large tendency to expect more from older looking 6-month-olds but also overestimated their abilities, judging them as higher than the abilities typical of 6-month-olds.[32] Because babyfaceness and attractiveness are positively correlated in infancy, the older looking infants in this research were less attractive than their younger looking peers. Also, the parents who were evaluating them not only thought they looked older but also believed that they actually were older. This fact, of course, makes it possible that parents' expectations reflected their perceptions of the infants' age or attractiveness rather than facial maturity per se. However, other research that disentangled the effects of infants' facial maturity, perceived age, and attractiveness still found strong effects of infants' facial maturity on adults' expectations. Six-month-old mature-faced infants were perceived as more likely to know that it is naughty to do certain things and less likely to be fooled into thinking a hidden toy is gone than babyfaced infants who were equated in attractiveness and known to be the same age.[33]

Parents also attributed higher abilities to mature-faced than babyfaced 11-year-olds, knowing full well that these children were all the same age. When parents were asked how they would divide a number of chores among four boys or four girls at summer camp, the children's facial maturity, as depicted in photographs, had a large effect on their decisions. Parents allocated more demanding tasks to mature-faced children than to babyfaced children even when they were told that the children were all 11 years old. The mature-faced children were given chores such as editing the camp newspaper or being cashier in the camp store. The babyfaced children were given less cognitively demanding chores such as leading grace at the table or making sandwiches. Not only were the children in this study all known to be the same age, but also they were equal in facial attractiveness.[34] Student teachers also have been found to demand less of babyfaced children. They not only engage in more affectionate-sounding baby talk, as noted previously, but also show a strong tendency to speak more slowly to more babyfaced children.[35]

It is important to note that the effects of appearance on teacher expectancies can be outweighed by other information. In one study, teachers evaluated a student on the basis of a report card that included not only academic grades but also conduct grades, such as for personal and social growth, work habits, and attitudes. Physical attractiveness had no effect on teachers' estimates of the student's IQ or the level of educational attainment they expected, whereas conduct grades did have an effect.[36] These results are consistent with the argument that the positive social outcomes generally predicted for attractive individuals derive from a facial fit effect. When teachers have concrete information about children's traits, they predict outcomes that fit those traits and disregard attractiveness.

Conditions Conducive to Self-Fulfilling and Self-Defeating Prophecies

We have seen that a person's babyfaceness or attractiveness may influence the warmth and intellectual challenge of the person's social environment. The question remains as to whether these or other, as yet undemonstrated, environmental effects of appearance feed into self-fulfilling or self-defeating prophecies. It turns out that self-fulfilling prophecies are not as readily produced as Figure 8.3 suggests they are. Rather, several conditions must be met.

Self-Fulfilling Prophecies.   The first step in a self-fulfilling prophecy is that a person's appearance must create strong expectancies in the perceiver regarding that person's likely behavior. Second, the perceiver must act on those expectancies in a way that is likely to elicit the expected behavior. Third, the target must respond to these actions with confirming behavior. Fourth, the perceiver's expectancies must in fact be the cause of the target's behavior rather than merely predicting it. When these conditions are met, there will be a circumscribed self-fulfilling prophecy. That is, a perceiver's expectations will be fulfilled in a particular context. For a more global self-fulfilling prophecy to occur, whereby the target fulfills the same expectations across contexts, time, and interaction partners, two more conditions must be met: The appearance-based expectancies must be consistent across perceivers, and the person's appearance must be stable across time so that it consistently elicits the same expectations. When all six conditions are met, it can be concluded that the expectations have influenced the target's stable personality traits, which are often defined by personality theorists as a tendency to show consistent behaviors across contexts, time, and interaction partners. The expected behaviors may also become internalized into a person's self-concept. The result is a self-fulfilling prophecy that is self-perpetuating: The expected behavior occurs even in the absence of eliciting expectancies.

Factors Favoring Global Self-Fulfilling Prophecy Effects of Appearance. A strong consensus in expectancies about people who vary in attractiveness and babyfaceness coupled with evidence for the stability of appearance across the life span would provide two necessary conditions for global self-fulfilling prophecies. The strong consensus in expectancies has been amply demonstrated in earlier chapters, which revealed the universality and consistency of appearance stereotypes. The stability of appear-

171

Feiffer

FIGURE 8.3   *Feiffer.* © *Jules Feiffer. Reprinted with permission of Universal Press Syndicate. All rights reserved.*

ance has also been demonstrated using a data archive at the Institute of Human Development at the University of California, Berkeley. This archive includes the Intergenerational Studies of Development and Aging, which were initiated in the late 1920s and followed several hundred people from infancy or childhood until later adulthood. Among other things, these studies included photographs of the same individuals from age 4 through the late 50s. An investigation of the stability of appearance across five age transitions beginning at approximately 5 years of age and ending at approximately 58 revealed that the attractiveness of people of both sexes was stable across the life span. Facial maturity was also highly stable for people of both sexes during their years of maturation: age 5 through late adolescence. However, it was not stable after that for women, and it remained stable for men only until the early 30s. Since attractiveness and babyfaceness showed equal stability during the years of maturation, it was concluded that these two facial qualities have an equal potential to create strong self-fulfilling prophecy effects from childhood through adolescence, whereas attractiveness has a greater potential to produce such effects in adulthood.[37]

The finding that facial appearance is highly stable during the formative years indicates that people's facial appearance tends to elicit consistent expectations from others as they mature. Indeed, impressions of boys' and girls' submissiveness show moderate-to-strong consistency from childhood to late adolescence. Impressions of warmth also show strong consistency across this time span for girls and small-to-moderate consistency for boys.[38] To the extent that these expectations elicit confirming behaviors, a mere practice effect could foster a global self-fulfilling prophecy. For example, the expectancy that attractive people are warm and sociable may consistently elicit sociable behaviors, with the consequence that attractive people develop greater social skills. In addition to getting more opportunity to practice social skills, the experience of consistently showing sociable behavior should influence the self-concept of attractive people, also fostering a global effect. More attractive people will think of themselves as more sociable, which may cause them to behave consistently with this self-view.

Factors Impeding Global Self-Fulfilling Prophecies and Fostering Self-Defeating Ones. Although the foregoing considerations suggest that trait expectations based on appearance may yield global self-fulfilling prophecies, there is also reason to argue that global effects are uncommon. One reason for this is that the changes in self-concept that foster a global effect may require considerable time to develop inasmuch as they require repeated experiences in which the expected behavior is elicited. Indeed, although research has occasionally demonstrated self-fulfilling prophecy effects that carry over from the immediate situation, it has more often demonstrated only circumscribed effects. This was true in a classical self-fulfilling prophecy experiment that demonstrated behavioral confirmation of appearance-based expectancies in short-term social interactions between strangers.[39]

In that experiment, male college students interacted by telephone with a female student whom they believed to be attractive or unattractive as a result of being shown a bogus photograph of her. Before the telephone conversation, men who were shown photographs of physically attractive women demonstrated a large halo effect. They expected their partners to be more sociable, poised, humorous, and socially adept than did the men who had seen unattractive photographs. These expectations initiated a chain of events that served to confirm them. The men's side of the telephone conversation was rated by judges who had no idea whom the men were talking to. The men who thought they were interacting with attractive women were rated by these judges as being more sociable, sexually warm, interesting, humorous, and socially adept, as well as enjoying the conversation more and liking their partner more. The women responded in kind. Judges rated the women whom the men thought attractive as more confident, more animated, enjoying the conversation more, and liking their partner more. They also rated these women as more sociable, poised, humorous, and socially adept; these large effects revealed the very traits the men expected them to have.

Although the women in this study showed a circumscribed self-fulfilling prophecy effect, behaviorally confirming the perceivers' expectations in their telephone interactions, they showed no changes in their self-concepts. Of course, this was only a single interaction, and it is possible that self-concept change and resultant global self-fulfilling prophecy effects would occur if the behavioral confirmation were repeated over time, as one might expect for people who really do differ in attractiveness. However, there are factors in real-life social interactions that work against consistent behavioral confirmation effects. In particular, behavioral confirmation may fail to occur in real-life social interactions because (a) targets engage in self-verification, behaving in a manner that provides corrective feedback to the person with an erroneous expectation rather than confirming the expectation; (b) targets show compensatory behavior, behaving in a manner that defies an expectation that is disagreeable; or (c) perceivers show compensatory behavior, behaving in ways that do not elicit the behaviors they expect.[40] The latter two processes may foster self-defeating prophecies whereby the expectancy not only fails to be confirmed, but moreover, it initiates a chain of events that cause contradictory behavior.

Behavioral confirmation is less likely when the expected behaviors are socially undesirable and when targets know that the perceiver has a negative expectation.[41] Behavioral confirmation is also less likely when the target is motivated to get to know the perceiver, a goal that is often operative in everyday life.[42] Finally, behavioral confirmation is less likely when the target has a personality disposition that is strongly discrepant from the expectancy or one that makes confirmation difficult.[43] Someone who is genetically predisposed to be introverted and shy is unlikely to confirm the expectation that she is highly sociable. Similarly, people cannot confirm high performance expectations that are beyond their abilities. In general, behavioral confirmation appears to be rare, occurring only when perceivers have very strong expectations *and* targets are uncertain about their own traits. Moreover, it may not occur even when these conditions are met, because perceivers with strong expectations do not always behave in ways that elicit the behaviors they expect.

Perceivers who expect to interact with a cold person may behave more warmly than those expecting to interact with a warm person.[44] The consequence of this compensatory behavior by perceivers is the opposite of behavioral confirmation: a self-defeating prophecy effect in which people who were expected to be cold behave more warmly than those who were expected to be warm.[45] These results are consistent with other research showing that behavioral confirmation does not occur when perceivers have the goal of 'getting along with' someone about whom they have strong negative expectancies because perceivers act in ways that promote the goal of a smooth interaction.[46] In everyday life, people have many encounters with others who are motivated to get along with them. As such, perceivers' negative expectations often are not expressed, and behavioral confirmation does not occur. What this means for expectancies that are based on appearance is that those who are unattractive or mature-faced may often be treated no differently in one-to-one interactions from those who are attractive or babyfaced.

Even when behavioral confirmation of perceivers' expectations does occur and even when it appears to be global, manifested across contexts and perceivers, it may not reflect a true self-fulfilling prophecy effect. Rather, behavioral confirmation may occur because the perceiver's expectations are an *accurate reflection* of the target's behavioral tendencies rather than because those expectations have had a self-fulfilling causal influence on the target's behavior. Research in the domain of intellectual competence has shown that teachers' expectancies are confirmed primarily because they are accurate predictions of students' ability, although the expectancies also produce small self-fulfilling prophecy effects.[47] Similarly, it is possible that expectancies about attractive or babyfaced individuals are confirmed less because of self-fulfilling prophecy effects than because the expectancies accurately reflect the behavior of people who vary in appearance. Of course, if this is true, the question still remains as to why people who vary in appearance also vary in behavior.[48] Regardless of the source of the covariation, the possibility that expectancies accurately reflect rather than causally influence a target's behavior is an important caveat to consider when evaluating associations between appearance and actual behavior. To conclude that such associations reflect true self-fulfilling prophecy effects, it is necessary to examine the relationship between appearance and behavior over time, controlling for other factors that could also be influencing the later behavior.

Causal Influence of Early Appearance on Later Personality

The potential for appearance to have a formative influence on personality is exemplified by Frankenstein's monster. In the original story, which was a moral parable, the monster was not evil when it first came to life. Rather, it expressed the hope "to meet with beings who, pardoning my outward form, would love me for the excellent qualities I was capable of unfolding . . . ."[49] What happened, of course, was that the monster was shunned by all because his repulsive appearance made people fear he would harm them. Their prophecy was fulfilled. The creature developed an inner character congruent with its outer appearance, killing his creator and others. He says, "I was benevolent and good; misery made me a fiend. Make me happy, and I shall again be virtuous."[50]

In the same way that Frankenstein's monster became the evil creature he was expected to be, the lesser warmth and greater harshness displayed toward unattractive or mature-faced children may contribute to the development of hostile behavior. Indeed, research has shown that children who are treated more harshly do become more aggressive. Boys who are harshly disciplined by their parents are more likely to become juvenile delinquents than equally intelligent children from the same neighborhoods who are not harshly disciplined.[51] Similarly, children who are rejected by their peers are more likely to become delinquents than those who are accepted.[52] Although they are provocative, the foregoing findings do not establish the nature of the causal link between harsh treatment and antisocial behavior. For example, it may be that boys who are treated more harshly at a young age receive such treatment because their behavior warrants it: They are bad and they continue to be bad. Somewhat stronger evidence that harsh treatment is a cause rather than merely a consequence of children's antisocial behavior is provided by one study in which it was found that such treatment predicts adolescent delinquency among boys who were equivalent in childhood behavior problems.[53]

Although it has been shown that children who are less attractive or less babyfaced elicit less warmth and harsher treatment and that harsh treatment may influence the development of antisocial behavior, there is little research directly establishing a causal link from appearance to prosocial or antisocial behavior. One way to demonstrate such a link is to use a clever experimental paradigm, like the telephone study described earlier that showed that women who are perceived as attractive are treated more warmly, which in turn elicits the warm, prosocial behavior that is expected of them. Whereas this experimental paradigm has shown a self-fulfilling prophecy effect of appearance on situationally circumscribed behaviors, a longitudinal study is necessary to detect a self-fulfilling prophecy effect on global traits. An investigation using archival data from the Intergenerational Studies described previously has examined such global self-fulfilling prophecy effects.[54] Although this research has elucidated the influence of appearance on stable personality traits, something the experimental paradigm cannot accomplish, it has not revealed exactly what environmental consequences of appearance are responsible for its effect on behavior, something that the experimental paradigm could more readily show.

The Intergenerational Studies archive contains not only photographs of participants across the life span but also a number of personality measures including ratings by clinicians based on varied sources of information such as behavioral observations, school records, and interviews with the participants and their families. These personality ratings were used to construct two new personality scores for all participants: (a) the match between their personality and the stereotypical attractive person's personality and (b) the match between their personality and the stereotypical babyfaced person's personality. The relationships of these two scores with other measures revealed that sociability was the strongest component of the stereotypical attractive personality, whereas submissiveness and low hostility were most central to the stereotypical babyfaced personality.

If facial appearance at one point in time predicts subsequent changes in personality, it would appear that facial appearance has a causal impact on personality development, such as that shown in the self-fulfilling and self-defeating prophecy paths in Figure 8.1. An examination of the archival data at ages 9 through 18 revealed that boys and girls who were more attractive in childhood or puberty did not develop a more or less stereotypical attractive personality at adolescence, thus failing to support a self-fulfilling or self-defeating prophecy effect of attractiveness. However, boys who were more babyfaced at early ages developed a *less* stereotypical babyfaced personality in adolescence. This moderate effect suggests a self-defeating prophecy effect of babyfaceness. The specific traits that accounted for this effect were assertiveness and hostility. It appears that boys may respond negatively to the expectations associated with the babyface stereotype. To counteract the expectation that they will show "babyish" submissive, warm, and affectionate behavior, they may compensate by developing greater assertiveness and hostility than their more mature-faced peers, who have less need to prove their manhood. Babyfaced girls showed no comparable effect, suggesting that they may be less motivated than boys to compensate for the expectancy that they will be childlike, perhaps because childlike traits are more compatible with a feminine identity than a masculine one.[55] It is also possible that the lack of effect for girls was due to the cross-sex effect in reactions to babyfaced children that was mentioned earlier: the low expectations for babyfaced children are shown most strongly by parents of the opposite sex. Since fathers played a much smaller child-rearing role than mothers during the time when these children grew up, it may be that the expectancy that babyfaced children will be childlike was not communicated as strongly to girls as to boys.

When the effects of babyfaceness on personality development were examined from ages 18 to the late 50s, there was no evidence of a self-defeating prophecy effect for either men or women. Although this suggests that these groups are less motivated than adolescent boys to compensate for the infantilizing expectations that their appearance elicits, it may also reflect the fact that babyfaceness was not stable across the adult years. If a person's level of babyfaceness fluctuates, it may not elicit sufficiently consistent expectations to have an influence on personality development. What was observed for adult men was a small self-fulfilling prophecy effect of attractiveness, an appearance quality that was stable in adulthood. Men who were highly attractive in adolescence and their 30s developed a more stereotypical attractive personality in their 50s than did those who were less attractive at the earlier ages. This effect was largely due to a positive influence of early attractiveness on later sociability. Like Frankenstein's monster, men who were unattractive grew less sociable. However, they did not become more hostile. The finding that attractiveness produced a self-fulfilling prophecy effect in adulthood but not in childhood may be due to greater social consequences of attractiveness in adulthood. Babyfaceness may be a more salient determinant of reactions to boys than attractiveness is, whereas the reverse may be true for men. The restriction of the attractiveness self-fulfilling prophecy effect to adulthood may also reflect a cumulation of environmental effects that show up in personality only after many years.

It is surprising that attractiveness did not produce a self-fulfilling prophecy effect for adult women. This is particularly puzzling in light of the evidence discussed in Chapter 7 that indicated that attractiveness often has a greater effect on the social environments of women than men.

However, it is possible that the greater social consequences for women actually explain the lack of evidence for a self-fulfilling prophecy effect. In particular, there may be a countervailing compensation effect for unattractive women, who attempt to defeat the expectation that they will be unsociable, yielding no net effect of attractiveness on women's personality development. It is consistent with this suggestion that some research has found evidence of stereotype-defying compensation effects among physically unattractive women and girls.[56]

Causal Influence of Early Appearance on Later Intellectual Performance

As noted earlier, parents expect better performance from unknown attractive and mature-faced children. Moreover, the expectations that parents have about their own children, such as those based on sex stereotypes, influence the children's self-concepts and performance.[57] It seems reasonable to expect a parallel influence of facial stereotypes. A similar argument can be made regarding the effects of teacher expectations. Teachers expect better performance from attractive students, and although there is no direct evidence that these expectations influence attractive students' performance, it has been shown that expectations based on other factors can do so. In a classic study called "Pygmalion in the classroom," elementary school teachers were given bogus test results indicating that certain students would "bloom" during the upcoming school year. The students for whom high expectancies were induced showed greater gains on objective intelligence tests 8 months later than an equivalent group of students for whom no expectancies were induced.[58]

It should be noted that a causal influence of teacher expectancies on student achievement may be considerably weaker in the case of naturally occurring expectancies than for experimentally manipulated ones. This is because naturally occurring expectancies may accurately reflect the higher capabilities of certain children rather than simply causing them. Indeed, as noted earlier, teacher expectancies about students in their classes that are based on the students' records are confirmed primarily because they are accurate predictions of students' ability, quite apart from any direct influence that these expectancies may exert on the students' performance. Although there is some direct influence, this self-fulfilling prophecy effect is generally quite small in comparison with that shown in laboratory experiments and in comparison with the effects of accurate prediction on the behavioral confirmation of expectancies.

One study sought direct evidence of self-fulfilling prophecy effects of attractiveness in the intellectual domain.[59] This was accomplished by using the archival data described earlier to examine directly the effects of early appearance on the development of intellectual competence at a later age as assessed by IQ gains, motivational gains, and educational attainment. Although early attractiveness had no effect on later motivation or educational attainment for either males or females, there were effects of attractiveness on IQ development. Women who were more attractive than their peers in adolescence and their 30s had higher IQs in their 50s. Also, boys who were more attractive than their peers in childhood and puberty had higher IQs in adolescence—but only if they were also below average in height. The reverse relationship was shown for boys who were above average in height: Those who had been more attractive than their peers in childhood and puberty had *lower* IQs in adolescence. Optimal expectancies provide one possible explanation for this unexpected result. Since more intellectual competence is expected from children who are either attractive or tall, it may be that too much is expected of those who are both attractive *and* tall. These boys may be given tasks beyond their grasp, with the result that their ability does not develop as much as that of boys who are unattractive and tall and who consequently evoke more moderate positive expectations. The result is a self-defeating prophecy effect for tall, attractive boys. At the other end of the continuum are boys who are both unattractive and short. Because so little is expected of these boys, they may be given unchallenging tasks that do not develop their ability as much as that of boys who are attractive and short, who evoke moderately positive expectations that produce a self-fulfilling prophecy effect.

In considering what, if any, causal relationship to expect between facial maturity and intellectual competence, it should be recalled that a self-fulfilling prophecy chain begun by facial maturity has some uncertain links. Although facial maturity elicits positive expectancies, it is facial babyishness that tends to elicit most of the teacher behaviors that have been found to facilitate student achievement. In the list of helpful behaviors described earlier, the only one that is likely to be directed more at mature-faced children is the presentation of more material or more difficult material. Babyfaced children might therefore achieve more because their appearance elicits many warm and positive teacher behaviors. Alternatively, mature-faced children might achieve more because their appearance elicits high expectations accompanied by the presentation of difficult material. Finally, babyfaced and mature-faced children might not differ in achievement insofar as each elicits some of the teacher behaviors that help students to "flower."

It is surprising that the one study that examined consequences of instructional behavior directed toward babyfaced children found that the more affectionate baby talk—high pitch and changing intonation—had no impact on performance, whereas the slower, simpler speech, which could convey negative expectancies, resulted in superior learning of the task.[60] Therefore, rather than a self-fulfilling prophecy, whereby children who are treated as if they are expected to be incompetent perform accordingly, we see a self-defeating prophecy: Children who were taught as if they would have difficulty understanding showed better performance than other children of the same age. Evidence for a self-defeating prophecy effect was also provided in the archival study. Although babyfaceness in childhood and puberty did not predict IQ at adolescence for either boys or girls, it did predict higher motivation for boys. Moreover, this effect was not due to initial differences in motivation or IQ between the more and less babyfaced boys, and it was not due to socioeconomic differences. More babyfaced boys, who look less competent, developed higher motivation, a small effect that could reflect either their receipt of more effective teaching or their efforts to compensate for the low expectations they encountered. Not only did more babyfaced boys become more ambitious at adolescence, but also boys who were more babyfaced at adolescence achieved higher levels of education, again defying the babyface stereotype. Whereas this effect was moderate for boys who had been stable in babyfaceness from childhood to adolescence, it was absent for those whose appearance was unstable. It therefore appears to require some time for the environmental effects of a babyface to influence the development of traits that foster educational attainment

The Path from Early Traits to Later Appearance

Early Environmental Effects of Psychological Traits

Before summarizing some of the research evidence for the influence of early psychological traits on the social environment, it is important to consider how environmental effects of traits may contribute to changes in appearance. Although research has rarely addressed this question, it seems reasonable to suggest that hostile individuals may become less attractive over time and sociable individuals may become more attractive, consistent with a Dorian Gray effect. This change may be a direct effect of personality on appearance, resulting from habitual facial expressions that ultimately become etched into the permanent lines on the face. However, it could also be an indirect effect, resulting from the social environments into which people's traits place them or from the reactions that their traits elicit from others. For example, adolescents who are sociable and outgoing may be more likely than shy teens to go to dances, to join various clubs, or to socialize with friends, and these social experiences may provide them with more knowledge about how to improve their appearance. On the other hand, if a woman's hostility produces downward social mobility through a less felicitous marriage, she may become less attractive than her peers because she has fewer resources to spend on beauty aids.

Similarly, if a shy woman does not venture into the work world, she may become less attractive than her working peers because she has less incentive to apply makeup or to try new, fashionable hairstyles.

Research on the traits of shyness and hostility, which used data from the Intergenerational Studies archive, has illustrated the foregoing environmental effects of personality. Boys who were shy in childhood, according to ratings by their mothers and teachers, took longer than their more extraverted peers to enter new and unfamiliar social environments in adulthood, including marriage, parenthood, and stable careers. The shy dispositions of these boys apparently made it more difficult for them to initiate courtship and to take the initiative necessary to pursue stable careers. Girls who were shy in childhood also appeared to have more difficulty entering the labor force. These girls, who came of age in the late 1940s when women did not typically pursue careers, were even more likely than their more extraverted peers to have no work history or to fail to reenter the labor force after their children were grown. However, shy girls were not delayed in entering the traditional female environments of marriage and motherhood. Indeed, they were more likely to lead the familiar "feminine" life of marriage and homemaking that was typical for women of their era.[61]

Research using the archival data has also shown environmental effects of early hostility. Boys who were hostile in childhood, as indicated by frequent, severe temper tantrums at ages 8–10, left the social environment of formal education at an earlier age than their more even-tempered peers. This departure consigned the more hostile boys to low-status occupations. Boys who were hostile in childhood also had more erratic work histories, an effect that appeared to be caused by their ill-tempered nature rather than by the particular jobs that they held. Also, hostile boys were more than twice as likely as their more even-tempered peers to be divorced by age 40. Similarly, women who had been ill-tempered in childhood were more than twice as likely to be divorced by midlife, and husbands of those who had not divorced reported more marital conflicts and more marital dissatisfaction. More ill-tempered girls also tended to marry men with lower occupational status, and they consequently showed downward social mobility as compared with their own father's occupational status.[62]

Conditions Conducive to Dorian Gray and Artifice Effects

Several conditions are necessary to foster an effect of personality on the development of a congruent appearance (the Dorian Gray effect) or an incongruent appearance (the artifice effect). First, the personality trait in question must have some visible manifestations that can match or mismatch perceivers' expectations. The research on consensus at zero acquaintance that was discussed in Chapter 3 suggests that the traits of extraversion, dominance, sexual availability, honesty, and conscientiousness are prime candidates, since each is conveyed by appearance. Second, more malleable appearance qualities will be more subject to an influence of personality. Traits that are shown in appearance qualities that are highly malleable, such as hairstyles, facial hair, or expressive behavior, are more likely to produce Dorian Gray or artifice effects than traits that are manifested in less malleable qualities, such as facial lines or bone structure. Finally, certain effects of personality on appearance may require personality stability. Insofar as Dorian Gray effects reflect the influence of personality on facial lines and wrinkles or habitual facial expressions and mannerisms, an unstable personality trait is unlikely to have a consistent enough influence on appearance to produce a congruence between the two. Similarly, personality stability seems to be an important precondition for an artifice effect if it rests on the acquisition of stable facial qualities that convey a misleading impression. On the other hand, it is possible that even unstable personality traits could influence appearance, since certain appearance changes do not require years to develop, such as those produced by makeup, hairstyles, and facial hair.

There is considerable evidence for personality stability across the life span. As noted previously, individuals who were shy and reserved in late childhood continued to show reluctance to enter unfamiliar social settings as adults, being later than their peers to enter marriage, parenthood, and stable careers. This consistency of personality continues into later adulthood, with personality measures of sociability and introversion showing considerable stability.[63] There is also evidence for continuity in shyness very early in life, as shown by infant predictors of an inhibited, shy temperament in childhood.[64] Similar evidence for the stability of personality across the life span exists for other traits, including aggression, conscientiousness, agreeableness, neuroticism, and openness to experience.[65] This evidence indicates that personality is sufficiently stable to influence appearance via Dorian Gray or artifice effects, even when those effects involve changes in appearance that take considerable time to develop. At the same time, personality stability is far from perfect, and there are large differences from one person to another. The changes that do occur provide an opportunity for appearance to influence personality via self-fulfilling or self-defeating prophecy effects.

Causal Influence of Early Traits on Later Appearance

The Dorian Gray effect and the artifice effect have received almost no attention in psychological research. However, examples of these effects can be readily found in folklore and in literary works. The cartoon in Figure 8.4 captures the familiar parental admonition to "wipe that look off your face

GEE... MY MOTHER ALWAYS SAID IF I KEPT MAKING UGLY FACES, SOMEDAY IT COULD STICK LIKE THAT ... I GUESS SHE'S RIGHT!

FIGURE 8.4   *Mother Goose and Grimm. Reprinted by permission of Tribune Media Services.*

before it freezes." This homage to a Dorian Gray effect is also captured in the novel for which the effect is named as well as in other novels and folktales. For example, in *Dr. Jekyll and Mr. Hyde*, the ugly form of Mr. Hyde becomes more and more predominant with increases in the antisocial behavior of this split personality. Similarly, in *Beauty and the Beast*, the ugly form of the beast is replaced by a handsome prince when he shows warm and loving behavior. Literature and folklore also provide examples of the artifice effect. The prototype is the parable of the wolf in sheep's clothing or the wolf in grandmother's clothing in *Little Red Riding Hood*. Artifice is also seen in the *Wizard of Oz*, where an inept man's deceptively powerful and wise personas enable him to dominate others, and in the *Scarlet Pimpernel*, where a heroic man's deceptively weak and stupid demeanor enables him to carry out heroic acts without arousing suspicion.

A study mentioned in Chapter 3 provided indirect support for a Dorian Gray effect in the finding that older people's faces looked like their personalities. Those who had a hostile personality looked angry even when trying to pose a neutral expression; those who had an anxious personality looked fearful when posing a neutral expression; and so on.[66] Although these results are provocative, they do not provide conclusive evidence for an effect of earlier personality on later appearance. It is possible, for example, that personality and appearance are congruent not because personality has influenced appearance but because appearance has influenced personality or because both have been influenced by some other factor, such as a warm or hostile environment. To conclude that such correlations reflect true Dorian Gray effects, it is necessary to examine the relationship between personality and appearance over time, controlling for other factors that could also be influencing the later appearance. This has been done for the appearance qualities of attractiveness and babyfaceness using the data archive described earlier[67]

Both Dorian Gray and artifice effects have been found, albeit only for women and only for attractiveness. Women whose personality matched that of the stereotypical attractive person when they were in adolescence and their 30s became more attractive in their late 50s. This reflected an influence of early sociability on later attractiveness rather than an influence of the other facets of the stereotypical attractive personality, such as dominance, responsibility, low hostility, or high honesty. Indeed, honesty in the early years was associated with an artifice effect rather than a Dorian Gray effect. Early *dis*honesty predicted higher later attractiveness, which in turn was positively related to perceived honesty.[68] These results suggest that women who are relatively dishonest may manipulate their appearance so they can get away with deceptive behavior.[69] The fact that the traits of sociability and dishonesty are both conducive to the development of a more attractive appearance in women may reflect a tendency for women with either of these traits to be more concerned with impression management than their less sociable or more honest counterparts. Whereas sociability consequently fosters the development of an appearance that is congruent with social expectations—a Dorian Gray effect—dishonesty fosters the development of an appearance that is incongruent with expectations—an artifice effect.

The effects of women's personality on their later attractiveness contrasts with the absence of such effects for men. One possible reason for this is that women may be more dependent on appearance qualities to achieve their social goals. Women who are highly sociable may need to cultivate high attractiveness to maintain an active social life, whereas this may be less important for highly sociable men. Also, women who are highly dishonest may need to use their appearance to achieve their goals, whereas dishonest men have other sources of power. Another factor that may foster effects of personality on the appearance of women, but not of men, is the greater ability of women to alter their appearance deliberately. Indeed, it was the greater use of makeup by women with a stereotypical attractive personality that accounted for their greater attractiveness in later life.

Whereas early personality can influence subsequent attractiveness, at least in women, the existing research has provided no evidence for an influence of early personality on later babyfaceness. One possible explanation for this result is that the qualities of appearance that contribute to babyfaceness may be less malleable than those that contribute to attractiveness. However, this explanation seems unlikely both because babyfaceness was less stable across the life span than attractiveness was, indicating that it is mutable, and also because makeup, which accounted for the Dorian Gray effect on attractiveness, can readily alter features central to babyfaceness, such as eye size and eyebrow height. Another possible explanation for the failure to find Dorian Gray effects on babyfaceness is that the visible effects of personality on babyfaceness may be revealed only in moving faces, whereas the effects on attractiveness can be detected in still photographs. Thus, highly sociable women became more attractive owing to greater use of makeup, something that can be detected in the photographs that were used in this study. It is possible that women with a babyfaced personality did become more babyfaced, but this may be manifested in facial mannerisms, such as raising one's eyebrows or widening one's eyes, that can be detected only in videotapes or live interactions.

Accuracy of Appearance Stereotypes

The developmental relationships between appearance and behavior that have been discussed in this chapter have implications for the accuracy of appearance stereotypes. Developmental processes that produce self-fulfilling prophecies or Dorian Gray effects may contribute to accurate facial stereotypes, whereas those that produce self-defeating prophecies or artifice effects may contribute to inaccurate stereotypes.

The Attractiveness Halo

There is little evidence to support the stereotype of attractive people as more dominant and intelligent than their less attractive peers.[70] There is also no consistent evidence that attractive people are more ambitious.[71] Thus, the fact that they are advantaged when competing for leadership positions and that they complete more years of education with somewhat higher grades seems to reflect biased treatment rather than the accuracy of stereotypes concerning dominance and ability. However, it is important to note that research has not examined the accuracy of these stereotypes for different subtypes of attractive people, such as those mentioned in Chapters 6 and 7. Such an analysis may reveal that certain subtypes, such as "sophisticated," *are* more dominant and ambitious, whereas the "cute" types are not. Even when all subtypes are grouped together, there is considerable evidence for the accuracy of the stereotype that attractive people are warm and socially skilled. There is also some evidence that attractive people are less likely to show "bad" behavior.

It has been well established that attractive people are more popular. Moreover, there is some evidence to indicate that this derives from their greater social competence. In particular, more attractive children are seen by their classmates as showing more prosocial behavior, such as being kind and not fighting, and more attractive children show less aggressive behavior. Similarly, more attractive girls are less likely to show severe or frequent temper tantrums in childhood and puberty.[72] There is also some evidence for a negative relationship between attractiveness and delinquency, although shortcomings in these studies make it difficult to draw firm conclusions.[73]

The association of attractiveness with socially skilled behavior is seen in adults as well as in children.[74] Not only do attractive adults show a moderate-to-strong tendency to be more popular, but also they show a small tendency to be less troubled by loneliness, by social anxiety with the opposite sex, and by social anxiety in general. Although attractive people do not report more permissive sexual attitudes, they do report more sexual experiences. Although these are small effects, they are consistent with the perception that attractive people have greater sexual warmth. The greater sexual experience and social skills of attractive individuals may at least partially explain people's accuracy in perceiving the sexual availability and extraversion of strangers that was discussed in Chapter 3. They may use attractiveness as a valid cue when judging these traits.[75]

The question remains as to whether the more sociable behavior of attractive children and adults reflects a circumscribed effect or a more global one. That is, do attractive and unattractive individuals show a global tendency to display different behaviors in the absence of differential treatment by their peers, or are the behavioral differences a circumscribed reaction to treatment differences? A review of many studies concerning adolescents and young adults found no tendency for attractive individuals to score higher on personality measures of sociability, although they are more socially skilled in dyadic interactions, in which they are responding to others' expectations. These results suggest that the relationship between attractiveness and sociable behavior is a circumscribed one.[76] On the other hand, an investigation of the accuracy of the attractiveness stereotype across the life span did provide evidence that the attractiveness stereotype has global accuracy for certain groups of people.[77] More attractive women in their 50s had personalities more like the stereotypical attractive person, and this moderate effect was due to the women whose appearance or personality had been stable since adolescence. Similar, albeit weak, accuracy was found for adolescent boys and girls who had been attractive since childhood and men in their 50s who had been attractive since adolescence. On the other hand, the attractiveness stereotype was not accurate for adolescents or adults in their 50s whose previous level of attractiveness or personality had been unstable. The fact that the attractiveness stereotype was accurate only for those whose attractiveness or personality was consistent across time suggests that stereotype accuracy occurs only when there has been sufficient opportunity for appearance to influence personality via a self-fulfilling prophecy effect or for personality to influence appearance via a Dorian Gray effect. Finally, it should be recalled that the stereotype that attractive people are more sociable holds true primarily for the "cute" attractive types. More evidence of accuracy might be revealed if the traits of people representing this type of attractiveness were examined.

The Babyface Stereotype

Whereas there is much research bearing on the relationship of attractiveness to personality traits, there is less evidence bearing on the accuracy of the babyface stereotype. A study mentioned in Chapter 5, which found that babyfaced college men reported higher self-disclosure and greater intimacy in their social interactions, can be taken as evidence not only for greater warmth directed toward babyfaced people but also for their reciprocal warmth.[78] Warmth is also indicated by a small tendency for babyfaced people to be rated as more agreeable by people who know them well and also by themselves.[79] Evidence for accuracy of the stereotype that babyfaced people are warm and submissive is also provided by a medium-to-large tendency for babyfaced college men to score lower on a personality test of aggression.[80]

The traits of high warmth and low aggressiveness are related to the personality trait of agreeableness, which is one of the Big Five, and as discussed in Chapter 3, there is some evidence for accuracy in perceiving the agreeableness of unknown college students when their faces can be seen.[81] An interesting question is whether babyfaceness is a valid cue that contributes to this accuracy. The answer is, as yet, unclear. One study found that people did use the valid cue of a childlike face when accurately perceiving the agreeableness of strangers who did not vary in age or sex.[82] However, other research has provided inconsistent evidence regarding the contribution of babyfaceness to accurate perceptions of strangers' warmth and aggressiveness.[83] The fact that babyfaceness does not reliably explain accurate perceptions of these traits may be because not all babyfaced people have these traits.

The traits of babyfaced and mature-faced individuals who are equally attractive do not always match the babyface stereotype.[84] For females, no evidence for stereotype accuracy has been found in childhood, puberty, adolescence, or the 30s. For women in their 50s, the stereotype was accurate only for those who had been babyfaced since adolescence. The restriction of stereotype accuracy to these women is consistent with the suggestion that accuracy is produced by self-fulfilling prophecy effects: Such effects would not operate as strongly for those whose appearance had been unstable. In contrast to the accuracy of the babyface stereotype for this subgroup of adult women, the stereotype was inaccurate for boys. Compared with mature-faced boys, those who were more babyfaced showed more negativity in childhood and puberty, more quarrelsomeness and lying in puberty, and *less* stereotypical babyfaced personalities in adolescence, an effect that was due to their higher assertiveness and higher hostility. The latter effects were due to those high in babyfaceness showing a worse match to the babyface stereotype than boys who were average or low in babyfaceness. Moreover, the tendency for babyfaced adolescent boys to have less babyfaced personalities was true only for those who had been babyfaced since childhood. This moderate effect suggests that the self-defeating prophecy effect for babyfaceness contributes to an inaccurate babyface stereotype for these boys, since the self-defeating prophecy would not operate as strongly for those whose appearance had been unstable.

Babyfaced individuals may deviate from the appearance stereotype in their intellectual abilities as well as in their personality traits. In particular, more babyfaced boys had higher IQs than their mature-faced peers in puberty and adolescence even when researchers controlled for other variables that may influence intelligence, including attractiveness, weight, height, and socioeconomic status.[85] Moreover, the effects were attributable to the greater intelligence of the most babyfaced individuals: Those who were average and low in babyfaceness did not differ in IQ. Since babyfaced individuals are expected to be less intellectually astute than their more mature-faced peers, the positive relationship between babyfaceness and IQ suggests a self-defeating prophecy effect. Indeed, babyfaced boys appear to obtain higher IQ scores because they are more ambitious, a personality trait that may derive from their efforts to refute negative expectancies about their competence. The fact that babyfaced girls showed neither greater ambition nor higher IQs may reflect differential sex-role expectations, which lead girls to be less motivated to refute negative expectancies about their competence.

Summary

Because social expectations have environmental effects that can elicit confirming behaviors, there is reason to believe that what begins as an appearance stereotype may become a social reality. However, self-fulfilling prophecy effects are elusive owing to a number of factors that work against the conversion of expectancies to reality. There is considerable evidence to indicate that our expectancies about people who vary in attractiveness or babyfaceness can have a strong impact on their social environments, and more attractive people may show greater social competence when they are reacting to positive expectancies in a circumscribed setting. However, current evidence for a self-fulfilling prophecy effect on global personality traits is limited. Although further research is needed before any firm conclusions can be drawn, the existing evidence suggests that appearance must be stable over time if its environmental effects are to influence personality development. Moreover, the effects of appearance on personality development sometimes show self-defeating rather than self-fulfilling prophecies. In particular, rather than fulfilling the expectation

that they are submissive, nonthreatening, and lacking in intellectual astuteness, babyfaced boys become more assertive, hostile, and intelligent
than their more mature-faced peers. The available evidence also suggests
that personality may be as likely to affect the development of appearance
as vice versa. Just as stereotypes about attractive and babyfaced people
create self-fulfilling prophecy effects over time for only certain groups of
people, only certain groups confirm the accuracy of these stereotypes at
any one point in time. Thus, accuracy of the attractiveness halo or the
babyface overgeneralization effect is likely to account for only a small
portion of the accuracy in personality impressions that was documented
in Chapter 3. Given the scant evidence for accuracy of these facial stereotypes, it seems important to reduce their influence. Chapter 9 considers
various tactics that may be useful in achieving this goal.

9

Phasing Out
Face Effects

I ran against a Prejudice
That quite cut off the view.

— **C. P. Gilman, *In This Our World: An Obstacle*[1]**

The prejudgments of people that are manifested in facial stereotypes can indeed cut off our view, specifically, our view of psychological traits. We are blinded by beauty and babyfaceness. By responding strongly to these qualities despite the unreliability of the trait information they provide, we may fail to use more diagnostic information. Whether other facial qualities provide such information remains an open question that will be resolved not by scorning the physiognomists but by conducting further research. Worse than the potential of facial stereotypes to hinder accurate impressions is their ability to foster inaccurate ones. Few would condone the social consequences of appearance stereotypes that have been documented in this book. Indeed, it has even been suggested that they be legislated away. As mentioned earlier, a note in the *Harvard Law Review* argued that the Rehabilitation Act of 1973 "should be construed to protect people against employment discrimination on the basis of largely immutable aspects of bodily and facial appearance."[2] Even if implemented, a legal remedy for facial stereotyping would address its effects only in certain public domains. Moreover, to implement remedies in these domains, be they courtrooms or schools or the workplace, requires ameliorative behaviors by those in positions of leadership. Such behavior change also is needed in interpersonal relationships that do not come within the purview of the law. Although the "face effects" detailed in this book may be grounded in fundamental human tendencies to overgeneralize adaptive responses to babies' faces and genetically fit faces, as well as to respond with positive affect to attractive faces, people *can* control these effects. This chapter considers tactics available to perpetrators and targets of facial stereotyping, who are likely to be one and the same. It also considers tactics suggested by observations of cultural influences on facial stereotyping.[3] Although the recommendations made in this chapter focus on tactics available to individuals, they need to be implemented through policy changes at an institutional level if they are to have far-reaching effects.

Perceiver Contributions to Face Effects

Even if innate influences render the impressions of people's traits from their facial appearance to be as automatic and uncontrollable as perceptions of emotions, age, or sex, perceivers can go beyond these first impressions. Indeed, perceivers differ in their susceptibility to face effects depending on their motivation and attention, awareness of appearance stereotypes, and personality traits.

Motivational Effects

People's motives can influence the likelihood of forming stereotyped trait impressions as well as the likelihood of eliciting expectancy-confirming behaviors from others. As noted in Chapter 8, those who have the goal of "getting along with" someone about whom they have strong negative expectancies act in ways that promote the goal of a smooth interaction, and behavioral confirmation does not occur. Indeed, one study found that those who expected to interact with a cold person behaved more warmly than those expecting to interact with a warm person, creating a self-*defeating* prophecy effect: Targets behaved more warmly toward those who expected them to be cold than toward those who expected them to be warm. We therefore may be able to forestall the behavioral effects of our negative expectancies if we are motivated to prevent them from being confirmed.[4]

There are many venues in which a properly motivated perceiver can reduce face effects by altering discriminatory behavior. A simple example is the tendency to avoid sitting next to a facially disfigured person on a commuter train.[5] It may be difficult for people to alter their immediate feelings about such a person or even their impressions of the person's traits, but they can voluntarily alter their behavior by changing where they sit. Doing such things on repeated occasions may mitigate negative reactions to unattractive people via the effects of familiarity that were discussed in Chapter 6. Similarly, although it may take a leap of faith to give babyfaced people tasks that do not "fit" their appearance, this may be easier than changing the initial impression about the match between the person and the task. Taking such actions may do much to change that impression if the person successfully completes the task.

Differential behavior toward those who vary in appearance may be easier to change than more subjective reactions. For example, even when people with negative expectations of others behave in ways that do not elicit expectancy-confirming behavior, their judgments of target persons may continue to reflect their initial expectations. In the self-defeating prophecy effect that was just discussed, perceivers' impressions of targets moved in the direction of targets' actual behavior, and thus away from initial expectancies, but there still remained an influence of initial expectations. However, appropriately motivated perceivers may be able to escape even this remnant of biased impressions. In particular, appropriately motivated perceivers are capable of resisting "primacy effects" in impression formation, a type of bias that encompasses face effects. The primacy effect occurs when people give heavy emphasis to the first information they receive about someone (which may be appearance) and are relatively unresponsive to later information. Accountability can prevent first impressions from dominating final judgments.

When people were asked to evaluate someone's competence, they were less influenced by early information or by ethnic stereotypes if they expected to justify their judgments and to find out whether their judgments agreed with those of experts.[6] Even the simple goal to form as accurate an impression as possible sufficed to induce perceivers to evaluate a former mental patient's likability on the basis of relevant personal information rather than on the basis of stereotypes about schizophrenics.[7] In general, those who are motivated to be accurate and to feel accountable for their judgments rely more on objective data and less on the first information they receive or their own preconceptions about people in a particular group.[8] Therefore, accountable perceivers should be less likely to show an unthinking attractiveness halo or babyface overgeneralization effect and more likely to use available behavioral information that is pertinent to the trait judgments being made.

People may be motivated to avert primacy effects for reasons other than accountability. Feeling interdependent with the target is another motivation. When women were asked to make judgments about a man whom they had seen in a photo, they showed a strong tendency to make more accurate use of the available information about him if they had agreed to have several dates with him than if they did not anticipate any future interactions.[9] When students were dependent on the skills of a former mental patient for them to complete a task successfully and win a monetary prize, they paid more attention to personal information about the patient. Moreover, their judgments of his likability depended more on the positivity of the information and less on his negative patient status.[10] When it is important for people to make an accurate judgment because the target's traits will affect them in some way, they are more likely to form impressions on the basis of later behavioral data than solely on the basis of salient physical qualities like attractiveness or babyfaceness.[11]

Attentional Effects

Even when people are not particularly motivated to be accurate in their impressions of others, there is evidence that the presence of behavioral information can reduce the effects of stereotypes on their impressions.[12] However, the provision of behavioral data is not a panacea. There is often sufficient ambiguity in behavioral data for people to attend selectively to the evidence that confirms their initial expectancy. To effectively fight face effects, therefore, we must consider the evidence impartially. For example, to find out whether a first impression of an attractive person as sociable and outgoing is indeed correct, we need to probe for evidence of introversion and shyness as well as for confirmatory evidence. In developing this tactic, it is helpful to think of reasons that an attractive person might in fact be introverted and shy, since it has been found that when people create explanations for opposite relationships between particular types of people and particular behaviors, they are more likely to abandon their initial impressions in the face of disconfirming evidence.[13]

We can fight face effects not only by attending to behaviors that can disconfirm our expectancies but also by forming impressions of a person's specific behavioral tendencies rather than more global impressions. When people judged the behavior of an adult interacting with an infant, there were strong effects of the adult's attractiveness on global ratings, with an attractive caretaker perceived as more effective in holding the baby, in engaging the baby in play with a toy, and in stimulating the baby. However, the attractiveness halo had no effect on perceptions of specific behaviors such as the frequency with which the baby was held in various ways, how much the toy was shown to the baby, or how much touching and rocking and physical restraint the baby received.[14] The implication of these results is that to make unbiased judgments about people's assertiveness, warmth, or other traits requires attending to specific behaviors, like the frequency with which they offer a differing opinion or how much they smile, rather than simply forming global impressions. For this reason, perceivers who are lacking in attentional resources may show stronger face effects than those who are less busy.[15]

Insofar as facial stereotypes represent a primacy effect in impression formation—that is, more weight is given to early information—the most straightforward way to counteract them is to access information about people's behavioral and psychological attributes *before* viewing their face. Indeed, when men were asked to indicate their interest in dating women who varied in attractiveness and personality traits, the timing of the information was crucial. Although attractive women were preferred regardless of the timing, trait information also had an effect when it was shown before the face was seen but not when it was shown afterward. Women with positive traits were preferred to those with negative traits when the trait information was shown 3 seconds before the face, whereas traits had no effect on men's preferences if they saw the face first.[16]

If a delay of only 3 seconds between substantive information and facial appearance can make a difference, it seems likely that we can make significant headway against face effects if we get to know something about a person before meeting her face-to-face. Those involved in personnel selection will be less biased if they interview job candidates face-to-face after examining resumes that do not have photographs attached or after a preliminary phone interview. Educators will be less biased if they assess the work of their students before linking a face to it. Those involved in jury selection will be less biased by face effects if initial queries of potential jurors are conducted with their faces out of view. Physicians may be less biased if they read a patient's medical record and an account of current symptoms before meeting the patient face-to-face. Finally, although appearance is certainly viewed as valid information to use when selecting a date, those who do not want to be overly biased by face effects would do well to make their selections through the personal ads, which are based on written or phone messages (that almost always say the person is "attractive"), rather than through video dating services. If the latter are used, attending to the written protocols before examining photographs or videotapes may weaken the biasing effects of facial appearance.

Awareness

It seems reasonable to suggest that increasing people's awareness of the effects of appearance on social judgments and social outcomes would ameliorate those effects. This is true not only because most people find such effects objectionable, but also because people generally are not aware of them. As noted in Chapter 1, face readers cannot articulate the bases for their impressions even when those impressions are systematically related to physical differences among the faces being judged. People also cannot accurately report the effects of attractiveness on their trait impressions. One study found no relationship between subjective estimates of stereotyping and actual stereotyping of the sociability of attractive versus unattractive targets.[17] Another study found that people reported a greater effect of attractiveness than it actually had on some trait judgments and a positive effect rather than the true negative effect for others.[18] Other evidence that people are unaware of the influence of appearance on their impressions is provided by the finding that men continued to show the attractiveness halo as well as confidence in their impressions of an attractive woman's traits even when they were convinced that their judgments of her attractiveness were highly subjective.[19]

Although it appears that use of the attractiveness stereotype is covert and not readily influenced by beliefs about the subjectivity of attractiveness judgments, it is possible that the use of facial stereotypes could be reduced if people were made aware of the stereotypes themselves. Indeed, that is a goal of this book. However, there are pitfalls in the attempt to ameliorate facial stereotypes by increasing perceivers' awareness of them. First, although awareness of facial stereotypes may be sufficient to overcome differential responding to those who are at the extremes of attractiveness or babyfaceness, it may be insufficient to overcome the documented tendency to respond to small differences in appearance. Second, there is the possibility of an overcompensation effect such that the normal bias is reversed rather than neutralized.[20] Finally, awareness is more apt to ameliorate facial stereotypes if it is accompanied by knowledge of accurate nonverbal cues to traits so that perceivers have some other basis for forming impressions. Unfortunately, as discussed in Chapter 3, research cannot yet provide people with knowledge of such cues.

Personality Effects

Although the personality differences that influence facial stereotyping may not be readily controlled, they are discussed here because they make clear that such stereotyping is not inevitable.

Belief in a just world is one personality trait that may affect attractiveness stereotyping. Those who strongly believe that we live in a just world where people get what they deserve are more likely to believe that men who have "gotten" the positive life outcomes associated with an attractive appearance have deserving personality traits. People who do not believe that this is a just world do not show as strong an attractiveness halo as believers do.[21]

Another personality variable that contributes to face effects is self-monitoring. High self-monitors, as assessed by a self-report questionnaire, are individuals who carefully monitor their behavior, adjusting it to fit the requirements of the particular situation in which they find themselves to control the image they project. Low self-monitors, on the other hand, are less concerned with matching their behavior to the particular situation. Rather, their behavior conveys their own stable disposition and attitudes. The tendency for high self-monitors to focus on their public image and low self-monitors to convey their true disposition is paralleled by their reactions to others. When choosing a potential date from information about 50 different women, men who were high self-monitors spent more time looking at pictures of the women than did low self-monitors, who spent more time looking at descriptions of the personality attributes of their potential dates. Moreover, these strong effects recurred when men were asked to choose between two dates: High self-monitors preferred an attractive woman who had undesirable personal qualities over an unattractive women with more desirable traits. Low self-monitors showed the opposite preference.[22]

High self-monitors' concern with appearance extends beyond the dating domain. When deciding which job applicants should be hired, there is a strong tendency for high self-monitors to be more influenced by appearance than low self-monitors, who are more influenced by personality traits. High self-monitors consequently preferred an applicant with unsuitable personality traits and an appearance that was either attractive or befitting the job over one with a suitable personality but an unattractive or unsuitable appearance. Low self-monitors showed the reverse pattern, preferring an applicant with suitable personality traits despite an unattractive or unsuitable appearance.[23] It is interesting that high self-monitors were aware of the influence that appearance had on their choices. The majority of these individuals acknowledged that the photographs of the potential dates and job applicants had influenced them, something that most low self-monitors correctly denied. This awareness, which is often absent in facial stereotyping, should make it relatively easy for high self-monitors to desist from "face effects" if they are motivated to do so.

Additional personality effects have been demonstrated in research comparing people who vary in how sex-typed they are. The rationale for this research derives from the fact that individuals who are strongly sex typed—very feminine women and very masculine men—are more likely to organize information in terms of sex-linked associations than are androgynous individuals, who have a mixture of feminine and masculine traits. Because an attractive appearance is prototypical for a person's sex, the salience of sex-linked associations may cause sex-typed individuals to be more sensitive to variations in attractiveness. Consistent with this reasoning, sex-typed individuals were found to display more discriminatory behavior toward those who vary in attractiveness both in job rankings and in getting-acquainted conversations.[24] Whereas sex-typed and androgynous individuals differed in the likelihood of exhibiting discriminatory behavior, they did not show consistent differences in their trait impressions.[25] It thus appears that androgyny has a more consistent effect on behaviors that are likely to be under conscious control than it does on more automatic trait inferences.

The fact that androgyny influences the differential treatment of attractive and unattractive individuals suggests that this personality variable may influence the likelihood of producing self-fulfilling prophecy effects. Indeed, sex-typed women elicited behavior that was more congruent with the attractiveness stereotype when they interacted with targets whom they thought were attractive than when they interacted with presumably unattractive targets. This large effect was reversed when androgynous women interacted with attractive and unattractive targets. This suggests that androgynous individuals may be motivated to compensate for appearance stereotypes, producing a "bending over backward" effect that creates a self-defeating prophecy. It is consistent with this suggestion that androgynous women were in fact slightly more responsive to unattractive than attractive targets, an effect that is also consistent with the effects of perceiver motivation that were discussed previously.

Target Contributions to Face Effects

Potential targets of facial stereotyping may want to make their own efforts to fight face effects rather than relying on the good will of perceivers. Fortunately, there are some effective actions to take, ranging from actual changes in facial appearance to adjustments in behavior, changes in public image, and changes in self-image.

Adjustments to Facial Appearance

The most direct way to fight face effects is to change facial appearance through use of cosmetics or plastic surgery, each of which can modify facial attractiveness and facial maturity. The impact of cosmetics on attractiveness supports the million dollar cosmetic industry and may seem rather obvious. Still, it is worth noting that systematic research has shown a positive impact of facial makeup on judgments of women's attractiveness. Makeup has a moderate-to-strong effect on ratings of women photographed with and without their usual cosmetics, with the made-up women seen as more attractive.[26] Makeup also has a strong effect on attractiveness judgments made by the photographed women themselves, who thought they would be seen as more attractive when wearing their customary makeup.[27] Even someone who is already highly attractive shows a strong benefit of cosmetics: Women rated a professional model as more attractive when she wore moderate or heavy cosmetics than when she wore none.[28]

Cosmetics may affect not only a woman's attractiveness but also her facial maturity. Although using makeup to accentuate cheekbones or to darken eyebrows yields a less babyfaced appearance, cosmetics primarily serve to make a woman more babyfaced. Babies have lighter skin, larger eyes, redder and poutier lips, and rosier cheeks than adults, and eyeliner, powder, lipstick, and rouge all serve to mimic these infantile facial attributes. Of course, to have this effect the makeup must be applied with subtlety. Heavily made-up women look anything but babyfaced.

In addition to augmenting a woman's attractiveness and babyfaceness, cosmetics may also influence impressions of her traits. Although the effects on trait impressions are less reliable than those on attractiveness, more made-up women are frequently perceived as more popular, sociable, and talkative, as well as more secure, poised, and confident.[29] Some of these impressions suggest that more made-up women are perceived as conforming more to sex-role stereotypes. There is some evidence that this can be a negative factor when applying for certain jobs, perhaps because the made-up woman is assimilated to the stereotype of an incompetent female.[30] To the extent that made-up women look more babyfaced, one would also expect them to be perceived as having more childlike traits, which as noted in Chapter 5 are similar to stereotypical feminine traits.

Like cosmetics, hairstyle can influence women's appearance and perceived traits. An extreme example is the use of hair to hide an unattractive face. Lucy Grealy, whose face was deformed by cancer, wrote the following:

> I walked around with my head bent, my dark blond hair covering half my face. . . . The simple act of lifting my hair and exposing my face was among the hardest things I ever had to do. . . . I gladly would have undergone any amount of physical pain to keep my hair down . . . sometimes men would whistle at me from a distance. . . . My long blond hair, when I bothered to brush it, was pretty. I would walk as fast as possible, my head bent down . . . .[31]

Hairstyle can influence babyfaceness as well as attractiveness. One study found a large effect on judgments of facial maturity, with higher ratings given to women when their hair was stylishly combed than when it was casually arranged. There was also a strong tendency to judge those with stylish hair as more reliable, a mature-faced trait.[32] Since a baby's hair is often in disarray, this may reflect the babyface overgeneralization effect. However, those with stylish hair were also seen as warmer, kinder, and more caring, traits that are not typically ascribed to more mature-faced individuals. As noted earlier, stereotypes of blonds versus brunettes may also reflect the babyface overgeneralization effect. Women who want to avoid the babyface stereotype may do well to select stylish hairdos and to avoid bleaching their hair. Like cranial hair, facial hair can also influence women's babyfaceness and attractiveness. Women who pluck or wax their eyebrows and bleach or wax their upper lips make themselves look more babyfaced as well as more attractive.

Men are unlikely to use cosmetics to fight face effects, and there isn't too much that they can do with hairstyles. However, they can use toupees or other means to increase their cranial hair. There is some evidence that bald men look babyfaced, and adding cranial hair has the surprising effect of making men look both chronologically younger and more mature-faced. Bald men, like babyfaced men, are perceived as relatively timid, naive, gentle, submissive, weak, and nonaggressive. Babyfaced men who are balding can fight the double whammy effect of their facial structure and their hair loss on these trait impressions by adding cranial hair through a toupee or other means, which will also serve to increase their attractiveness.[33]

Men also can use facial hair to control face effects. A weak-chinned, babyfaced man can create the impression of greater dominance by growing a beard that augments his jawline. Indeed, research has revealed a moderate-to-strong tendency for men to be judged as more mature and dominant when bearded than when clean-shaven.[34] Some research also has found a small tendency for bearded men to be judged as more competent on measures such as industry, expertise, education level, and intelligence, although these findings are less reliable. A beard not only may modify impressions of maturity and associated traits, but also it may modify impressions of attractiveness, although here the findings are inconsistent. When the same men were rated before and after shaving their beards, they were judged to be moderately better looking in their unshaven state.[35] However, these were men who had chosen to grow a beard, and they may have done so with the goal of concealing an unattractive face. Another study found that men were judged as more attractive when they were clean-shaven than when they wore fake beards, but this could reflect the artificiality of those beards.[36] Other studies examining the attractiveness of schematic faces with and without beards have yielded mixed results.[37] It should be noted that the impressions created by beards may vary as a function of how fashionable they are at a particular time in history. However, the effects on trait impressions reviewed here were consistent from the early 1970s, when beards were commonplace among "hippies," to the early 1990s, when a clean-shaven look was more in vogue.

Plastic surgery is a more extreme solution to face effects but one that is increasingly popular. Many procedures are designed to reverse the effects of aging; these tend to create a more attractive appearance in our youth-oriented culture as well as a more babyfaced appearance. For example, eyelid surgery to eliminate sagging upper eyelids and bags under the eyes creates the wide-eyed appearance that is both attractive and babyfaced. Similarly, procedures to remove wrinkles, such as dermabrasion and chemical peels, create a smooth-skinned appearance that is both attractive and babyfaced. The person who has such procedures may subsequently be perceived to have traits more in keeping with the attractiveness halo and the babyface stereotype. Whereas the former effect may be a uniformly desired outcome, the latter may not. For example, male executives are increasingly electing cosmetic surgery to give themselves a more energetic and youthful appearance. They would probably not be pleased if their surgery also produced a more submissive and naive appearance.

In addition to the use of plastic surgery by older individuals who wish to counteract the effects of aging, younger individuals may elect various procedures to alter their facial structure. A "nose job" is the most common of these. Those who have a large, high-bridged nose, like the woman in the "before" picture in Figure 9.1, may have it reduced to a shape that is culturally attractive. This new nose may be more babyish as well as more attractive, and those who wish to avoid the trait impressions associated with the babyface stereotype would do well to avoid an upturned nose with a concave bridge. Those who already have such a nose, like the man in the "before" picture in Figure 9.1, could elect surgery to fashion a larger nose with a more prominent bridge in order to be perceived as more dominant and shrewd. Jaw reconstruction is another option for individuals who wish to alter their facial appearance. Such surgery often has medical justification, since it may serve to correct misalignment of the upper and lower teeth. A receding chin may be made more prominent, thereby increasing attractiveness as well as facial maturity. An overly prominent chin may be reduced in size, which can increase attractiveness and babyfaceness.

Behavioral Adjustments

Plastic surgery is an expensive and rather extreme method for fighting face effects, and there is only so much that one can do with cosmetics or hair. Fortunately there are other, more readily accessible, means to combat facial stereotypes. Just as perceivers can fight face effects by focusing attention more on people's behavior than on their appearance, so can targets fight face effects by modifying their behavior. Indeed, as noted in Chapter 5, individuals were perceived as less babyfaced when they showed high than low academic achievement.[38] In addition to counteracting facial stereotypes by behaving in ways that directly contradict them—babyfaced individuals taking on achieving, leadership roles or unattractive individuals developing good social skills—targets can also make more subtle behavioral adjustments.

Smiling or frowning can counteract facial stereotypes by influencing impressions of facial appearance or by directly influencing trait impressions. Smiling increases attractiveness as does high nonverbal expressive-

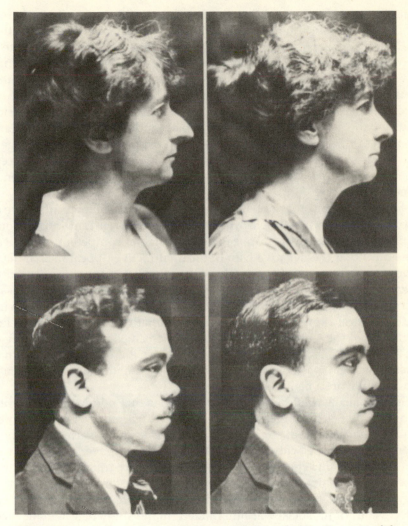

FIGURE 9.1   *Before and after nasal surgery. Patients of Dr. Bourguet of the French Academy of Medicine, 1924. Radio Times Hulton.*

ness in general, whereas frowning decreases attractiveness compared with a neutral expression. Although a smile can moderately augment attractiveness, it is unfortunately not worth too much in terms of how people rank in attractiveness when they smile versus when they do not. When smiling pictures of people were compared to pictures of 29 others who had neutral expressions, the smilers tended to be ranked only about two places higher in attractiveness than they were ranked on the basis of a picture with a neutral expression.[39]

It was recently reported that children laugh 400 times a day, whereas adults laugh only 15 times.[40] Although no one has investigated whether the childlike behavior of laughing increases how babyfaced someone is perceived to be, a study has examined the effects of smiling by comparing judgments of babyfaced and mature-faced schematic faces shown with a smiling, neutral, or frowning expression. Whereas the structure of these faces had a large effect on how babyfaced they looked, facial expression had only a small effect, with smiling faces judged slightly more baby-faced than those with neutral or frowning expressions.[41] Similarly, general facial structure was found to have a large effect on adults' perceptions of infants' cuteness, whereas facial expression had only a moderate effect.[42]

Although a smile may not make people appear much more attractive or babyfaced, it can nevertheless have direct effects on trait impressions. Smiling can make people appear more sociable, competent, or honest, thus offsetting the negative halo of an unattractive appearance. Indeed, when an unattractive fictitious female college student was accused of cheating on an exam, she was seen as less responsible by judges who saw a smiling schematic drawing of her than by judges who saw a drawing with a neutral expression. Not only did an unattractive woman look less guilty when she smiled, but also she was perceived as no more guilty of cheating than a smiling attractive woman. On the other hand, an unattractive woman was perceived as more guilty than an attractive woman when both wore a neutral expression.[43]

Smiling also has effects on trait impressions that mimic the effects of a babyface. Just as babyfaced people are seen as warmer and more friendly than the mature-faced, so are smiling people seen as warmer and more friendly than those with a neutral expression. Moreover, a smiling mature-faced person is perceived as warmer and more friendly than a baby-faced person with a neutral or a frowning expression.[44] Merely by smiling, the mature-faced person can compensate greatly for the negative impressions of his social warmth. Indeed, in the study of schematic faces described earlier, facial expression had a large effect on judgments of social warmth, whereas facial structure had only a small effect.

Whereas facial expression can offset the impressions of coldness created by a mature face, it is less successful in offsetting the impressions of weakness created by a babyface. Just as being more babyfaced creates the impression of greater dependence, submissiveness, and naivete, so does more smiling. However, a frowning babyfaced person continued to be seen as weaker than a mature-faced person with a neutral or a frowning expression and was seen as no stronger than the mature-faced person who wore a smile.[45] Thus, manipulations of facial expression are insufficient to create an impression of greater strength in a babyfaced than a mature-faced person. Indeed, facial expression had only a small effect on judgments of the social weakness of schematic faces, whereas facial structure had a moderate effect.

A number of nonverbal behaviors besides facial expression can be perceived as quickly as babyfaceness and attractiveness and can therefore offset the primacy of facial structure. Although the feasibility of using these behaviors to manage impressions is limited by the fact that some may be difficult to control consciously, those who are very babyfaced can counteract the impression of submissiveness that their face creates by nonverbal behaviors that signal dominance.[46] These include sitting at the head of the table in a group setting, making a lot of eye contact, lowering one's eyebrows, using expansive and relaxed body movements, showing an erect posture, and exhibiting a powerful-looking gait. Such a gait is rapid, forward leaning, and loose-jointed with a large arm swing and stride length, considerable hip sway, knee bending, picking up of feet, and a relatively bouncy rhythm.[47] Those who are concerned that their high facial maturity is threatening to others can counteract the impression of dominance that their face creates by nonverbal behaviors that signal deference: gaze aversion, raised eyebrows, constrained and tight body movements, a stooped posture, and a weak-looking gait. Nonverbal behaviors that counteract the impression of coldness that a mature face creates include smaller interpersonal distances.[48] Finally, those who are concerned that their lack of attractiveness creates the impression of low social competence may find that gesturing and facial expressiveness will help, since such nonverbal behaviors augment impressions of attractiveness and social competence.[49]

Vocal behaviors can also offset face effects, although these do not have the advantage of primacy that is provided by facial expressions and gestures.[50] People may offset the effects of low attractiveness on impressions of their social competence by increasing how much they talk; it has been found that job applicants who talk a lot during an interview are perceived as more socially competent than those who talk less.[51] People may also increase impressions of their social competence by speaking louder, since those with louder voices are seen as friendlier and more extraverted. Using a relatively loud voice also signals dominance, as does a low-pitched voice and taking control of the topics of conversation; speaking rapidly signals competence (at least to Westerners). These verbal styles can offset the effects of a babyface or an unattractive face. On the other hand, soft, slow, or high-pitched speech will offset the impressions of dominance or coldness created by a mature face. The ability of vocal qualities to counteract face effects appears to be greater for impressions of weakness than for impressions of warmth, an effect demonstrated in research on the content as well as the style of speech. Greater use of words expressing positive emotion and of self-referents (e.g., *I, me,* and *my*) decreases impressions of a person's social power but has no effect on impressions of warmth and likability.[52] Therefore, by avoiding positive emotion words and self-referents in their speech, unattractive or babyfaced people may offset the impression that they are low in power. The same effect may be achieved by using a mature-sounding voice—clear and low-pitched.[53]

Adjusting the Company One Keeps

There is a tendency to judge people as less attractive after looking at other, highly attractive, individuals. This is called the "successive contrast effect."[54] The implication for targets desiring to control face effects is to avoid introductions to people right after those people have been talking to or looking at someone who is gorgeous. Of course, this is not a very feasible strategy to implement. However, there is another effect of social context that is more controllable: the "simultaneous assimilation effect."[55] Judgments of a person's attractiveness move toward the attractiveness of the people who are seen at the same time. An average-looking person is judged as moderately more attractive when her face is shown at the same time as two highly attractive faces than when it is shown at the same time as two unattractive faces. Those who keep company with attractive people, therefore, are likely to be seen as more attractive themselves. In addition, being seen with a set of friends of even average looks increases how attractive someone is perceived to be as opposed to being seen with average-looking strangers.[56] This effect represents the attractiveness halo operating in reverse: The person who appears to be socially competent is perceived as more attractive.

Adjusting One's Public Image

The motto "dress for success" has merit. Clothing and eyeglasses can influence people's judgments of facial appearance and traits. People are judged to be less attractive when wearing glasses. This effect occurs as early as first grade, and it tends to be small-to-medium for judgments of males and medium-to-large for judgments of females.[57] Those in need of corrective lenses can avoid a negative halo effect by electing to wear contact lenses. However, donning spectacles may have some beneficial effects for those who are already relatively unattractive: When people are shown wearing glasses, they are judged to be more intelligent and conscientious than when they are shown without glasses.[58] Although images of bespectacled "nerds" as well as the old adage "men seldom make passes at girls who wear glasses" suggest that wearing glasses will not offset a negative halo on judgments of social competence, it may offset a negative halo on judgments of intellectual competence. However, such benefits may be short-lived. Although the initial impression of greater intelligence in the bespectacled is maintained when perceivers observe them sitting alone for up to 2 minutes, this impression can be undone when perceivers observe their behavior during an interview.[59]

The particular style of glasses an individual wears is also significant in determining trait impressions. It is consistent with the roundness of a babyface as well as with evidence that angular forms are seen as more threatening than curvilinear ones that people wearing square glasses are perceived as more mature-faced than those wearing round ones. Moreover, babyfaced people wearing square glasses are seen as less warm, naive, submissive, and honest than those wearing round glasses. Thus, those who are babyfaced may be able to offset the babyface stereotype by wearing square glasses. However, wearing round glasses does not seem to be useful in offsetting the mature-face stereotype, perhaps because glasses of any sort lend a mature appearance to the face.[60]

Clothing is another attribute that can modify the first impressions created by facial appearance.[61] There is considerable consensus regarding the personal qualities that are conveyed by particular clothes. For example, people agree that certain clothes are likely to be worn by women who are snobbish, with other clothes likely to be worn by those who are fun loving or shy or sophisticated or rebellious. Researchers have categorized women's clothing styles into four groups, examples of which are shown in Figure 9.2.[62] Dramatic styles reflect extremes in fashion and are characterized by bold or severe design lines. Natural dress is informal, casual, and comfortable apparel with minimal ornamentation. Romantic clothing has gently curved lines that convey a feminine air. Classic styles are characterized by simple, conservative, and tailored lines.

Babyfaced women who wish to look less submissive and naive would do well to wear the classic style, which is seen as the most dominant and sophisticated of the four and yields higher ratings of a newscaster's credibility than other styles. They would also be wise to avoid the romantic and natural styles, which are seen as the most submissive and unsophisticated, respectively. Mature-faced women who wish to look less threatening should wear the romantic style, which appears the most approachable, and they should avoid the classic style, which looks least approachable.

Although research has focused more on the effects of women's than men's clothing, there is reason to believe that men too can counteract face effects by wearing certain clothes. More formal dress is likely to create an aura of authority that can counteract the babyface stereotype. Candid camera-type studies of jaywalking have shown that the good example set

DRAMATIC   NATURAL

ROMANTIC   CLASSIC

FIGURE 9.2 *Women's clothing styles. C. Jackson (1980).* Color me beautiful. *New York: Ballantine Books. Adapted by M. R. Solomon (Eds.). (1985).* The psychology of fashion *(p. 324). Lexington Books. Reprinted with permission.*

by a man who does not cross against the light is more often followed by others if the man is wearing a business suit and tie than if he is wearing a work shirt and trousers. Similarly, pedestrians are more likely to comply with a request to participate in a survey if the interviewer is well dressed rather than poorly dressed.[63]

Among the image-making devices that people may use to fight face effects is their name. Willy Smith was acquitted of rape. Ollie North was exonerated of treason. Perhaps William and Oliver, babyfaced though they may be, would have been viewed as more culpable. Perhaps James Carter would have been viewed as a stronger leader than Jimmy was. In short, a childlike nickname may create impressions similar to those created by a babyface, whereas a more mature-sounding, formal name may create the opposite impressions. Babyfaced people who want to appear more dominant and shrewd may do well to use the formal version of their name. Mature-faced people who want to appear more honest and approachable may do well to use a diminutive nickname.

It is consistent with the foregoing recommendation that warm names, like a babyface, have been found to augment impressions of warmth and honesty, whereas cold names, like a mature face, augmented impressions of strength and leadership. This was true even when the two sets of names included no nicknames or diminutives. Moreover, mature-faced job applicants with warm-sounding names were perceived as less powerful than those with colder names and also as more suited to jobs requiring warmth, such as teacher's aide at a day care center or counselor at a homeless shelter. Indeed, mature-faced and babyfaced applicants were equally likely to be recommended for such jobs when both had warm names but not when both had cold names. Name warmth was also capable of offsetting the positive effects of applicants' facial maturity on their judged suitability for jobs requiring administrative and decision-making competence. Mature-faced applicants with warm names and babyfaced applicants with cold names were recommended equally for such jobs.[64]

Adjustments to Self-Image

It is interesting that there is only a moderate relationship between people's attractiveness as judged by others and their self-ratings of attractiveness. There are a goodly number of very attractive people who do not perceive themselves as attractive, and there are many rather homely people who think they look just fine. Similarly, people who are viewed by others as babyfaced do not necessarily see themselves this way.[65] What may sustain these self-perceptions is a tendency for people's self-views to influence the way they think others view them.[66] Moreover, the way people think they look can have at least as much influence on their personal and social outcomes as their "objective" appearance has. Those who feel more attractive are more popular, sociable, and dominant, effects that reflect their higher self-esteem. Moreover, self-ratings of attractiveness predict popularity just as well as more objective ratings, and self-ratings are even better predictors of sociability and dominance.[67] Although these effects are small, they may cause those who feel attractive to be judged similarly to those who in fact are attractive. Comparable effects have been found for self-perceptions of babyfaceness. Regardless of whether a woman looks babyfaced to others, if she perceives herself as babyfaced she is less assertive, less socially powerful, and more feminine according to standard personality tests. Moreover, self-ratings of babyfaceness are more strongly related to actual assertiveness and social power than are ratings by others. Men who perceive themselves as babyfaced are also more feminine than those who perceive themselves as mature-faced.[68] These small-to-moderate effects may cause those who feel they are babyfaced to be judged similarly to those who in fact are babyfaced. The implication of these findings is that "you are what you think you are."

Cultural Contributions to Face Effects

It has been shown that perceivers and targets can vary in their susceptibility to face effects. An examination of cultural contributions to these effects provides additional insights into the factors that can make perceivers and targets more or less vulnerable to facial stereotyping.[69]

Contributions of Parents

Evidence suggesting an effect of parental socialization on face effects is provided by the finding that children whose fathers expect them to prefer to play with an attractive rather than an unattractive peer are more likely to do so. More direct evidence that such preferences may be influenced by parents' expectations is provided by the finding that parents communicate physical appearance stereotypes to their children when they are asked to tell impromptu stories about a child going to school for the first time. For example, if the story character is depicted as obese, a greater proportion of the descriptions of him are negative ones than if he is depicted as normal weight. Also, the stories report more negative peer reactions to obese children, who are more likely to be described as having low self-esteem.[70] Although parents may have the best of intentions—trying to teach their children to be kind to unattractive individuals—they may instead be unwittingly teaching their children the attractiveness halo. Stories featuring unattractive children who are popular and self-confident may ameliorate this tacit message.

Parents can influence not only their children's attitudes toward the appearance of others but also their attitudes toward their own appearance. Since, as noted earlier, there is only a moderate relationship between people's attractiveness as judged by others and their self-ratings of attractiveness, there should be ample opportunity for parents to influence their children's self-views. Parents who have failed to provide an attractive countenance to their children through their genes can more than make up for this by giving their children a positive self-regard. Indeed, it is possible that high self-esteem is central, with children who have high self-esteem, for whatever reason, coming to view themselves as attractive.[71] Similarly, parents whose genetic endowment has bestowed a babyface on their offspring may be able to offset the disadvantageous psychological and social consequences of this appearance by inculcating a feeling of self-efficacy. Fostering high self-esteem also should be advantageous to children whose appearance induces low expectancies—be they unattractive or babyfaced. Parents who produce children with high self-esteem in Western cultures are those who value high achievement. Lower self-esteem occurs among children who report that their parents value accommodation: characteristics like obedience, adjustment to others, and kindness.[72] This pattern of results may reflect the traits that are most valued in Western, individualistic cultures, which value individual achievement. The results may well be different in more collectivist societies, which value interdependence.

Contributions of Teachers

As discussed in Chapter 8, teachers are vulnerable to the attractiveness halo effect in their reactions to their students. Moreover, students are more likely to internalize teachers' expectations when the teachers' treatment of those in the class is highly differentiated.[73] Surely such behavior is unwitting, and most teachers, if aware, would attempt to be less biased. One way to reduce bias is for teachers to base their expectancies about students' performance on other, more diagnostic information. One researcher has also suggested some steps that teachers can take so that they will not give subtle messages to students about the value of beauty.[74]

First, it is recommended that teachers examine their own behavior. Specifically, teachers need to notice (and correct) any tendencies to (a) be more likely to develop special relationships with the attractive children in their classes, giving these children more smiles and other nonverbal reinforcers; (b) have higher expectations for the performance of attractive children and call on them more often; (c) compliment children on their appearance in ways that encourage comparisons among children or that relate beauty to goodness; (d) display on bulletin boards only stereotyped images of cute children and attractive adults. Second, a series of classroom activities is recommended to teach children the importance of respecting and accepting others for themselves rather than for their looks. One example is a mock election in which the teacher mounts on a bulletin board a series of pictures of boy and girl candidates of different races, body builds, clothing, and facial attractiveness. The children are then asked to vote for the candidate whom they think would make the best school president, secretary, and treasurer. After tallying and reporting the votes, the teacher can discuss with the children how they decided for whom to vote, whether this is a fair way to run an election, whether they think people often judge others by their appearance, and why "judging a book by its cover" is a form of prejudice.

Contributions of the Media

Whatever changes can be made by individual parents and teachers will be less than optimally effective unless there are concomitant changes in the media. The stories that parents have traditionally read to their children are rife with appearance stereotypes. The textbooks that children find in the classroom have not yet achieved sufficiently numerous and positive portrayals of females and racial minorities, much less such portrayals of the unattractive. Television advertising perpetuates the stereotype that babyfaced individuals are trustworthy and mature-faced individuals are knowledgeable, and advertisers in all media typically use attractive communicators.

Not only do advertisements portray predominantly attractive individuals, but also the verbal messages in these ads hammer home the importance of appearance. A systematic content analysis of over 4,000 television commercials revealed that more than one in four ads made a reference to some aspect of appearance, be it beauty, youth, weight, or style, and one in eleven made a reference to beauty in particular.[75] Given the amount of television viewed by most individuals, it has been estimated that we are exposed to over 5,000 appearance messages a year with close to 2,000 of these dealing specifically with beauty.

In addition to transmittal of the attractiveness halo by the media, the prevalence of beautiful people in magazines, books, and television may diminish individuals' evaluations of their own attractiveness. Indeed, consistent with the successive contrast effect noted earlier, college men judged an average-looking female peer as less attractive if they had just been watching *Charlie's Angels,* a once popular television show with three highly attractive female actors, than if they had not been watching TV or had been watching a different show.[76] Similar strong contrast effects were found when men judged the attractiveness of an average-looking woman after viewing a picture of a female magazine model and when men judged the attractiveness of a nude female after looking at nudes in the magazines *Playboy* and *Penthouse.*[77] Even women showed a successive contrast effect when judging the attractiveness of other women. It is not unreasonable to expect that people do likewise in their self-judgments. The portrayal of beautiful people in the media not only reinforces the view that more attractive individuals have more desirable traits but also can make viewers feel that they are not in that privileged group.

The media has responded to social pressures to change their portrayal of women and racial minorities over the past few decades. In the 1950s and early 1960s, one never saw a black person in a television commercial, and the only blacks to be found on TV programs appeared in highly stereotyped roles. Perhaps one day ordinary-looking and even unattractive people will appear on television programs in greater numbers than they currently do. Reducing the emphasis on a beautiful appearance in television commercials is likely to be more problematic in this society owing to vested economic interests in industries involved with cosmetics, perfume, apparel, hair care, and weight loss aids. However, advertisements for products that have nothing to do with appearance may not necessarily benefit from use of beautiful models. As suggested in Chapter 7, the fit between the model's assumed traits and the product may also be important such that an attractive, sexy model could be less of an asset in marketing chicken soup or floor cleaner than a homely, wholesome one.[78]

Contributions of Cultural Values

There is no evidence for cultural differences in the babyface overgeneralization effect, which is consistent with the argument that it derives from the universally adaptive value of responding to the needs of babies. The suggestion that the attractiveness halo is an overgeneralization of adaptive responses to facial indicators of fitness also argues for cultural universality of this facial stereotype. Although a halo effect has been found in all cultures that have been studied, its extent and content have been proposed to vary with cultural differences in individualism and collectivism.

Individualistic cultures are those that value personal autonomy, self-realization, and individual achievement. In such cultures, which include the United States, people's identity is based on their personal attributes. Collectivist cultures are those that value interdependence and group achievement. In such cultures, people's identity is based on their place in the social system. Because one's personal appearance has more significance for identity in individualistic cultures, it has been hypothesized that attractiveness stereotyping is more prevalent in such cultures. Because different traits are valued in individualistic and collectivist cultures, it also has been hypothesized that the halo effect is most pronounced for different traits in the two types of cultures. This hypothesis is consistent with the argument that the halo effect derives from the good feelings that an attractive face evokes in the beholder, since those feelings should produce positive evaluations only on culturally valued traits. There is as yet little research bearing on the two hypotheses regarding cultural differences. However, the available evidence suggests that cultural values can have an impact on appearance stereotyping both by influencing those traits that are captured by the attractiveness halo as well as by influencing those traits that are most likely to be spared from stereotyping when the motivation to be accurate is high.

When there is no particular motivation to be accurate, the attractiveness halo shows up on the traits that are most culturally valued. A moderate positive effect of attractiveness on Koreans' impressions of a person's integrity and concern for others and the lack of an effect on their impressions of dominance and assertiveness is consistent with the stress on harmonious relationships in collectivist cultures. The reverse pattern shown by Americans is consistent with the self-affirming traits most valued in individualistic cultures.[79] The finding that impressions of intelligence show a stronger attractiveness halo for Chinese than Americans, whereas the reverse is true for impressions of sociability, is also consistent with differences in cultural values.[80]

Although the attractiveness halo may be most pronounced for culturally valued traits when accuracy motivation is negligible, it may be least pronounced for these traits when accuracy motivation is high, since these are the traits that people make the most effort to judge in an unbiased fashion. Such an effect was shown by Chinese-Canadian college students who were highly involved in the local collectivist Chinese community and who had been singled out from a North American population to participate in "a study of person-perception involving Chinese students." As representatives of their culture, these students may have been highly motivated to make accurate judgments, and they did indeed show less influence of attractiveness on judgments of traits highly valued in collectivist cultures, such as consideration, kindness, and sincerity, than did Chinese students who were less involved in the collectivist culture.[81] On the other hand, these two groups showed equal attractiveness stereotyping in judgments of career achievement, popularity, and a happy life. Thus, although value differences between individualistic and collectivist cultures may influence the particular traits that are inferred from attractiveness, there is no evidence that they can altogether eliminate the halo effect.

Institutional "Faceism"

Evidence reviewed in earlier chapters makes abundantly clear that face effects are prevalent in various social institutions, ranging from business to the political arena to the courtroom to the doctor's office. Explicit recognition of this problem and the development of policies to counteract it is needed. At the same time, the development of such policies requires knowing what measures can be effective in changing the behavior of individuals. The recommendations made in this chapter can be used not only to reduce individual vulnerability to facial stereotypes but also to reduce institutional "faceism" by those in positions of leadership within various social institutions.

Summary

Although facial stereotypes run contrary to our cultural values of equal opportunity and outcomes based on merit, this book has shown that face effects are real and pervasive. Whereas platitudes like "pretty is as pretty does" will not eliminate these effects, there are a number of effective remedies. One attack can be mounted at the level of individual perceivers. A sense of accountability for one's social judgments, a feeling of interdependence with those being judged, and a concern with the inner disposition of people rather than their public appearance will serve to mitigate face effects. Other remedies include accessing information about people's behavioral and psychological attributes before viewing their faces and paying unbiased attention to specific behaviors, taking care not to be overly influenced by those that confirm expectations and looking for disconfirming ones. Targets of face effects can also take measures to combat them. Adjustments to facial appearance, through use of cosmetics, facial and cranial hair, or plastic surgery, do not so much eliminate face effects as harness them to the individual's advantage. Adjustments to behavior, on the other hand, fight face effects by an opposing influence on first impressions of gestures, posture, gait, facial expressions, or vocal qualities. Similarly, adjustments to one's public image provide a counter-influence on impressions of apparel, eyewear, and name. Targets also can combat face effects with a strong countervailing self-image. Finally, the tactics that perceivers and targets can undertake to fight face effects may be promoted in the wider culture through efforts to curtail facial stereotypes on the part of parents, teachers, the media, and those in positions of leadership within various social institutions.

10

Unmasking the Face

There is something in a face, an air, and a peculiar grace, which boldest painters cannot trace.

—**Somerville, *The Lucky Hit*, 1727**

Although painters may fail to capture exactly what a face reveals, the human face remains a favored subject. This is equally true for judges of human character. Face reading is universal but imperfect. The deficiencies are grounded in adaptive mechanisms and, as such, lead to shared stereotypes. Indeed, the opening chapter of this book argued that the consensus regarding the traits that a face reveals is so strong that it can serve as a basis for humor. Readers of this book should now have a deeper understanding of the cartoons shown in that chapter. The benign appearance of the spaniel shown in Figure 1.2 reflects the babyface overgeneralization effect. This pooch exemplifies use of key infantile stimuli to create lovable cartoon characters, as in the evolution of Mickey Mouse that was discussed in Chapter 4. However, this dog's disarming appearance is misleading, as Garfield learns to our amusement. So is the threatening appearance of the bulldog shown in Figure 1.3, which is belied by his gentle character. His extremely prominent, mature jaw and his small eyes make him look domineering, the converse of the babyface overgeneralization effect. The violation of these associations between facial structure and traits is amusing. The same is true for the man buried in the sand in Figure 1.4. His babyish round face, large eyes, and receding chin make him look weak and submissive, and the disconfirmation of these expectations is humorous. Similarly, people find it comical to suggest that a shrewd disposition characterizes the man in Figure 1.1, since quite a different impression is conveyed by his babyfaced profile with its round chin, full lips, and pug nose.

Humor is by no means the only consequence of peoples' proclivity to judge others by their appearance. As demonstrated in Chapter 4, people of all ages and racial backgrounds see a baby's face in individuals of all ages and races who are not babies but merely resemble them. They also form stereotyped trait impressions of these individuals. More specifically, people with babyish facial qualities are seen as warm and affectionate, submissive and weak, and naive and ingenuous. This babyface overgeneralization effect may account for the differing impressions of Rembrandt and Gauguin, shown in Figure 1.7. Rembrandt's more approachable look may derive from his more babyish facial qualities: a rounder face, a smaller nose bridge, and a less prominent jaw. People of all ages and racial backgrounds also can see attractiveness in the same faces. This is true regardless of the age or race of the face and despite some cultural differences in judgments of attractiveness. Moreover, people show a halo effect in their trait impressions of attractive individuals, who are perceived more positively than unattractive people on a variety of dimensions.

The babyface overgeneralization effect and the attractiveness halo have consequences beyond mere trait expectancies. Chapter 5 revealed that significant social outcomes can be predicted from stereotyped views of babyfaced people's personality traits in a variety of contexts, including personal relationships, social influence, occupational outcomes, and encounters with the law. Similarly, Chapter 7 revealed that significant social outcomes in these contexts can be predicted from stereotyped views of attractive people's traits. Many of the social outcomes of appearance are consistent with the facial fit principle, which holds that biased social outcomes can result from the match between social roles and the traits suggested by an individual's facial appearance. There also may be contrast effects when there is an extreme lack of fit between people's behavior and the traits suggested by their appearance. Behavior that disconfirms negative expectations can produce more positive outcomes than occur when that behavior is expected, and behavior that disconfirms positive expectations can produce more negative outcomes than occur when that behavior is expected.

The social consequences of facial appearance are not trivial, and the effects are comparable in magnitude to those of other, better established, influencing factors. The moderate-to-large positive effect of facial maturity on coital experience reported by high school boys was equal to the independent effect of pubertal development. The moderate-to-large effect of applicant babyfaceness on occupational outcomes in simulated personnel decisions was similar in magnitude to the effect of applicant sex. The moderate effect of facial maturity on the real jobs held by a random sample of women was comparable in magnitude to the effect of their personality traits. The effect of facial maturity on judgments of the suitability of men and women for sex-stereotyped occupations was sufficiently strong to override the effect of sex, with babyfaced men and mature-faced women seen as equally suited to "feminine" and "masculine" occupational roles. The effect of defendants' babyfaceness on trial outcomes in small claims court was comparable in magnitude to the effect of evidence presented to support their case. The social effects of attractiveness are also substantial.

It has been argued that the babyface overgeneralization effect may derive from the adaptive value of responding to the valid age information that faces can provide. The growth process from birth to maturity is accompanied by changes in the face that are reliable cues to age. Moreover, as described in Chapter 2, people show acute sensitivity to this age information and they do so as early as 4 months of age. Coupled with evidence for specific deficits in age recognition among brain-damaged patients, this suggests that such recognition may have an innate neural basis. Certainly, that would be adaptive, since appropriate responses to age-related facial cues facilitate evolutionarily important behaviors such as mating with the fertile and nurturing the young. Indeed, Chapter 4 chronicled cross-cultural and cross-species evidence that certain key stimuli in an infant's appearance deter aggression and elicit warm, affectionate, and protective responses. The evolutionary necessity of quick, reliable, and appropriate responses to the needs of babies may have predisposed us to respond in a similar fashion to those whose faces are even a partial match to key infantile stimuli. Recent evidence that the power of key stimuli to elicit nurturant responses in mice may be controlled by a specific gene is consistent with this argument, as is evidence that young infants respond positively not only to other babies but also to babyfaced adults.

It has been suggested that the attractiveness halo effect may derive from the adaptive value of responding to the valid fitness information that faces can provide, an instance of the sickness similarities overgeneralization effect. The components of attractiveness that were discussed in Chapter 6 suggest that attractiveness, as manifested in symmetry, averageness, youthfulness, and gender prototypicality, signals physical, psychological, and intellectual fitness. Although there is as yet little evidence that this is true within a normal population of individuals who are all the same age, it certainly is true when one considers the extremes. People who are beyond their reproductive years tend to be less attractive, as do those with genetic disorders that create various intellectual, psychological, and physical impairments. The perception that unattractive people are less socially and intellectually competent as well as less healthy and fertile than their more attractive peers may reflect the overgeneralization of evolutionarily adaptive responses to the unfit people whom unattractive individuals resemble. The evolutionary selection pressures that may produce a sickness similarities overgeneralization effect may also produce more positive affective responses to more attractive people. Such responses not only could foster social interactions that promote survival of the fittest but also could contribute to the attractiveness halo. Whether or not evolutionary selection is a viable explanation for the attractiveness halo, its early onset and cultural universality is consistent with the postulate that it is founded in some innate aesthetic preference, although social conditioning certainly may augment the effect.

Chapter 8 considered the interesting possibility that the attractiveness halo and the babyface overgeneralization effect are self-fulfilling: that those who are more attractive or more babyfaced are treated in ways that foster the very traits that are expected. Although there is abundant evidence for differential treatment of individuals who are more or less attractive or babyfaced, there is less support for the thesis that this treatment yields actual differences in traits. There does seem to be a kernel of truth to the stereotype that attractive people are more socially skilled, but this is most true in circumscribed social interactions when the people are responding directly to others' expectations. When global personality traits are examined, the attractiveness halo shows moderate accuracy only for individuals whose appearance has been stable over many years.

There is even less support for accuracy of the babyface stereotype. Although there is weak evidence for its accuracy among adult women who have been stable in babyfaceness since adolescence, babyfaced adolescent boys are just the opposite of what they appear to be. Rather than being submissive, nonthreatening, or lacking in intellectual astuteness as the babyface stereotype would suggest, they are more assertive, hostile, and intelligent than their more mature-faced peers. Although additional research is needed to replicate and fully explain these surprising effects, they suggest a self-defeating prophecy, whereby babyfaced boys develop compensatory patterns of behavior in order to refute unwanted expectations that they have childlike traits.

The remarkable strength of facial stereotypes is even more striking in light of the foregoing evidence that they are often wrong. The persistence of the strong perception that babyfaced people have childlike traits and that attractive people have socially desirable traits cannot be explained by the sorts of motivational factors that may contribute to the persistence of erroneous beliefs about the traits of individuals who vary in race, sex, or national origin. Rather, these perceptions must be grounded in strong associative links, perhaps innate, that can persist through perceptual biases such as illusory correlation effects. Such illusory effects can occur when there are strong associative connections between particular types of people and particular types of behavior. Perceivers pay more attention to the

people-behavior pairings that are strongly associated, and they consequently overestimate the relationship between them. For example, although babyfaced and mature-faced people may be equally likely to perform submissive and dominant behaviors, the strong association of
babyfaceness with submissiveness that is produced by the babyface overgeneralization effect may perpetuate the illusion of a correlation between
appearance and behavior that does not really exist.

Although facial stereotypes are strong enough to endure despite a lack
of confirmatory evidence, they can be overcome. Indeed, a major goal of
this book has been to provide readers with insights that can be used to
fight face effects. As discussed in Chapter 9, there are a number of malleable influences that can be used to combat facial stereotypes even
though those stereotypes may be grounded in evolutionarily adaptive reactions. Individual perceivers can employ a variety of mechanisms to
combat facial stereotypes, including making changes in institutional policies that foster "faceism." Targets of facial stereotypes can master them either by using them to their own advantage through alterations in their
appearance or by adjusting their behavior or self-concept to produce an
opposing influence on trait impressions. Finally, the support that society
adds to any innate basis for facial stereotypes can be weakened if parents,
teachers, and particularly, the media curtail their explicit or tacit encouragement of them.

This book has focused on attractiveness and babyfaceness because
these are the only two facial qualities that have received substantial attention in the research literature. However, as suggested in Chapter 3, there
are other possible bases of reading traits in faces that merit attention.
These include overgeneralized responses to facial qualities that accurately reveal other functionally significant attributes that were discussed
in Chapter 2: (a) *emotion overgeneralization effects*, whereby people are perceived to have traits that are associated with the emotional expressions
that their features resemble; (b) *mistaken identity effects*, whereby people
are perceived to have the same traits as the significant others or archetypes whom they resemble; and (c) *animal analogy effects*, whereby people
are perceived to have traits that are associated with the animal whom
their features resemble. There may also be *sickness similarity effects* in addition to those implicated in the attractiveness halo effect, such that people are perceived to have traits that are associated with a specific physical
or mental disorder that their facial features resemble. Finally, the age information in faces may yield not only a babyface overgeneralization effect
but also an *elderly overgeneralization effect*, whereby our reactions to old
people are overgeneralized to those who look old owing to premature
gray hair, balding, or wrinkles.

A final possible basis of reading psychological traits in faces is *accuracy*. Although attractiveness and babyfaceness do not appear to be very accurate indicators of traits, other facial qualities may conceivably provide more accurate trait information. Indeed, Chapters 3 and 8 considered four possible routes to a true relationship between appearance and behavior: (a) common biological influences, (b) common environmental influences, (c) influences of behavior on appearance (Dorian Gray and artifice effects), and (d) influences of appearance on behavior (self-fulfilling and self-defeating prophecy effects). Moreover, evidence that those who "judge a book by its cover" can be accurate is provided by strangers' consensual judgments of people's traits on the basis of limited nonverbal cues that are corroborated by various kinds of validity evidence.

Despite these reasons to consider seriously the possibility that facial features accurately convey psychological traits, considerable research will be necessary before any clear conclusions can be drawn. For one thing, as discussed in Chapter 3, the available research has not clarified the extent to which facial cues (as opposed to body and gestural cues) contribute to accurate judgments. In addition, the limited research examining facial cues to accuracy has yielded a chaotic array of correlations, reflecting two shortcomings in that research. First, it lacks a guiding theory for predicting what facial cues will communicate what psychological qualities. Second, it has focused on isolated facial features rather than the configural facial qualities that are likely to provide a more coherent story, akin to that revealed in this saga of babyfaceness and attractiveness.

Research has helped us to understand what psychological traits we see in faces that vary in babyishness or attractiveness, the causes of these perceptions, and their social and psychological consequences. A face can reveal important qualities, lending truth to Walt Whitman's metaphor, "In the faces of men and women, I see God." Continued efforts to unmask the face will serve to further disclose nature's secrets and to caution those who would fall prey to facial stereotypes.

Notes

Chapter One

1. C. A. Darwin, *Autobiography*. Cited in J. Liggett (1974), *The human face* (p. 215). New York: Stein & Day.

2. Aristotle, *Historia animalium*. Cited in Liggett (1974), *The human face*, p. 181.

3. *Physiognomics*, attributed to Aristotle. Cited in J. Wechsler (1982), *A human comedy: Physiognomy and caricature in 19th century Paris* (p. 15). Chicago: University of Chicago Press.

4. A. Brandt (1980, December), Face reading: The persistence of physiognomy. *Psychology Today*, p. 93.

5. Liggett (1974), *The human face*, p. 190.

6. Liggett (1974), *The human face*, p. 227.

7. J. Wechsler (1982), *A human comedy: Physiognomy and caricature in 19th century Paris* (p. 94). Chicago: University of Chicago Press.

8. J. C. Lavater (1789), *Essays on physiognomy, for the promotion of the knowledge and the love of mankind*. Quoted in Wechsler (1982), *A human comedy*, p. 94.

9. Wechsler (1982), *A human comedy*, p. 143.

10. J. C. Lavater (1879), *Essays on physiognomy* (16th ed., p. 16). Translated from the German by Thomas Holcroft. London: William Tegg.

11. T. Landau (1989), *About faces* (p. 198). New York: Doubleday.

12. *The New York Times* (1989, October 29), p. 41.

13. H. de Balzac, *The girl with the golden eyes* (p. 320). Quoted in Wechsler (1982), *A human comedy*, p. 29.

14. H. de Balzac, *The girl with the golden eyes* (p. 319). Quoted in Wechsler (1982), *A human comedy*, p. 29.

15. C. Dickens (1991), *David Copperfield* (p. 47). New York: Knopf.

16. C. Dickens (1986), *The Pickwick papers* (p. 36). Oxford, England: Oxford University Press.

17. A. M. Glenberg & T. Grimes (1994), Memory and faces: Pictures help you remember who said what. *Personality and Social Psychology Bulletin, 21*, 196–206.

18. S. T. Fiske & M. G. Cox (1979), Person concepts: The effect of target familiarity and descriptive purpose on the process of describing others. *Journal of Personality, 47*, 136–161. W. J. Livesley & D. B. Bromley (1973), *Person perception in childhood and adolescence*. London: Wiley.

19. P. F. Secord, W. F. Dukes, & W. W. Bevan (1954), Personalities in faces: I. An experiment in social perceiving. *Genetic Psychology Monographs, 49,* 231–279. P. F. Secord & J. E. Muthard (1955), Personalities in faces: IV. A descriptive analysis of the perception of women's faces and the identification of some physiognomic determinants. *Journal of Personality, 39,* 269–278.

20. J. Hochberg & R. E. Galper (1974), Attribution of intention as a function of physiognomy. *Memory and Cognition, 2,* 39–42.

21. S. M. Kassin (1977), Physical continuity and trait inference: A test of Mischel's hypothesis. *Personality and Social Psychology Bulletin, 3,* 637–640.

22. W. M. Evans (1975), The question of Emma's eyes. *Romance Notes, XVI,* 274–277.

23. O. Wilde (1974), *The picture of Dorian Gray* (I. Murray, Ed., pp. 90–91). London: Oxford University Press. (Original work published 1891)

24. P. C. Bowman (1979), Physical constancy and trait attribution: Attenuation of the primacy effect. *Personality and Social Psychology Bulletin, 5,* 61–64.

25. B. Lyman, D. Hatelid, & C. Macurdy, C. (1981), Stimulus person cues in first impression attraction. *Perceptual and Motor Skills, 52,* 59–66. E. Berscheid & E. Walster (1974), Physical attractiveness. In L. Berkowitz (Ed.), *Advances in experimental social psychology* (Vol. 7, pp. 158–216). New York: Academic Press.

26. Secord, Dukes, & Bevan (1954), *Personalities in faces*: I.

27. J. J. Gibson (1979), *The ecological approach to visual perception.* Boston: Houghton Mifflin. L. Z. McArthur & R. M. Baron (1983), Toward an ecological theory of social perception. *Psychological Review, 90,* 215–238.

28. L. A. Zebrowitz (1990), *Social perception.* Pacific Grove, CA: Brooks/Cole.

29. J. Cohen (1977), *Statistical power analysis for the behavioral sciences* (Rev. ed., pp. 24–27). New York: Academic Press.

Chapter Two

1. P. Ekman (1978), Facial signs: Facts, fantasies, and possibilities. In T. Sebeok (Ed.), *Sight, sound, and sense* (pp. 124–156). Bloomington: Indiana University Press.

2. D. H. Enlow (1982), *Handbook of facial growth* (pp. 9–23). Philadelphia: Saunders.

3. D. S. Berry (1990), What can a moving face tell us? *Journal of Personality and Social Psychology, 58,* 1004–1014.

4. R. Henss (1991), Perceiving age and attractiveness in facial photographs. *Journal of Applied Social Psychology, 21,* 933–946.

5. C. P. Edwards (1984), The age group labels and categories of preschool children. *Child Development, 55,* 440–452. G. Jones & P. K. Smith (1984), The eyes have it: Young children's discrimination of age in masked and unmasked facial photographs. *Journal of Experimental Child Psychology, 38,* 328–337. N. Kogan, J. Stevens, & F. C. Shelton (1961), Age differences: A developmental study of discriminability and affective response. *Journal of Abnormal Social Psychology, 62,* 221–230.

6. J. M. Montepare & L. Z. McArthur (1986), The influence of facial characteristics on children's age perceptions. *Journal of Experimental Child Psychology, 42,* 303–314.

7. Jones & Smith (1984), The eyes have it, p. 336.

8. G. Tiberghien & I. Clerc (1986), The cognitive locus of prosopagnosia. In R. Bruyer (Ed.), *The neuropsychology of face perception and facial expression* (pp. 39–62). Hillsdale, NJ: Erlbaum.

9. R. E. Lasky, R. E. Klein, & S. Martinez (1974), Age and sex discriminations in five- and six-month-old infants. *Journal of Psychology, 88,* 317–324. R. B. McCall & C. B. Kennedy (1980), Attention of 4-month infants to discrepancy and babyishness. *Journal of Experimental Child Psychology, 29,* 189–201.

10. J. Brooks & M. Lewis (1976), Infants' responses to strangers: Midget, adult, and child. *Child Development, 47,* 323–332.

11. G. A. Borkan, S. S. Bachman, & A. H. Norris (1982), Comparison of visually estimated age with physiologically predicted age as indicators of rates of aging. *Social Science and Medicine, 16,* 197–204.

12. P. L. van den Berghe & P. Frost (1986), Skin color preference, sexual dimorphism and sexual selection: A case of gene culture co-evolution? *Ethnic and Racial Studies, 9,* 87–113.

13. Enlow (1982), *Handbook of facial growth,* pp. 6–9.

14. J. L. Gewirtz, R. A. Weber, & M. Nogueras (1990, April), *The role of facial characteristics in neonatal gender discrimination from photographs.* Paper presented at the International Conference on Infant Studies, Montreal, Canada. J. M. Haviland (1976, April), *Sex differences in the presentation and perception of the human face.* Paper presented at the symposium, "The Communication of Sex-Roles," Eastern Psychological Association, New York.

15. Berry (1990), What can a moving face tell us?

16. Tiberghien & Clerc (1986), The cognitive locus of prosopagnosia.

17. Lasky et al. (1974), Age and sex discrimination.

18. M. D. Leinbach (1983), *Gender discrimination in toddlers: Identifying pictures of male and female children and adults.* Paper presented at the biennial meeting of the Society for Research in Child Development, Detroit.

19. Is Mona Lisa da Vinci? (1986, December 19). *Boston Globe,* p. 3, col. 5.

20. A. Mazur (1973), The role of predisposition in identifying Jews. *Jewish Social Studies, 35,* 290–291. L. D. Savitz & R. F. Tomasson (1959), The identifiability of Jews. *American Journal of Sociology, 64,* 468–475.

21. Enlow (1982), *Handbook of facial growth,* pp. 2–6, 230–231, 268–275.

22. Enlow (1982), *Handbook of facial growth,* p. 12.

23. E. Huber (1981), *Evolution of facial musculature and facial expression.* Baltimore: Johns Hopkins University Press.

24. H. P. Bahrick, P. O. Bahrick, & R. P. Wittlinger (1975), Fifty years of memory for names and faces: A cross-sectional approach. *Journal of Experimental Psychology: General, 104,* 54–75.

25. E. Bronte (1991), *Wuthering Heights.* New York: Knopf. (Original work published 1847)

26. T. Anthony, C. Copper, & B. Mullen (1992), Cross-racial facial identification: A social cognitive integration. *Personality and Social Psychology Bulletin, 18,* 296–301. P. N. Shapiro & S. Penrod (1986), Meta-analysis of facial identification studies. *Psychological Bulletin, 100,* 139–156. J. Shepherd (1981), Social factors in face recognition. In G. Davies, H. Ellis, & J. Shepherd (Eds.), *Perceiving and remembering faces* (pp. 55–80). San Diego, CA: Academic Press.

27. J. C. Brigham & R. S. Malpass (1985), The role of experience and contact in the recognition of faces of own- and other-race persons. *Journal of Social Issues, 41,* 139–155.

28. G. C. Baylis, E. T. Rollis, & C. M. Leonard (1985), Selectivity between faces in the responses of a population of neurons in the cortex in the superior temporal sulcus of the monkey. *Brain Research, 342,* 91–102. R. Desimone (1991), Face-selective cells in the temporal cortex of monkeys. *Journal of Cognitive Neuroscience, 3,* 1–8. D. I. Perrett, E. T. Rolls, & W. Caan (1982), Visual neurones responsive to faces in the monkey temporal cortex. *Experimental Brain Research, 47,* 329–342.

29. K. M. Kendrick & B. A. Baldwin (1987), Cells in the temporal cortex of sheep can respond preferentially to the sight of faces. *Science, 236,* 448–450.

30. I. W. R. Bushnell, F. Sai, & J. T. Mullin (1989), Neonatal recognition of the mother's face. *British Journal of Developmental Psychology, 7,* 3–15. T. M. Field, D. Cohen, R. Garcia, & R. Greenberg (1985), Mother-stranger face discrimination by the newborn. *Infant Behavior and Development, 7,* 19–25. G. E. Walton, N. J. A. Bower, & T. G. R. Bower (1992), Recognition of familiar faces by newborns. *Infant Behavior and Development, 15,* 265–269.

31. A. R. Damasio & H. Damasio (1986), The anatomical substrate of prosopagnosia. In R. Bruyer (Ed.), *The neuropsychology of face perception and facial expression* (pp. 31–38). Hillsdale, NJ: Erlbaum.

32. Cited in O. Sacks (1987), *The man who mistook his wife for a hat* (pp. 21–22). New York: Harper & Row.

33. H. Ellis & A. W. Young (1989), Are faces special? In A. W. Young & H. D. Ellis (Eds.), *Handbook of research on face processing* (pp. 1–26). Amsterdam: North Holland. N. L. Etcoff, R. Freeman, & K. R. Cave (1991), Can we lose memories of faces? Content specificity and awareness in a prosopagnosic. *Journal of Cognitive Neuroscience, 3,* 25–41. Tiberghien & Clerc (1986), The cognitive locus of prosopagnosia.

34. P. Ekman, W. V. Friesen, & P. Ellsworth (1982), Does the face provide accurate information? In P. Ekman (Ed.), *Emotion in the human face* (2nd ed., pp. 56–97). Cambridge, England: Cambridge University Press.

35. N. H. Frijda (1953), An understanding of facial expression of emotion. *Acta Psychologica, 9,* 294–362.

36. J. Bassili (1979), Emotion recognition: The role of facial movement. *Journal of Personality and Social Psychology, 37,* 2049–2058.

37. J. Aronoff, A. M. Barclay, & L. A. Stevenson (1988), The recognition of threatening facial stimuli. *Journal of Personality and Social Psychology, 54,* 647–655.

38. P. Ekman, W. V. Friesen, & P. Ellsworth (1982). What are the similarities and differences in facial behavior across cultures? In P. Ekman (Ed.), *Emotion in the human face* (2nd ed.). Cambridge, England: Cambridge University Press. P. Ekman & W. V. Friesen (1986), A new pan-cultural facial expression of emotion. *Motivation and Emotion, 10,* 159–168.

39. For a pertinent review, see L. A. Zebrowitz (1990), *Social perception* (chap. 4). Pacific Grove, CA: Brooks/Cole.

40. L. L. Benowitz, D. M. Bear, R. Rosenthal, M. M. Mesulam, E. Zaidel, & R. W. Sperry (1983), Hemispheric specialization in nonverbal communication. *Cortex, 19,* 5–11.

41. H. Buchtel, F. Campari, C. DeRisio, & R. Rota (1978), Hemispheric difference in the discrimination reaction time to facial expressions. *Italian Journal of Psychology, 5*, 159–169.

42. R. G. Ley & E. Strauss (1986), Hemispheric asymmetries in the perception of facial expressions by normals. In R. Bruyer (Ed.), *The neuropsychology of face perception and facial expression* (pp. 269–289). Hillsdale, NJ: Erlbaum.

43. C. A. Nelson (1987), The recognition of facial expression in the first two years of life: Mechanisms of development. *Child Development, 58*, 889–909.

44. M. T. Balaban (1995), Affective influences on startle in five-month-old infants: Reactions to facial expressions of emotion. *Child Development, 66*, 28–36.

45. G. M. Schwartz, C. E. Izard, & S. E. Ansul (1985), The 5-month-old's ability to discriminate facial expressions of emotion. *Infant Behavior and Development, 8*, 65–77.

46. J. F. Sorce, R. N. Emde, J. J. Campos, & M. D. Klennert (1985), Maternal emotional signalling: Its effects on the visual cliff behavior of 1-year-olds. *Developmental Psychology, 21*, 195–200.

47. M. D. Klinnert, R. N. Emde, P. Butterfield, & J. J. Campos (1985), Social referencing: The infant's use of emotional signals from a friendly adult with mother present. *Developmental Psychology, 22*, 427–432.

48. P. Ekman, W. V. Friesen, & M. O'Sullivan (1988), Smiles when lying. *Journal of Personality and Social Psychology, 54*, 414–420.

49. C. F. Bond, Jr., K. N. Kahler, & L. M. Paolicelli, (1985), The miscommunication of deception: An adaptive perspective. *Journal of Experimental Social Psychology, 21*, 331–345.

50. P. Ekman & M. O'Sullivan (1991), Who can catch a liar? *American Psychologist, 46*, 913–920.

51. B. M. De Paulo, G. D. Lassiter, & J. I. Stone (1982), Attentional determinants of success at detecting deception and truth. *Personality and Social Psychology Bulletin, 8*, 273–279.

52. T. B. Harbottle (1958), *Dictionary of quotations (classical)*. New York: Frederick Ungar.

53. S. K. Clarren, P. D. Sampson, J. Larsen, D. J. Donnell, H. M. Barr, F. L. Bookstein, D. C. Martin, & A. P. Streissguth (1987), Facial effects of fetal alcohol exposure: Assessment by photographs and morphometric analysis. *American Journal of Medical Genetics, 26*, 651–666. D. W. Smith (1982), *Recognizable patterns of human malformation: Genetic, embryologic, and clinical aspects* (3rd ed.). Philadelphia: Saunders.

54. S. K. Clarren (1981), Recognition of fetal alcohol syndrome. *Journal of the American Medical Association, 245*, 2436–2437.

55. A. P. Streissguth, C. S. Herman, & D. W. Smith (1978), Intelligence, behavior, and dysmorphogenesis in the fetal alcohol syndrome: A report on 20 patients. *The Journal of Pediatrics, 92*, 363–367.

56. C. Cummings, D. Flynn, & M. Preus (1982), Increased morphological variants in children with learning disabilities. *Journal of Autism and Developmental Disorders, 12*, 373–383. J. P. Krouse & J. M. Kauffman (1982), Minor physical anomalies in exceptional children: A review and critique of research. *Journal of Abnormal Child Psychology, 10*, 247–264.

57. R. Thornhill & A. P. Møller (in press), Developmental stability, disease and medicine. *Quarterly Review of Biology.*

58. R. Krafft-Ebing (1879), *Textbook of insanity* (C. G. Chaddock, Trans.; p. 124). Philadelphia: Davis.

59. E. Kretschmer (1936), *Physique and character: An investigation of the nature of constitution and of the theory of temperament* (2nd ed., chap. 3, pp. 38–55). London: Routledge & Kegan Paul.

60. American Psychiatric Association. (1994). *Diagnostic and statistical manual of mental disorders* (4th ed.). Washington, DC: Author.

61. P. Ekman & A. J. Fridlund (1987), Assessment of facial behavior in affective disorders. In J. D. Maser (Ed.), *Depression and expressive behavior.* Hillsdale NJ: Erlbaum. A. W. Siegman (1985), Expressive correlates of affective states and traits. In A. W. Siegman & S. Feldstein (Eds.), *Multichannel integrations of nonverbal behavior.* Hillsdale, NJ: Erlbaum. R. A. Knight & J. B. Valner (1993), Affective deficits in schizophrenia. In C. G. Costello (Ed.), *Symptoms of schizophrenia.* New York: Wiley.

62. M. Campbell, B. Geller, A. M. Small, T. A. Petti, & S. H. Ferris (1978), Minor physical anomalies in young psychotic children. *American Journal of Psychiatry, 135,* 573–575. Thornhill & Møller (1996), Developmental stability, disease, and medicine.

63. T. K. Shackelford & R. J. Larsen (in press), Facial asymmetry as an indicator of psychological, emotional, and physiological distress. *Journal of Personality and Social Psychology.*

64. M. A. Chesney, P. Ekman, W. V. Friesen, G. W. Black, & M. H. L. Hecker (1990), Type A behavior pattern: Facial behavior and speech components. *Psychosomatic Medicine, 52,* 307–319.

65. C. Z. Malatesta, R. Jonas, & C. E. Izaard (1987), The relation between low facial expressivity during emotional arousal and somatic symptoms. *British Journal of Medical Psychology, 60,* 169–180.

66. G. Draper, C. W. Dupertuis, J. L. Caughey, Jr. (1944), *Human constitution in clinical medicine* (pp. 118–119, 186–206). New York: Hoeber.

67. B. Teaton, quoted in C. Stern (1995, February 19), You don't have to live with it. *Parade Magazine,* p. 8

68. S. M. Kalick, L. A. Zebrowitz, J. H. Langlois, & R. M. Johnson (1997), *Does human facial attractiveness honestly advertise health?* Longitudinal data on an evolutionary question. *Psychological Science,* in press.

Chapter Three

1. J. C. Lavater (1772), *Hanoverian Magazine, 10,* 148. Cited in S. L. Gilman (1982), *Seeing the insane* (p. 62). New York: Wiley.

2. J. C. Lavater (1879), *Essays on physiognomy* (16th ed., p. 39). Translated from the German by Thomas Holcroft. London: William Tegg.

3. Lavater (1879), *Essays on physiognomy,* p. 38.

4. J. J. Gibson (1979), *The ecological approach to visual perception.* Boston: Houghton Mifflin. L. Z. McArthur & R. M. Baron (1983), Toward an ecological theory of social perception. *Psychological Review, 90,* 215–238.

5. E. Langer & R. P. Abelson (1974), A patient by any other name . . . : Clinician group differences in labeling bias. *Journal of Consulting and Clinical Psychology, 42,* 4–9.

6. D. S. Berry (1991), Accuracy in social perception: Contributions of facial and vocal information. *Journal of Personality and Social Psychology, 61,* 298–307. P. Borkenau & A. Liebler (1992), Trait inferences: Sources of validity at zero acquaintance. *Journal of Personality and Social Psychology, 62,* 645–657. P. Borkenau & A. Liebler (1993), Convergence of stranger ratings of personality and intelligence with self-ratings, partner ratings, and measured intelligence. *Journal of Personality and Social Psychology, 65,* 546–553. D. C. Funder & C. D. Sneed (1993), Behavioral manifestations of personality: An ecological approach to judgmental accuracy. *Journal of Personality and Social Psychology, 64,* 479–490. R. Gifford & B. O'Connor (1987), The interpersonal circumplex as a behavior map. *Journal of Personality and Social Psychology, 52,* 1019–1026. D. A. Kenny, L. Albright, T. E. Malloy, & D. A. Kashy (1994), Consensus in interpersonal perception: Acquaintance and the Big Five. *Psychological Bulletin, 116,* 245–258. M. J. Levesque & D. A. Kenny (1993), Accuracy of behavioral predictions at zero acquaintance: A social relations analysis. *Journal of Personality and Social Psychology, 65,* 1178–1187. D. S. Moskowitz (1990), Convergence of self-reports and independent observers: Dominance and friendliness. *Journal of Personality and Social Psychology, 58,* 1096–1106. D. Watson (1989), Strangers' ratings of the five robust personality factors: Evidence of a surprising convergence with self-report. *Journal of Personality and Social Psychology, 57,* 120–128.

7. D. A. Kenny, C. Horner, D. A. Kashy, & L. Chu (1992), Consensus at zero acquaintance: Replication, behavioral cues, and stability. *Journal of Personality and Social Psychology, 62,* 88–97.

8. L. Albright, D. A. Kenny, & T. E. Malloy (1988), Consensus in personality judgments at zero acquaintance. *Journal of Personality and Social Psychology, 55,* 387–395. Borkenau & Liebler (1993), Convergence of stranger ratings of personality. Kenny et al. (1992), Consensus at zero acquaintance. Kenny et al. (1994), Consensus in interpersonal perception. F. T. Passini & W. T. Norman (1966), A universal conception of personality structure? *Journal of Personality and Social Psychology, 4,* 44–49.

9. R. R. McCrae & P. T. Costa, Jr. (1989), The structure of interpersonal traits: Wiggin's circumplex and the five-factor model. *Journal of Personality and Social Psychology, 56,* 586–595.

10. D. R. Omark & M. S. Edelman (1976), The development of attention structures in young children. In M. R. A. Chance & R. R. Larsen (Eds.), *The structure of social attention.* London: Wiley.

11. D. S. Berry (1990), Taking people at face value: Evidence for the kernel of truth hypothesis. *Social Cognition, 8,* 343–361. Berry (1991), Accuracy in social perception. L. A. Zebrowitz (1995), *Accuracy of perceived warmth and dominance across the lifespan.* Unpublished research, Brandeis University, Waltham, MA.

12. P. D. Cherulnik, J. H. Way, S. Ames, & D. B. Hutto (1981), Impressions of high and low Machiavellian men. *Journal of Personality, 49,* 388–400.

13. P. D. Cherulnik, L. C. Turns, & S. K. Wilderman, (1990), Physical appearance and leadership: Exploring the role of appearance-based attribution in leader emergence. *Journal of Applied Social Psychology, 20,* 1530–1539.

14. A. Kalma (1991), Hierarchisation and dominance assessment at first glance. *European Journal of Social Psychology, 21,* 165–181.

15. N. Ambady & R. Rosenthal (1992), Thin slices of expressive behavior as predictors of interpersonal consequences: A meta-analysis. *Psychological Bulletin, 111,* 256–274.

16. Berry (1990), Taking people at face value. Berry (1991), Accuracy in social perception. Gifford & O'Connor (1987), The interpersonal circumplex. D. S. Moskowitz (1990), Convergence of self-reports and independent observers.

17. S. W. Gangestad, J. A. Simpson, K. DiGeronimo, & M. Biek (1992), Differential accuracy in person perception across traits: Examination of a functional hypothesis. *Journal of Personality and Social Psychology, 62,* 688–698.

18. C. Hull (1928), *Aptitude testing* (p. 122). Yonkers-on-Hudson, NY: World Book.

19. Borkenau & Liebler (1993), Convergence of stranger ratings.

20. C. F. Bond, K. N. Kahler, & L. M. Paolicelli (1985), The miscommunication of deception: An adaptive perspective. *Journal of Experimental Social Psychology, 21,* 331–345. M. Zuckerman, R. S. DeFrank, J. A. Hall, D. T. Larrance, & R. Rosenthal (1979), Facial and vocal cues of deception and honesty. *Journal of Experimental Social Psychology, 15,* 378–396.

21. C. F. Bond, Jr., D. S. Berry, & A. Omar (1994), The kernel of truth in judgments of deceptiveness. *Basic and Applied Social Psychology, 15,* 523–534.

22. L. A. Zebrowitz, L. Voinescu, & M. A. Collins (1996), "Wide-eyed" and "crooked-faced": Determinants of perceived and real honesty across the lifespan. *Personality and Social Psychology Bulletin, 22,* 1258–1269.

23. C. F. Bond, Jr., A. Omar, A. Mahmoud, & R. N. Bonser (1990), Lie detection across cultures. *Journal of Nonverbal Behavior, 14,* 189–204.

24. V. A. Battistich & J. Aronoff (1985), Perceiver, target, and situational influences on social cognition: An interactional analysis. *Journal of Personality and Social Psychology, 49,* 788–798.

25. A. Kruglanski & T. Freund (1983), The freezing and unfreezing of lay inferences: Effects on impressional primacy, ethnic stereotyping, and numerical anchoring. *Journal of Experimental Social Psychology, 19,* 448–468. P. E. Tetlock & J. I. Kim (1987), Accountability and judgment processes in a personality prediction task. *Journal of Personality and Social Psychology, 52,* 700–709.

26. Borkenau & Liebler (1992), Trait inferences. P. Borkenau & A. Liebler (1993), Consensus and self-other agreement for trait inferences from minimal information. *Journal of Personality, 61,* 477–496. P. Borkenau & A. Liebler (1995), Observable attributes as manifestations and cues of personality and intelligence. *Journal of Personality, 63,* 1–25. Gangestad et al. (1992), Differential accuracy in person perception across traits.

27. S. Stewart-Brown, M. N. Haslum, & N. Butler (1985), Educational attainment of 10-year-old children with treated and untreated visual defects. *Developmental Medicine and Child Neurology, 27,* 504–513.

28. Hull (1928), *Aptitude testing,* pp. 131–138.

29. C. Goring (1913), *The English convict.* London: H. M. Stationery Office. Cited in D. G. Paterson (1930), Personality and physique. In J. A. Harris, C. M. Jackson,

D. G. Paterson, & R. E. Scammon (Eds.), *The measurement of man* (chap. 3, pp. 130–131). Minneapolis: University of Minnesota Press.

30. D. E. Clayson & M. R. C. Maughan (1986), Redheads and blonds: Stereotypic images. *Psychological Reports, 59*, 811–816. E. D. Lawson (1971), Hair color, personality, and the observer. *Psychological Reports, 28*, 311–322.

31. C. F. Bond & M. Robinson (1988). The evolution of deception. *Journal of Nonverbal Behavior, 12*, 295–307. L. A. Zebrowitz et al. (1996), Wide-eyed and crooked-faced.

32. Borkenau & Liebler (1992), Trait inferences. P. Secord, W. F. Dukes, & W. Bevan (1954), Personalities in faces: I. An experiment in social perceiving. *Genetic Psychology Monographs, 49*, 231–279.

33. A. Rosenberg & J. Kagan (1987), Iris pigmentation and behavioral inhibition. *Developmental Psychobiology, 20*, 377–392.

34. A. Markle, R. O. Rinn, & C. Bell (1984), Eye color as a predictor of outcomes in behavior therapy. *Journal of Clinical Psychology, 40*, 489–495. M. Worthy (1974), *Eye color, sex and race: Keys to human and animal behavior.* Anderson, SC: Droke House/Hallux.

35. M. Kushi (1978), *Oriental diagnosis: What your face reveals.* London: Sunwheel Publications. T. T. Mar (1974), *Face reading: The Chinese art of physiognomy.* New York: Dodd, Mead.

36. D. Arcus & J. Kagan (1995), Temperament and craniofacial variation in the first two years. *Child Development, 66*, 1529–1540.

37. R. W. Squier & J. R. C. Mew (1981), The relationship between facial structure and personality characteristics. *British Journal of Social Psychology, 20*, 151–160.

38. Hull (1928), *Aptitude testing.*

39. R. Q. Bell & M. F. Waldrop (1982), Temperament and minor physical anomalies. In R. Porter & G. M. Collins (Eds.), *Temperamental differences in infants and young children: CIBA Symposium No. 89* (pp. 206–220). London: Pitman. D. L. Paulhus & C. L. Martin (1986), Predicting adult temperament from minor physical anomalies. *Journal of Personality and Social Psychology, 50*, 1235–1239. M. F. Waldrop & C. F. Halverson (1972), Minor physical anomalies: Their incidence and relation to behavior in a normal and a deviant sample. In R. C. Smart & M. S. Smart (Eds.), *Readings in child development and relationships* (pp. 146–155). New York: Macmillan.

40. M. A. Chesney, P. Ekman, W. V. Friesen, G. W. Black, & M. H. L. Hecker (1990), Type A behavior pattern: Facial behavior and speech components. *Psychosomatic Medicine, 52*, 307–319.

41. C. F. Keating, A. Mazur, M. H. Segall, P. G. Cysneiros, W. T. Divale, J. E. Kilbride, S. Komin, P. Leahy, B. Thurman, & R. Wirsing (1981), Culture and the perception of social dominance from facial expression. *Journal of Personality and Social Psychology, 40*, 615–626.

42. For a related discussion, see G. Lindzey (1967), Behavior and morphological variation. In J. N. Spuhler (Ed.), *Genetic diversity and human behavior* (pp. 227–240). Chicago: Aldine.

43. H. D. Winston & G. Lindzey (1964), Albinism and water escape performance in the mouse. *Science, 144*, 189–191.

44. Rosenberg & Kagan (1987), Iris pigmentation.

45. R. Saltus (1995, November 20), Rare mutant gene may help in probing origins of cancer. *The Boston Globe*, Health/Science, pp. 33, 37.

46. R. B. Zajonc, P. K. Adelmann, S. T. Murphy, & P. M. Niedenthal (1987), Convergence in the physical appearance of spouses. *Motivation and Emotion, 11,* 335–346.

47. G. Orwell (1949, April 17), Closing words, MS notebook. Cited in *The Oxford dictionary of quotations* (1989, 3rd ed., p. 365). Oxford, England: Oxford University Press.

48. C. Z. Malatesta, M. J. Fiore, & J. J. Messina (1987), Affect, personality, and facial expression characteristics of older people. *Psychology and Aging, 2,* 64–69.

49. T. F. Cash (1990), The psychology of physical appearance: Aesthetics, attributes, and images. In T. F. Cash & T. Pruzinsky (Eds.), *Body images: Development, deviance, and change* (pp. 51–79). New York: Guilford Press. T. F. Cash & D. W. Cash (1982), Women's use of cosmetics: Psychosocial correlates and consequences. *International Journal of Cosmetic Science, 4,* 1–14.

50. D. S. Berry & J. L. Finch-Wero (1993), Accuracy in face perception: A view from ecological psychology. *Journal of Personality, 61,* 497–520.

51. For related discussions, see A. Caspi, D. J. Bem, & G. H. Elder, Jr. (1989), Continuities and consequences of interactional styles across the life course. *Journal of Personality, 57,* 375–406. S. Scarr & K. McCartney (1983), How people make their own environments: A theory of genotype-environment correlations. *Child Development, 40,* 424–435.

52. T. Hill, P. Lewicki, M. Czyzewska, & G. Schuller (1990), The role of learned inferential encoding rules in the perception of faces: Effects of nonconscious self-perpetuation of a bias. *Journal of Experimental Social Psychology, 26,* 350–371.

53. M. T. Balaban (1995), Affective influences on startle in five-month-old infants: Reactions to facial expressions of emotion. *Child Development, 66,* 28–36. A. Ohman & U. Dimberg (1978), Facial expressions as conditioned stimuli for electrodermal responses: A case of preparedness? *Journal of Personality and Social Psychology, 36,* 1251–1258.

54. S. T. Fiske (1982), Schema-triggered affect: Applications to social perception. In M. S. Clark & S. T. Fiske (Eds.), *Affect and cognition: The seventeenth annual Carnegie Symposium on Cognition* (p. 66). Hillsdale, NJ: Erlbaum.

55. P. F. Secord & S. M. Jourard (1956), Mother-concepts and judgments of young women's faces. *Journal of Abnormal and Social Psychology, 52,* 246–250.

56. S. M. Andersen & S. W. Cole (1990), "Do I know you?": The role of significant others in general social perception. *Journal of Personality and Social Psychology, 59,* 384–399. S. M. Andersen, N. S. Glassman, S. Chen, & S. W. Cole (1995), Transference in social perception: The role of chronic accessibility in significant-other representations. *Journal of Personality and Social Psychology, 69,* 41–67.

57. Fiske (1982), Schema-triggered affect.

58. P. Lewicki (1985), Nonconscious biasing effects of single instances on subsequent judgments. *Journal of Personality and Social Psychology, 48,* 563–574.

59. T. Hill et al. (1990), The role of learned inferential encoding rules.

60. G. della Porta (1655), *De humana physiognomica.* Quoted in J. Wechsler (1982), *A human comedy: Physiognomy and caricature in 19th century Paris* (chap. 1, p. 179, footnote 12). Chicago: University of Chicago Press.

61. J. C. Lavater (1804). Quoted in D. G. Paterson (1930), *Personality and physique*. In J. A. Harris, C. M. Jackson, D. G. Paterson, & R. E. Scammon (Eds.), *The measurement of man* (p. 121). Minneapolis: University of Minnesota Press.

62. G. M. Fess (1924), *The correspondence of physical and material factors with character in Balzac*. A thesis in Romance languages presented to the faculty of the graduate school of the University of Pennsylvania, Philadelphia, pp. 87–88.

63. Quotation from a cook at a Massachusetts restaurant cited in *The Boston Globe*, February 4, 1992, p. 49.

64. Y. Peng, personal communication, 1992.

65. K. Szymanski & L. A. Zebrowitz (1987), *Personality impressions of lion-faced and foxed-faced men*. Unpublished research, Brandeis University, Waltham, MA.

66. P. S. Laser & V. A. Mathie (1982), Face facts: An unbidden role for features in communication. *Journal of Nonverbal Behavior, 7*, 3–19. Secord et al. (1954), Personalities in faces.

67. Keating et al. (1981), Culture and the perception of social dominance.

68. Malatesta, Fiore, & Messina (1987), Affect, personality, and facial expression characteristics of older people.

Chapter Four

1. J. C. Peery & D. Stern (1976), Gaze duration frequency distributions during mother-infant interactions. *Journal of Genetic Psychology, 129*, 45–55.

2. C. A. Ferguson (1964), Baby talk in six languages. In J. J. Gumperz & D. Humes (Eds.), *The ethnography of communication, 66*, 103–114. D. L. Grieser & P. K. Kuhl (1988), Maternal speech to infants in a tonal language: Support for universal prosodic features in motherese. *Developmental Psychology, 24*, 14–20.

3. M. Schleidt, W. Schiefenhovel, K. Stanjek, & R. Krell (1980), "Caring for a baby" behavior: Reactions of passersby to a mother and baby. *Man-Environment Systems, 10*, 73–82.

4. V. McCabe (1982), Invariants and affordances: An analysis of species-typical information. *Ethology and Sociobiology, 3*, 88.

5. Sylvia Warren (a geriatric nurse), personal communication, April 21, 1996.

6. R. B. McCall & C. B. Kennedy (1980), Attention of 4-month infants to discrepancy and babyishness. *Journal of Experimental Child Psychology, 29*, 189–201.

7. D. Stern (1977), *The first relationship: Infant and mother*. Cambridge, MA: Harvard University Press.

8. J. B. Lancaster (1972), Play-mothering: The relations between juvenile females and young infants among free-ranging vervet monkeys. In F. E. Poirier (Ed.), *Primate socialization* (pp. 83–104). New York: Random House.

9. G. P. Sackett (1973), Monkeys reared in isolation with pictures as visual input: Evidence for an innate releasing mechanism. In T. E. McGill (Ed.), *Readings in animal behavior* (2nd ed., pp. 263–269). New York: Holt, Rinehart & Winston.

10. J. S. Rosenblatt (1967), Nonhormonal basis of maternal behavior in the rat. *Science, 156*, 1512–1514.

11. J. R. Brown, H. Ye, R. T. Bronson, P. Dikkes, & M. E. Greenberg (1996), A defect in nurturing in mice lacking the immediate early gene Fos B. *Cell, 86*, 297–310.

12. For a pertinent review, see I. Eibl-Eibesfeldt (1970), *Ethology: The biology of behavior*. New York: Holt, Rinehart and Winston.

13. N. R. Carlson (1986), *Physiology of behavior* (p. 302). Boston: Allyn & Bacon.

14. K. Z. Lorenz (1943), Die angeborenen Formen möglicher Vererbung. *Zeitschrift für Tierpsychologie, 5*, 235–409. Cited in R. Shaw & J. Bransford (Eds.). (1977), *Perceiving, acting, and knowing: Toward an ecological psychology* (p. 125). Hillsdale, NJ: Erlbaum.

15. Jay (1962), Aspects of maternal behavior among langurs. *Annals of the New York Academy of Science, 102*, 468–476. McCabe (1982), Invariants and affordances.

16. T. W. Ransom & T. E. Rowell (1972), Early social development of feral baboons. In F. E. Poirier (Ed.), *Primate socialization* (pp. 105–144). New York: Random House.

17. G. Mitchell, & E. M. Brandt (1972), Paternal behavior in primates. In F. E. Poirier (Ed.), *Primate socialization* (pp. 173–206). New York: Random House.

18. McCabe (1982), Invariants and affordances.

19. P. L. van den Berghe & P. Frost (1986), Skin color preference, sexual dimorphism, and sexual selection: A case of gene culture co-evolution? *Ethnic and Racial Studies, 9*, 87–113.

20. Lorenz (1943), Die angeborenen Formen Möglicher Vererbung.

21. I. Eibl-Eibesfeldt (1989), *Human ethology* (p. 205). New York: Aldine de Gruyter.

22. M. S. Banks & P. J. Bennett (1988), Optical and photoreceptor immaturities limit the spatial and chromatic vision of human neonates. *Journal of the Optical Society of America: A. Optics and Image Science, 5*, 2059–2079.

23. R. D. Guthrie (1976), *Body hot spots: The anatomy of human social organs and behavior*. New York: Van Nostrand Reinhold.

24. D. H. Enlow (1982), *Handbook of facial growth* (2nd ed.). Philadelphia: Saunders.

25. R. Shaw & J. B. Pittenger (1977), Perceiving the face of change in changing faces: Implications for a theory of object perception. In R. Shaw & J. Bransford (Eds.). (1977), *Perceiving, acting, and knowing: Toward an ecological psychology* (p. 126). Hillsdale, NJ: Erlbaum.

26. D. S. Berry & L. Z. McArthur (1986), Perceiving character in faces: The impact of age-related craniofacial changes on social perception. *Psychological Bulletin, 100*, 3–18.

27. T. R. Alley (1983), Infantile head shape as an elicitor of adult protection. *Merrill-Palmer Quarterly, 29*, 411–427.

28. Eibl-Eibesfeldt (1970), *Ethology: The biology of behavior*, p. 68.

29. T. R. Alley (1981), Head shape and the perception of cuteness. *Developmental Psychology, 17*, 650–654. K. A. Hildebrandt & H. E. Fitzgerald (1979), Facial feature determinants of perceived infant attractiveness. *Infant Behavior and Development, 2*, 329–339. S. H. Sternglanz, J. L. Gray, & M. Murakami (1977), Adult preferences for infantile facial features: An ethological approach. *Animal Behavior, 25*, 108–115.

30. K. A. Hildebrandt & H. E. Fitzgerald (1983), The infant's physical attractiveness: Its effect on bonding and attachment. *Infant Mental Health Journal, 4*, 3–12.

31. A. M. Frodi, M. E. Lamb, L. A. Leavitt, W. L. Donovan, C. Neff, & D. Sherry (1978), Fathers' and mothers' responses to the faces and cries of normal and pre-

mature infants. *Developmental Psychology, 14*, 490–498. M. Klein & L. Stern (1971), Low birthweight and the battered child syndrome. *American Journal of Disorders of Childhood, 122*, 15–18. R. A. Maier, D. L. Holmes, F. L. Slaymaker, & J. N. Reich (1984), The perceived attractiveness of preterm infants. *Infant Behavior and Development, 7*, 403–414.

32. P. Spindler (1961). Cited in Eibl-Eibesfeldt, *Ethology: the biology of behavior*, p. 432.

33. D. Csermey & D. Mainardi (1983), Infant signals. In A. Oliverio & M. Zappella (Eds.), *The behavior of human infants* (pp. 1–19). New York: Plenum Press.

34. J. B. Pittenger (1990), Body proportions as information for age and cuteness: Animals in illustrated children's books. *Perception and Psychophysics, 48*, 124–130.

35. S. J. Gould (1979), Mickey Mouse meets Konrad Lorenz. *Natural History, 88*, 30–36.

36. R. A. Hinde & L. A. Barden (1985), The evolution of the teddy bear. *Animal Behaviour, 33*, 1371–1373.

37. Eibl-Eibesfeldt (1989), *Human ethology*, p. 60. B. T. Gardner & L. Wallach (1965), Shapes of figures identified as a baby's head. *Perceptual and Motor Skills, 20*, 135–142.

38. Eibl-Eibesfeldt (1970), *Ethology: The biology of behavior*, p. 82.

39. N. Tinbergen (1953), *The herring gull's world: A study of the social behaviour of birds* (p. 158). London: Collins.

40. D. Csermey & D. Mainardi (1983), Infant signals. In A. Oliverio & M. Zappella (Eds.), *The behavior of human infants* (pp. 1–19). New York: Plenum Press.

41. L. A. Zebrowitz & J. M. Montepare (1992), Impressions of babyfaced males and females across the life span. *Developmental Psychology, 28*, 1143–1152.

42. M. R. Cunningham, A. R. Roberts, A. P. Barbee, P. B. Druen, & C. H. Wu (1995), "Their ideas of beauty are, on the whole, the same as ours": Consistency and variability in the cross-cultural perception of female physical attractiveness. *Journal of Personality and Social Psychology, 68*, 261–279. L. Z. McArthur & D. S. Berry (1987), Cross-cultural agreement in perceptions of babyfaced adults. *Journal of Cross-Cultural Psychology, 18*, 165–192. L. A. Zebrowitz, J. M. Montepare, & H. K. Lee (1993), They don't all look alike: Differentiating same versus other race individuals. *Journal of Personality and Social Psychology, 65*, 85–101.

43. S. Kramer, L. A. Zebrowitz, J. P. San Giovanni, & B. Sherak (1995), Infants' preferences for attractiveness and babyfaceness. In B. G. Bardy, R. J. Bootsma, & Y. Guiard (Eds.), *Studies in perception and action: III* (pp. 389–392). Hillsdale, NJ: Erlbaum.

44. J. M. Montepare & L. Z. McArthur (1986), The influence of facial characteristics on children's age perceptions. *Journal of Experimental Child Psychology, 42*, 303–314.

45. J. M. Montepare & L. Zebrowitz-McArthur (1989), Children's perceptions of babyfaced adults. *Perceptual and Motor Skills, 69*, 467–472.

46. Zebrowitz & Montepare (1992), Impressions of babyfaced males and females.

47. Enlow (1982), *Handbook of facial growth*, pp. 6–7.

48. Zebrowitz et al. (1993), They don't all look alike.

49. Enlow (1982), *Handbook of facial growth*, pp. 12–20.

Chapter Five

1. J. C. Lavater (1879), *Essays on physiognomy* (16th ed., pp. 381–382). Translated from the German by Thomas Holcroft. London: William Tegg.

2. L. Z. McArthur & K. Apatow (1983–1984). Impressions of baby-faced adults. *Social Cognition, 2,* 315–342.

3. G. H. LeBarr (1922). *Why you are what you are* (pp. 63–64). Boston: Author.

4. McArthur & Apatow (1983–1984), Impressions of baby-faced adults.

5. Lavater (1879), *Essays on physiognomy,* p. 384.

6. G. Tytler (1982), *Physiognomy in the European novel* (p. 211). Princeton: Princeton University Press.

7. C. F. Keating, A. Mazur, M. H. Segall, P. G. Cysneiros, W. T. Divale, J. E. Kilbride, S. Komin, P. Leahy, B. Thurman, & R. Wirsing (1981), Culture and the perception of social dominance from facial expression. *Journal of Personality and Social Psychology, 40,* 615–626.

8. Lavater (1879), *Essays on physiognomy,* p. 389.

9. H. Melville (1971), *Pierre; or The ambiguities. The writings of Herman Melville* (Vol. 7, p. 314). Evanston, IL: Northwestern University Press.

10. Lavater (1879), *Essays on physiognomy,* p. 383.

11. Lavater (1879), *Essays on physiognomy,* p. 299.

12. E. D. Lawson (1971), Hair color, personality, and the observer. *Psychological Reports, 28,* 311–322.

13. D. H. Enlow (1982), *Handbook of facial growth* (p. 16). Philadelphia: Saunders.

14. McArthur & Apatow (1983–1984), Impressions of baby-faced adults.

15. Lavater (1879), *Essays on physiognomy,* p. 391.

16. C. F. Keating (1985), Gender and the physiognomy of dominance and attractiveness. *Social Psychology Quarterly, 48,* 61–70. C. F. Keating, A. Mazur, M. H. Segall (1981), A cross-cultural exploration of physiognomic traits of dominance and happiness. *Ethology and Sociobiology, 2,* 41–48.

17. Lavater (1879), *Essays on physiognomy,* p. 391.

18. Lavater (1879), *Essays on physiognomy,* p. 394.

19. G. M. Fess (1924), *The correspondence of physical and material factors with character in Balzac* (p. 50). Philadelphia: University of Pennsylvania Press. J. W. Mileham (1982), *The conspiracy novel: Structure and metaphor in Balzac's Comedie Humaine* (pp. 67–68). Lexington, KY: French Forum Publishers.

20. LeBarr (1922), *Why you are,* p. 73.

21. D. S. Berry & L. Z. McArthur (1986), Perceiving character in faces: The impact of age-related craniofacial changes on social perception. *Psychological Bulletin, 100,* 3–18.

22. C. F. Keating, A. Mazur, M. H. Segall (1981), A cross-cultural exploration of physiognomic traits of dominance and happiness. *Ethology and Sociobiology, 2,* 41–48. P. Borkenau & A. Liebler (1995), Observable attributes as manifestations and cues of personality and intelligence. *Journal of Personality, 63,* 1–25.

23. LeBarr (1922), *Why you are,* pp. 26–27.

24. Lavater (1879), *Essays on physiognomy,* p. 396.

25. McArthur & Apatow (1983–1984), Impressions of baby-faced adults.

26. D. S. Berry & L. Z. McArthur (1985), Some components and consequences of a babyface. *Journal of Personality and Social Psychology, 48,* 312–323. L. A. Zebrowitz

& J. M. Montepare (1992), Impressions of babyfaced males and females across the lifespan. *Developmental Psychology, 28,* 1143–1152.

27. L. Zebrowitz-McArthur & J. M. Montepare (1989), Contributions of a baby-face and a childlike voice to impressions of moving and talking faces. *Journal of Nonverbal Behavior, 13,* 189–203.

28. Zebrowitz & Montepare (1992), Impressions of babyfaced males and females.

29. L. A. Zebrowitz, J. M. Montepare, & H. K. Lee (1993), They don't all look alike: Differentiating same versus other race individuals. *Journal of Personality and Social Psychology, 65,* 85–101.

30. C. F. Keating & D. L. Bai (1986), Children's attributions of social dominance from facial cues. *Child Development, 57,* 1269–1276.

31. J. M. Montepare & L. Zebrowitz-McArthur (1989), Children's perceptions of babyfaced adults. *Perceptual and Motor Skills, 69,* 467–472.

32. H. Gray (1985), *Anatomy of the human body* (p. 178). Philadelphia: Lea & Febiger,

33. M. J. Guyton (1993), *The relative importance of facial maturity and emotional expression in decisions about an unidentified infant's sex.* Unpublished master's thesis, Brandeis University, Waltham, MA.

34. H. Friedman & L. A. Zebrowitz (1992), The contribution of facial maturity to sex-role stereotypes. *Personality and Social Psychology Bulletin, 18,* 430–438.

35. J. E. Williams & D. L. Best (1982), *Measuring sex stereotypes: A thirty-nation study.* Beverly Hills, CA: Sage.

36. A. Eagly (1987), *Sex differences in social behavior: A social role interpretation.* Hillsdale, NJ: Erlbaum.

37. E. Rafford, personal communication, October 30, 1995.

38. A. Zitner (1993, December 12), The disarming dean. *The Boston Globe,* p. 81.

39. This principle is an extension of the "lack of fit" model that was initially proposed by Heilman to account for gender biases in the workplace: M. Heilman (1983), Sex bias in work settings: The lack of fit model. *Research in Organizational Behavior, 5,* 269–298.

40. M. Manis & J. R. Paskewitz (1984), Judging psychopathology: Expectation and contrast. *Journal of Experimental Social Psychology, 20,* 363–381.

41. D. S. Berry & J. C. Landry (1997), *Social perception in the real world: Facial maturity and daily social interaction. Journal of Personality and Social Psychology,* in press.

42. A. Mazur, C. Halpern, & J. R. Udry (1994), Dominant looking male teenagers copulate earlier. *Ethology and Sociobiology, 15,* 87–94.

43. S. B. Hadden & S. Brownlow (1991, March 20–24), *The impact of facial structure and assertiveness on dating choice.* Poster presented at the annual meeting of the Southeastern Psychological Association, New Orleans.

44. S. Brownlow & L. A. Zebrowitz (1990), Facial appearance, gender, and credibility in television commercials. *Journal of Nonverbal Behavior, 14,* 51–60.

45. M. R. Solomon, R. D. Ashmore, & L. C. Longo (1992), The beauty match-up hypothesis: Congruence between types of beauty and product images in advertising. *Journal of Advertising, XXI,* 23–34.

46. S. Brownlow & L. A. Zebrowitz (1990), Facial appearance, gender, and credibility in television commercials. *Journal of Nonverbal Behavior, 14,* 51–60.

47. S. Brownlow (1992), Seeing is believing: Facial appearance, credibility, and attitude change. *Journal of Nonverbal Behavior, 16*, 101–115.

48. P. D. Cherulnik, L. C. Turns, & S. K. Wilderman (1990), Physical appearance and leadership: Exploring the role of appearance-based attribution in leader emergence. *Journal of Applied Social Psychology, 20*, 1530–1539.

49. N. Costrich, J. Feinstein, L. Kidder, J. Maracek, & L. Pascale (1975), When stereotypes hurt: Three studies of penalties for sex-role reversals. *Journal of Experimental Social Psychology, 11*, 520–530. A. H. Eagly, M. G. Makhijani, & B. G. Klonsky (1992), Gender and the evaluation of leaders: A meta-analysis. *Psychological Bulletin, 111*, 3–22.

50. L. A. Zebrowitz, D. R. Tenenbaum, & L. H. Goldstein (1991), The impact of job applicants' facial maturity, sex, and academic achievement on hiring recommendations. *Journal of Applied Social Psychology, 21*, 525–548.

51. J. E. Copley & S. Brownlow (1995), The interactive effects of facial maturity and name warmth on perceptions of job candidates. *Basic and Applied Social Psychology, 16*, 251–265.

52. M. A. Collins & L. A. Zebrowitz (1995), The contributions of appearance to occupational outcomes in civilian and military settings. *Journal of Applied Social Psychology, 25*, 129–163.

53. H. Friedman & L. A. Zebrowitz (1992), The contribution of facial maturity to sex-role stereotypes. *Personality and Social Psychology Bulletin, 18*, 430–438.

54. A. Mazur, J. Mazur, & C. Keating (1984), Military rank attainment of a West Point Class: Effects of cadets' physical features. *American Journal of Sociology, 90*, 125–150. U. Mueller & A. Mazur (1996), Facial dominance in West Point cadets predicts military rank 20+ years later. *Social Forces, 74*, 823–850.

55. Collins & Zebrowitz (1995), The contributions of appearance to occupational outcomes. Because this contrast effect is shown on the objective measure of winning an award, it is likely to reflect a true higher regard for valorous baby-faced men rather than the "shifting standards" phenomenon that occurs when people make subjective ratings such as "he is brave," which could mean "he is brave for a babyfaced person." This same argument applies to other contrast effects discussed in this chapter. For a fuller discussion of this issue, see M. Biernat (1996), The shifting standards model: Implications of stereotype accuracy for social judgment. In Y. T. Lee, L. J. Jussim, & C. R. McCauley (Eds.), *Stereotype accuracy: Toward appreciating group differences* (pp. 87–114). Washington, DC: American Psychological Association.

56. R. D. Masters & D. G. Sullivan (1989), Facial displays and political leadership in France. *Behavioural Processes, 19*, 1–30.

57. *The Boston Globe*, March 17, 1992, p. 35.

58. S. T. Fiske, D. N. Bersoff, E. Borgida, K. Deaux, & M. E. Heilman (1991), Social science research on trial: The use of sex stereotyping research in *Price Waterhouse v. Hopkins. American Psychologist, 46*, 1049–1060.

59. J. Steinbeck (1952), *East of Eden* (p. 58). New York: Viking Press.

60. D. Schaap (1992, September 13), Profile on Billy Crystal. *Parade Magazine. The Boston Globe*, p. 5.

61. *The Boston Globe*, April 5, 1992, p. 67.

62. C. Lombroso & W. Ferrero (1895), *The female offender*. London: T. Fisher Unwin.

63. A. Goldstein, J. Chance, & B. Gilbert (1984), Facial stereotypes of good guys and bad guys: A replication and extension. *Bulletin of the Psychonomic Society, 22*, 549–552.

64. D. Shoemaker, D. South, & J. Lowe (1973), Facial stereotypes of deviants and judgments of guilt or innocence. *Social Forces, 51*, 427–433.

65. J. Robinson (1978), *Catching criminals: Some basic skills*. London: Police Review Publications.

66. *The Boston Globe*, July 11, 1987, p. 9.

67. D. S. Berry & L. Z. Zebrowitz-McArthur (1988), What's in a face? Facial maturity and the attribution of legal responsibility. *Personality and Social Psychology Bulletin, 14*, 23–33.

68. L. A. Zebrowitz, & S. M. McDonald (1991), The impact of litigants' babyfacedness and attractiveness on adjudications in small claims courts. *Law and Human Behavior, 15*, 603–623.

69. A. C. Downs & P. M. Lyons (1991), Natural observations of the links between attractiveness and initial legal judgments. *Personality and Social Psychology Bulletin, 17*, 541–547.

Chapter Six

1. J. Liggett (1974), *The human face* (chaps. 3 and 4). New York: Stein & Day.

2. J. Langlois, L. Kalakanis, A. Rubenstein, A. Larson, M. Hallam, & M. Smoot (1996, June 29–July 2), *The myths of beauty: A meta-analytic review*. Paper presented at the eighth annual meeting of the American Psychological Society, San Francisco.

3. L. A. Zebrowitz, K. Olson, & K. Hoffman (1992), Stability of babyfaceness and attractiveness across the lifespan. *Journal of Personality and Social Psychology, 64*, 453–466.

4. A. G. Goldstein & J. Papageorge (1980), Judgments of facial attractiveness in the absence of eye movements. *Bulletin of the Psychonomic Society, 15*, 269–270.

5. M. R. Cunningham, A. R. Roberts, A. P. Barbee, P. B. Druen, & C. H. Wu (1995), Their ideas of beauty are, on the whole, the same as ours: Consistency and variability in the cross-cultural perception of female physical attractiveness. *Journal of Personality and Social Psychology, 68*, 261–279. D. F. Johnson & J. B. Pittenger (1984), Attribution, the attractiveness stereotype, and the elderly. *Developmental Psychology, 20*, 1168–1172. Langlois et al., *The myths of beauty*. J. G. Martin (1964), Racial ethnocentrism and judgment of beauty. *Journal of Social Psychology, 63*, 59–63. L. A. Zebrowitz & J. M. Montepare (1992), Impressions of babyfaced males and females across the lifespan. *Developmental Psychology, 28*, 1143–1152. L. A. Zebrowitz, J. M. Montepare, & H. K. Lee (1993), They don't all look alike: Individuated impressions of other racial groups. *Journal of Personality and Social Psychology, 65*, 85–101.

6. G. I. Schulman & M. Hoskins (1986), Perceiving the male versus the female face. *Psychology of Women Quarterly, 10*, 141–154.

7. I. H. Bernstein, T. D. Lin, & P. McClellan (1982), Cross- vs. within-racial judgments of attractiveness. *Perception and Psychophysics, 32*, 495–503. Cunningham et al. (1995), Their ideas of beauty. Zebrowitz et al. (1993), They don't all look alike.

8. A. H. Iliffe (1960), A study of preferences in feminine beauty. *British Journal of Psychology, 51*, 267–273.

9. Zebrowitz et al. (1993), They don't all look alike.

10. M. R. Cunningham, R. A. Roberts, T. P. Richardson, A. P. Barbee, C. H. Wu, & D. D. Dehart (1991, August), *A psycho-evolutionary, multiple-motive interpretation of physical attractiveness.* Paper presented at the symposium Sex and Mating: Evolutionary Perspectives, at the 99th annual convention of the American Psychological Association, San Francisco.

11. Johnson & Pittenger (1984), Attribution, the attractiveness stereotype, and the elderly.

12. K. K. Dion (1973), Young children's stereotyping of facial attractiveness. *Developmental Psychology, 9*, 183–188. J. H. Langlois (1986), From the eye of the beholder to behavioral reality: Development of social behaviors and social relations as a function of physical attractiveness. In C. P. Herman, M. P. Zanna, & E. T. Higgins (Eds.), *Physical appearance, stigma, and social behavior: The Ontario Symposium.* (Vol. 3., pp. 23–52). Hillsdale, NJ: Erlbaum.

13. J. H. Langlois, J. M. Ritter, L. A. Roggman, & L. S. Vaughn (1991), Facial diversity and infant preferences for attractive faces. *Developmental Psychology, 27*, 79–84. S. Kramer, L. A. Zebrowitz, J. P. San Giovanni, & B. Sherak (1995), Infants' preferences for attractiveness and babyfaceness. In B. G. Bardy, R. J. Bootsma, & Y. Guiard (Eds.), *Studies in perception and action: III* (pp. 389–392). Hillsdale, NJ: Erlbaum.

14. T. Hardy (1988), *Tess of the D'Ubervilles* (p. 20). Oxford, England: Oxford University Press. (Original work published 1891)

15. F. Dostoyevsky (1976), *The brothers Karamazov* (p. 19). The Constance Garnett translation. New York: Norton. (Original work published 1879–1880)

16. A. Pope (1711), An essay on criticism, part II, line 45. Quoted in J. Bartlett (1980), *Bartlett's familiar quotations* (15th ed., p. 333). Boston: Little, Brown.

17. Computer simulations designed to study how perceptual biases may influence mate selection across many generations have demonstrated the "evolution" of overgeneralizations. M. Enquist & A. Arak (1993), Selection of exaggerated male traits by female aesthetic senses. *Nature, 361*, 446–448.

18. T. Woolnoth (1865), *The study of the human face* (pp. 181–244). London: Tweedie. Cited in H. Peck & S. Peck (1970), A concept of facial esthetics. *Angle Orthodontics, 40*, 289.

19. G. W. Lucker & L. W. Graber (1980), Physiognomic features and facial appearance judgments in children. *Journal of Psychology, 104*, 261–268.

20. Peck & Peck (1970), A concept of facial esthetics.

21. J. Dongieux & V. Sassouni (1980), The contribution of mandibular positioned variation to facial esthetics. *Facial Esthetics, 50*, 334–339.

22. C. Carello, A. Grosofsky, R. E. Shaw, J. B. Pittenger, & L. S. Mark (1989), Attractiveness of facial profiles is a function of distance from archetype. *Ecological Psychology, 1*, 227–251.

23. Carello et al. (1989), Attractiveness of facial profiles.

24. Dongieux & Sassouni (1980), The contribution of mandibular positioned variation. G. W. Lucker (1981), Esthetics and a quantitative analysis of facial appearance. In G. W. Lucker, K. A. Ribbens, & J. A. McNamara, Jr. (Eds.), *Psychological aspects of facial form* (pp. 49–79). Center for Human Growth and Development, University of Michigan, Ann Arbor.

25. Lucker (1981), Esthetics and a quantitative analysis of facial appearance. R. M. Ricketts (1982), The biologic significance of the divine proportion and Fibonacci series. *American Journal of Orthodontics, 81*, 351–370.

26. Dongieux & Sassouni (1980), The contribution of mandibular positioned variation.

27. Ricketts (1982), The biologic significance of the divine proportion.

28. M. H. Bornstein, Ferdinandsen, & C. G. Gross (1981), Perception of symmetry in infancy. *Developmental Psychology, 17*, 82–86.

29. W. C. Shaw (1988), Social aspects of dentofacial anomalies. In T. R. Alley (Ed.), *Social and applied aspects of perceiving faces* (pp. 191–216). Hillsdale, NJ: Erlbaum.

30. K. Grammer & R. Thornhill (1994), Human (*Homo sapiens*) facial attractiveness and sexual selection: The role of symmetry and averageness. *Journal of Comparative Psychology, 108*, 233–242. Zebrowitz, L. Voinescu, & M. A. Collins (in press), Wide-eyed and crooked-faced: Determinants of perceived and real honesty across the lifespan. *Personality and Social Psychology Bulletin.*

31. P. R. N. Sutton (1968), Lateral facial asymmetry: Methods of assessment. *The Angle Orthodontist, 38*, 82–92. Unlike facial asymmetry, bodily asymmetry appears to decrease from birth to adulthood, which suggests that one should be wary of drawing conclusions about the meaning of facial asymmetry from research investigating correlates of body asymmetry. See J. M. Wilson & J. T. Manning (in press), Fluctuating asymmetry and age in children: Evolutionary implications for the control of developmental stability. *Journal of Human Evolution.*

32. G. Rhodes, F. Proffitt, J. Grady, & A. Sumich (1996), *Facial symmetry and the biology of beauty.* Unpublished manuscript, University of Canterbury, New Zealand.

33. R. Kowner (1996), Facial asymmetry and attractiveness judgment in developmental perspective. *Journal of Experimental Psychology: Human Perception and Performance, 22*, 662–675. J. H. Langlois, L. A. Roggman, & L. Musselman (1994), What is average and what is not average about attractive faces? *Psychological Science, 5*, 214–220. Rhodes et al. (1996), *Facial symmetry and the biology of beauty.* C. A. Samuels, G. Butterworth, T. Rogerts, L. Graupner, & G. Hole (1994), Facial aesthetics: Babies prefer attractiveness to symmetry. *Perception, 23*, 823–831. J. P. Swaddle & I. C. Cuthill (1995), Asymmetry and human facial attractiveness: Symmetry may not always be beautiful. *Proceedings of the Royal Society of London, Series B, 261*, 111–116.

34. Grammer & Thornhill (1994), Human (*Homo sapiens*) facial attractiveness. Thornhill & S. W. Gangestad (1993), Human facial beauty: Averageness, symmetry, and parasite resistance. *Human Nature, 4*, 237–269.

35. M. Ridley (1992), Swallows and scorpionflies find symmetry is beautiful. *Science, 257*, 327–328. J. P. Swaddle & I. C. Cuthill (1994), Preference for symmetric males by female zebra finches. *Nature, 367*, 165–166.

36. R. Thornhill & S. W. Gangestad (1994), Human fluctuating asymmetry and sexual behavior. *Psychological Science, 5,* 297–302.

37. C. Darwin (1871), *The descent of man, and selection in relation to sex.* London: Murray.

38. For a comprehensive review of research relating symmetry to health, see R. Thornhill & A. P. Møller (in press), Developmental stability, disease, and medicine. *Quarterly Review of Biology.*

39. T. K. Shackelford & R. J. Larsen (1997), *Facial asymmetry as an indicator of psychological, emotional, and physiological distress. Journal of Personality and Social Psychology,* in press.

40. S. M. Kalick, L. A. Zebrowitz, J. H. Langlois, & R. M. Johnson (1997). *Does human facial attractiveness honestly advertise health?* Longitudinal data on an evolutionary question. *Psychological Science,* in press.

41. M. R. Cunningham (1986), Measuring the physical in physical attractiveness: Quasi-experiments on the sociobiology of female facial beauty. *Journal of Personality and Social Psychology, 50,* 925–935.

42. M. Enquist & A. Arak (1994), Symmetry, beauty, and evolution. *Nature, 372,* 169–172. R. A. Johnstone (1994), Female preference for symmetrical males as a by-product of selection for mate recognition. *Nature, 372,* 172–175.

43. Johnstone, Female preference for symmetrical males.

44. C. Packer & A. E. Pusey (1993), Should a lion change its spots? *Nature, 362,* 595.

45. J. Brophy (1946), *The human face* (p. 77). New York: Prentice-Hall.

46. Zebrowitz et al. (1993), Stability of babyfaceness and attractiveness.

47. T. R. Alley & K. A. Hildebrandt (1988), Determinants and consequences of facial aesthetics. In T. A. Alley (Ed.), *Social and applied aspects of perceiving faces* (pp. 101–140). Hillsdale, NJ: Erlbaum. R. Bull & G. Shead (1979), Pupil dilation, sex of stimulus, and age and sex of observer. *Perceptual and Motor Skills, 49,* 27–30. Cunningham (1986), Measuring the physical in physical attractiveness. M. R. Cunningham, A. P. Barbee, & C. L. Pike (1990), What do women want? Facialmetric assessment of multiple motives in the perception of male physical attractiveness. *Journal of Personality and Social Psychology, 59,* 61–72. Cunningham et al. (1995), Their ideas of beauty. E. H. Hess (1975), The role of pupil size in communication. *Scientific American, 233,* 110–119. C. Keating (1985), Gender and the physiognomy of dominance and attractiveness. *Social Psychology Quarterly, 48,* 61–70. L. Z. McArthur & K. Apatow (1983–1984) Impressions of babyfaced adults. *Social Cognition, 2,* 315–342. Zebrowitz et al., (1993), They don't all look alike.

48. D. S. Berry (1991), Attractive faces are not all created equal: Joint effects of facial babyishness and attractiveness on social perception. *Personality and Social Psychology Bulletin, 17,* 523–531.

49. Cunningham et al. (1995), Their ideas of beauty.

50. M. R. Solomon, R. D. Ashmore, & L. C. Longo (1992), The beauty match-up hypothesis: Congruence between types of beauty and product images in advertising. *Journal of Advertising, 21,* 23–34. L. Wheeler & H. Eghrari (1986), *Sexy, sophisticated, or wholesome: Perceptions of different types of attractive females.* Unpublished manuscript, University of Rochester, Rochester, NY.

51. Cunningham (1986), Measuring the physical in physical attractiveness. Cunningham et al. (1990), What do women want? Cunningham et al. (1995), Their ideas of beauty. K. T. Mueser, B. W. Grau, S. Sussman, & A. J. Rosen (1984), You're only as pretty as you feel: Facial expression as a determinant of physical attractiveness. *Journal of Personality and Social Psychology, 46,* 469–478. Schulman & Hoskins (1986), Perceiving the male versus the female face. Zebrowitz et al. (1996), Wide-eyed and crooked-faced.

52. Cunningham (1986), Measuring the physical in physical attractiveness. Cunningham et al. (1990), What do women want? Cunningham et al. (1995), Their ideas of beauty. J. E. Meerdink, C. P. Garbin, & D. W. Leger (1990), Cross-gender perceptions of facial attributes and their relation to attractiveness: Do we see them differently than they see us? *Perception and Psychophysics, 48,* 227–233. Zebrowitz et al. (1993), They don't all look alike.

53. T. R. Alley (1988), The effects of growth and aging on facial aesthetics. In T. R. Alley (Ed.), *Social and applied aspects of perceiving faces* (pp. 51–62). Hillsdale, NJ: Erlbaum. K. M. Korthase & I. Trenholme (1983), Children's perceptions of age and physical attractiveness. *Perceptual and Motor Skills, 56,* 895–900. Zebrowitz et al. (1993), Stability of babyfaceness and attractiveness.

54. Zebrowitz et al. (1993), Stability of babyfaceness and attractiveness.

55. Alley (1988), The effects of growth and aging on facial aesthetics. F. M. Deutsch, C. M. Zalenski, & M. E. Clark (1986), Is there a double standard of aging? *Journal of Applied Social Psychology, 16,* 771–785.

56. D. M. Buss (1989), Sex differences in human mate preferences: Evolutionary hypotheses tested in 37 cultures. *Behavioral and Brain Sciences, 12,* 1–49.

57. D. T. Kenrick & M. R. Trost (1988), A reproductive exchange model of heterosexual relationships: Putting proximate economics in ultimate perspective. In C. Hendrick (Ed.), *Review of personality and social psychology* (Vol. 10, pp. 92–118). Newbury Park, CA: Sage.

58. J. H. Langlois & L. A. Roggman (1990), Attractive faces are only average. *Psychological Science, 1,* 115–121.

59. S. Feinman & G. W. Gill (1978), Sex differences in physical attractiveness preferences. *The Journal of Social Psychology, 105,* 43–52. E. D. Lawson (1971), Hair color, personality, and the observer. *Psychological Reports, 28,* 311–322. J. Meyerowitz (1991), *Redheads.* New York: Rizzoli International Publications.

60. Langlois & Roggman (1990), Attractive faces are only average.

61. G. Rhodes & T. Tremewan (1996), Averageness, exaggeration, and facial attractiveness. *Psychological Science, 7,* 105–110.

62. T. R. Alley & M. R. Cunningham (1991), Averaged faces are attractive, but very attractive faces are not average. *Psychological Science, 2,* 123–125.

63. Johnstone (1994), Female preference for symmetrical males.

64. J. Aronoff, A, M. Barclay, & L. A. Stevenson (1988), The recognition of threatening facial stimuli. *Journal of Personality and Social Psychology, 54,* 647–655. J. Aronoff, B. A. Woike, & L. M. Hyman (1992), Which are the displays of anger and happiness? Configurational bases of emotion recognition. *Journal of Personality and Social Psychology, 62,* 1050–1056.

65. Alley & Cunningham (1991), Averaged faces are attractive.

66. J. H. Langlois, L. A. Roggman, & L. Musselman (1994), What is average and what is not average about attractive faces? *Psychological Science, 5*, 214–220.

67. E. Wagatsuma & C. L. Kleinke (1979), Ratings of facial beauty by Asian-American and Caucasian females. *Journal of Social Psychology, 109*, 299–300.

68. Martin (1964), Racial ethnocentrism and judgment of beauty. The attractiveness of body types also shows strong effects of culture and race that may reflect differences in population averages. See Cunningham (1995), Their ideas of beauty. A. Furnham & N. Alibhai (1983), Cross-cultural differences in the perception of female body shapes. *Psychological Medicine, 13*, 829–837.

69. D. I. Perrett & K. May (1994), Facial shape and judgements of female attractiveness. *Nature, 368*, 239–242.71.

70. F. Bacon (1625), Essays. Of beauty. Quoted in J. Bartlett (1980), *Bartlett's familiar quotations* (15th ed., p. 181). Boston: Little, Brown.

71. Alley & Cunningham (1991), Averaged faces are attractive.

72. Brophy (1946), *The human face*, p. 67.

73. Cunningham et al. (1986), Measuring the physical in physical attractiveness. Cunningham et al. (1990), What do women want? Cunningham et al. (1995), Their ideas of beauty. C. Keating (1985), Gender and the physiognomy of dominance and attractiveness. *Social Psychology Quarterly, 48*, 61–70. McArthur & Apatow (1983–1984), Impressions of babyfaced adults.

74. Wagatsuma & Kleinke (1979), Ratings of facial beauty.

75. McArthur & Apatow (1983–1984), Impressions of babyfaced adults. H. Friedman & L. A. Zebrowitz (1992), The contribution of typical sex differences in facial maturity to sex role stereotypes. *Personality and Social Psychology Bulletin, 18*, 430–438. Keating (1985), Gender and the physiognomy of dominance and attractiveness.

76. G. W. Lucker, L. W. Graber, & P. Pietromonaco (1981), The importance of dentofacial appearance in facial esthetics: A signal detection approach. *Basic and Applied Social Psychology, 2*, 261–274.

77. D. E. Carpenter (1979), Descriptive modes of physical beauty in Hispano-Arabic Muwassahat and Romance models. *Comparative Literature Studies, XVI*, 294–306.

78. P. L. van den Berghe & P. Frost (1986), Skin color preference, sexual dimorphism, and sexual selection: A case of gene culture co-evolution? *Ethnic and Racial Studies, 9*, 87–113.

79. Cunningham et al. (1995), Their ideas of beauty.

80. van den Berghe & Frost (1986), Skin color preference.

81. Cunningham (1986), Measuring the physical in physical attractiveness. Cunningham et al. (1990), What do women want? Cunningham et al. (1995), Their ideas of beauty. McArthur & Apatow (1983–1984), Impressions of babyfaced adults.

82. Just as people's faces are more attractive to the extent that they are prototypical for their gender, so are their bodies. See D. Singh (1993), Adaptive significance of female physical attractiveness: Role of waist-to-hip ratio. *Journal of Personality and Social Psychology, 65*, 293–307.

83. R. F. Bornstein (1989), Exposure and affect: Overview and meta-analysis of research, 1968–1987. *Psychological Bulletin, 106*, 265–289. R. B. Zajonc (1968), Atti-

tudinal effects of mere exposure. *Journal of Personality and Social Psychology, 9* [Monograph Supplement, no. 2, part 2].

84. T. H. Mita, M. Dermer, & J. Knight (1977), Reversed facial images and the mere-exposure hypothesis. *Journal of Personality and Social Psychology, 35,* 597–601.

85. R. L. Moreland & R. B. Zajonc (1979), Exposure effects may not depend on stimulus recognition. *Journal of Personality and Social Psychology, 37,* 1085–1089.

86. G. Orwell (1949), Closing words, MS notebook. Cited in *The Oxford dictionary of quotations* (1989, 3rd ed., p. 365). Oxford, England: Oxford University Press. Sappho (1965), Fragments 101. In *Poems and fragments.* Translated with an introduction by G. Davenport. Ann Arbor: University of Michigan press.

87. R. E. Nisbett & T. D. Wilson (1977), The halo effect: Evidence for unconscious alteration of judgments. *Journal of Personality and Social Psychology, 35,* 250–256.

88. R. Felson & G. Bohrnstedt (1979), Are the good beautiful or the beautiful good? *Social Psychology Quarterly, 42,* 386–392.

89. A. Gross & C. Crofton (1977), What is good is beautiful? *Sociometry, 40,* 85–90.

Chapter Seven

1. Because of the vast size of the research literature on the attractiveness halo, effect sizes are reported in this chapter only when they have been computed in meta-analyses by previous investigators. Also, research citations cannot be exhaustive. For comprehensive reviews of the literature on the attractiveness halo, see the following: R. Bull & N. Rumsey (1986), *The social psychology of facial appearance.* New York: Springer-Verlag. A. H. Eagly, R. D. Ashmore, M. G. Makhijani, & L. C. Longo (1991). "What is beautiful is good, but . . . ": A meta-analytic review of research on the physical attractiveness stereotype. *Psychological Bulletin, 110,* 109–128. A. Feingold (1992), Good-looking people are not what we think. *Psychological Bulletin, 111,* 304–341. E. Hatfield & S. Sprecher (1986), *Mirror, mirror . . . : The importance of looks in everyday life.* Albany: State University of New York Press. G. L. Patzer (1985), *The attractiveness phenomenon.* New York: Plenum Press. The reader may also be interested in the effects of attractive voices and bodies, as discussed in the following works: D. S. Berry (1990), Vocal attractiveness and vocal babyishness: Effects on stranger, self, and friend impressions. *Journal of Nonverbal Behavior,* 141–153. W. DeJong & R. E. Kleck (1986), The social psychological effects of overweight. In C. P. Herman, M. P. Zanna, & E. T. Higgins (Eds.), *Physical appearance, stigma, and social behavior: The Ontario Symposium* (Vol. 3, pp. 65–88). Hillsdale, NJ: Erlbaum. J. V. Roberts & C. P. Herman (1986), The psychology of height: An empirical review. In C. P. Herman, M. P. Zanna, & E. T. Higgins (Eds.), *Physical appearance, stigma, and social behavior: The Ontario Symposium* (Vol. 3, pp. 113–142). Hillsdale, NJ: Erlbaum. J. A. Shepperd & A. J. Strathman (1989), Attractiveness and height: The role of stature in dating preference, frequency of dating, and perceptions of attractiveness. *Personality and Social Psychology Bulletin, 15,* 617–627. M. Zuckerman, H. Hodgins, K. Miyake (1990), The vocal attractiveness stereotype: Replication and elaboration. *Journal of Nonverbal Behavior, 14,* 97–112.

2. G. M. Fess (1924), *The correspondence of physical and material factors with character in Balzac* (p. 53). Philadelphia: Publications of the University of Pennsylvania Department of Romanic Languages and Literatures, no. 10.

3. F. Dostoyevsky (1976), *The brothers Karamazov* (p. 17). The Constance Garnett translation. New York: Norton. (Original work published 1879–1880)

4. R. L. Stevenson (1985), *Dr. Jekyll and Mr. Hyde* (pp. 18, 22, 27). New York: Bantam Books. (Original work published 1886)

5. K. K. Dion, E. Berscheid, & E. Walster (Hatfield) (1972), What is beautiful is good. *Journal of Personality and Social Psychology, 24*, 285–290.

6. M. Dermer & D, Thiel (1975), When beauty may fail. *Journal of Personality and Social Psychology, 31*, 1168–1176.

7. Eagly et al. (1991), "What is beautiful is good, but . . . ." Feingold (1992), Good-looking people are not what we think.

8. L. C. Longo & R. D. Ashmore (1994), *What is beautiful is powerful.* Unpublished manuscript, Rutgers University, New Brunswick, NJ.

9. L. A. Zebrowitz & J. M. Montepare (1992), Impressions of babyfaced males and females across the lifespan. *Developmental Psychology, 28*, 1143–1152. L. A. Zebrowitz, J. M. Montepare, & H. K. Lee (1993), They don't all look alike: Individuated impressions of other racial groups. *Journal of Personality and Social Psychology, 65*, 85–101.

10. R. D. Ashmore & L. C. Longo (1996), Accuracy of stereotypes: What research on physical attractiveness can teach us. In Y. T. Lee, L. J. Jussim, & C. R. McCauley (Eds.), *Stereotype accuracy: Toward appreciating group differences* (pp. 63–86). Washington, DC: American Psychological Association. R. D. Ashmore, M. R. Solomon, & L. C. Longo (1996), Thinking about fashion models' looks: A multidimensional approach to the structure of perceived physical attractiveness. Unpublished manuscript, Rutgers University, New Brunswick, NJ. D. S. Berry (1991), Attractive faces are not all created equal: Joint effects of facial babyishness and attractiveness on social perception. *Personality and Social Psychology Bulletin, 17*, 523–531.

11. Eagly et al. (1991), "What is beautiful is good, but . . . ." Feingold (1992), Good-looking people are not what we think.

12. Longo & Ashmore (1994), What is beautiful is powerful.

13. B. Gillen (1981), Physical attractiveness: A determinant of two types of goodness. *Personality and Social Psychology Bulletin, 7*, 277–281.

14. D. F. Johnson & J. B. Pittenger (1984), Attribution, the attractiveness stereotype and the elderly. *Developmental Psychology, 20*, 1168–1172. J. H. Langlois (1986), From the eye of the beholder to behavioral reality: Development of social behaviors and social relations as a function of physical attractiveness. In C. P. Herman, M. P. Zanna, and E. T. Higgins (Eds.), *Physical appearance, stigma, and social behavior: The Ontario Symposium* (Vol. 3, pp. 23–52). Hillsdale, NJ: Erlbaum. L. A. Zebrowitz & J. M. Montepare (1992), Impressions of babyfaced males and females across the lifespan. *Developmental Psychology, 28*, 1143–1152.

15. J. H. Langlois, J. M. Ritter, L. A. Roggman, & L. S. Vaughn (1991), Facial diversity and infant preferences for attractive faces. *Developmental Psychology, 27*, 79–84. S. Kramer, L. A. Zebrowitz, J. P. San Giovanni, & B. Sherak (1995), Infants' preferences for attractiveness and babyfaceness. In B. G. Bardy, R. J. Bootsma, &

Y. Guiard (Eds.), *Studies in perception and action: III* (pp. 389–392). Hillsdale, NJ: Erlbaum.

16. J. H. Langlois, L. A. Roggman, & L. A. Rieser-Dannmer, (1990), Infants' differential social responses to attractive and unattractive faces. *Developmental Psychology, 26*, 153–159.

17. K. K. Dion (1973), Young children's stereotyping of facial attractiveness. *Developmental Psychology, 9*, 183–188. Langlois (1981), From the eye of the beholder to behavioral reality.

18. J. H. Langlois & C. Stephan (1977), The effects of physical attractiveness and ethnicity on children's behavioral attributions and peer preferences. *Child Development, 48*, 1694–1698. C. W. Stephan & J. H. Langlois (1984), Baby beautiful: Adult attributions of infant competence as a function of infant attractiveness. *Child Development, 55*, 576–585.

19. Zebrowitz et al. (1993), They don't all look alike.

20. L. Albright, Q. Dong, T. E. Malloy, D. A. Kenny, & D. Yu (1996), *Interpersonal perception at zero acquaintance in Chinese culture.* Unpublished manuscript, Westfield State College, Westfield, MA. L. Albright, T. E. Malloy, Q. Dong, X. Fang, L. Winquist, & D. A. Kenny (1996), *Cross-cultural consensus in personality judgments.* Unpublished manuscript, Westfield State College, Westfield, MA.

21. M. H. Bond (1991), *Beyond the Chinese face.* Hong Kong: Oxford University Press.

22. L. Wheeler & Y. Kim (1996), *The physical attractiveness stereotype has different content in collectivist cultures.* Unpublished manuscript, Department of Clinical and Social Sciences in Psychology, Rochester University, Rochester, NY.

23. Feingold (1992), Good-looking people are not what we think.

24. R. Thornhill & A. P. Møller (in press), Developmental stability, disease and medicine. *Quarterly Review of Biology.*

25. M. S. Clark & A. M. Isen (1982), Toward understanding the relationship between feeling states and social behavior. In A. Hastorf & A. M. Isen (Eds.), *Cognitive social psychology* (pp. 73–108). New York: Elsevier. J. A. Krosnick, A. L. Betz, L. J. Jussim, & A. R. Lynn (1992), Subliminal conditioning of attitudes. *Personality and Social Psychology Bulletin, 18*, 152–162.

26. J. P. Forgas (1991), Affect and person perception. In J. P. Forgas (Ed.), *Emotion and social judgments* (pp. 263–290). Oxford, England: Pergamon Pres. G. H. Bower (1991), Mood congruity of social judgments. In J. P. Forgas (Ed.), *Emotion and social judgments* (pp. 31–53). Oxford, England: Pergamon Press.

27. P. M. Niedenthal & N. Cantor (1986), Affective responses as guides to category-based inferences. *Motivation and Emotion, 10*, 217–232.

28. S. J. McKelvie (1993), Stereotyping in perception of attractiveness, age, and gender in schematic faces. *Social Behavior and Personality, 21*, 121–128.

29. D. T. Kenrick, D. R. Montello, S. E. Gutierres, & M. R. Trost (1993), Effects of physical attractiveness on affect and perceptual judgments: When social comparison overrides social reinforcement. *Personality and Social Psychology Bulletin, 19*, 195–199. Niedenthal & Cantor (1986), Affective responses as guides to category-based inferences.

30. The social outcomes of attractiveness are occasionally adverse. For example, contrast effects may cause attractive people to be given less credit for good performance and more blame for poor performance. Also, the positive reactions to their appearance can make attractive people wonder whether their other attributes are appreciated. Nevertheless, the predominant effects demonstrated for attractiveness have been advantageous, and these are the focus of this chapter.

31. E. Walster, E. Aronson, D. Abrahams, & L. Rottman (1966), The importance of physical attractiveness in dating behavior. *Journal of Personality and Social Psychology, 4*, 508–516.

32. Hatfield & Sprecher (1986), *Mirror, mirror,* chap. 4.

33. A. Feingold (1990), Gender differences in effects of physical attractiveness on romantic attraction: Comparison across five research domains. *Journal of Personality and Social Psychology, 59*, 981–993. R. Koestner & L. Wheeler (1988), Self-presentation in personal advertisements: The influence of implicit notions of attraction and role expectations. *Journal of Social and Personal Relationships, 5*, 149–160. M. Lynn & B. A. Shurgot (1984), Responses to lonely hearts advertisements: Effects of reported physical attractiveness, physique, and coloration. *Personality and Social Psychology Bulletin, 10*, 349–357.

34. R. E. Riggio & S. B. Woll (1984), The role of nonverbal cues and physical attractiveness in the selection of dating partners. *Journal of Social and Personal Relationships, 1*, 347–357.

35. Feingold (1992), Good-looking people are not what we think. S. K. Green, D. R. Buchanan, & S. K. Heuer (1984), Winners, losers, and choosers: A field investigation of dating initiation. *Personality and Social Psychology Bulletin, 10*, 502–511. D. Krebs & A. Adinolfi (1975), Physical attractiveness, social relations, and personality style. *Journal of Personality and Social Psychology, 31*, 245–253. C. Spreadbury & J. Reeves (1979), Physical attractiveness, dating behavior, and implications for women. *Personnel and Guidance Journal, 57*, 338–340.

36. D. M. Buss et al. (1990), International preferences in selecting mates. *Journal of Cross-cultural Psychology, 21*, 5–47.

37. S. Sprecher, Q. Sullivan, & E. Hatfield (1994), Mate selection preferences: Gender differences examined in a national sample. *Journal of Personality and Social Psychology, 66*, 1074–1080.

38. J. A. Howard, P. Blumstein, & P. Schwartz (1987), Social or evolutionary theories? Some observations on preferences in human mate selection. *Journal of Personality and Social Psychology, 53*, 194–200.

39. Buss et al. (1990), International preferences in selecting mates. Howard, Blumstein, & Schwartz (1987), Social or evolutionary theories? Sprecher, Sullivan, & Hatfield (1994), Mate selection preferences.

40. S. Holmes & C. E. Hatch (1938), Personal appearance as related to scholastic records and marriage selection in college women. *Human Biology, 10*, 65–76.

41. J. R. Udry & B. K. Eckland (1984), Benefits of being attractive: Differential payoffs for men and women. *Psychological Reports, 54*, 47–56.

42. D. Buss (1989), Sex differences in human mate preferences: Evolutionary hypotheses tested in 37 cultures. *Behavioral and Brain Sciences, 12*, 1–49.

43. G. H. Elder, Jr. (1969), Appearance and education in marriage mobility. *American Sociological Review, 34*, 519–533.

44. P. A. Taylor & N. D. Glenn (1976), The utility of education and attractiveness for females' status attainment through marriage. *American Sociological Review, 41,* 484–498.

45. H. Sigall & D. Landy (1973), Radiating beauty: Effects of having a physically attractive partner on person perception. *Journal of Personality and Social Psychology, 28,* 218–224.

46. A. Feingold (1988), Matching for attractiveness in romantic partners and same-sex friends: A meta-analysis and theoretical critique. *Psychological Bulletin, 104,* 226–235.

47. R. A. Price & S. G. Vandenberg (1979), Matching for physical attractiveness in married couples. *Personality and Social Psychology Bulletin, 5,* 398–400. R. L. Terry & E. Macklin (1977), Accuracy of identifying married couples on the basis of similarity of attractiveness. *Journal of Psychology, 97,* 15–20.

48. *Parade Magazine, The Boston Globe,* December 27, 1992, p. 8.

49. A. Aron (1988), The matching hypothesis reconsidered again: Comment on Kalick and Hamilton. *Journal of Personality and Social Psychology, 54,* 441–446. S. M. Kalick & T. E. Hamilton (1986), The matching hypothesis reexamined. *Journal of Personality and Social Psychology, 51,* 673–682. S. M. Kalick & T. E. Hamilton (1988), Closer look at a matching simulation: Reply to Aron. *Journal of Personality and Social Psychology, 54,* 447–451.

50. T. L. Huston (1973), Ambiguity of acceptance, social desirability and dating choice. *Journal of Experimental Social Psychology, 9,* 32–42.

51. For a pertinent review, see S. Chaiken (1986), Physical appearance and social influence. In C. P. Herman, M. P. Zanna, & E. T. Higgins (Eds.), *Physical appearance, stigma, and social behavior: The Ontario Symposium* (Vol. 3, pp. 143–177). Hillsdale, NJ: Erlbaum.

52. A. H. Eagly & S. Chaiken (1984), Cognitive theories of persuasion. In L. Berkowitz (Ed.), *Advances in experimental social psychology* (Vol. 17, pp. 267–359). New York: Academic Press.

53. M. R. Solomon, R. D. Ashmore, & L. C. Longo (1992), The beauty match-up hypothesis: Congruence between types of beauty and product images in advertising. *Journal of Advertising, XXI,* 23–34.

54. E. Goodman (1977, November 11), *The Boston Globe,* p. 15.

55. *Harvard Law Review,* 1987, p. 2035.

56. K. Swisher (1994, March 25), Her mustache or her job: Woman says facial hair resulted in firing from VA hotel. *The Washington Post,* p. B1.

57. For pertinent reviews, see the following: R. Bull & N. Rumsey (1988), *The social psychology of facial appearance* (Chapter 3). New York: Springer-Verlag. L. A. Jackson (1992), *Physical appearance and gender: Sociobiological and sociocultural perspectives* (Chapter 4). Albany: SUNY Press.

58. J. Klein (Producer), (1995, June 16), The value of beauty. 20/20, ABC News.

59. M. A. Collins & L. A. Zebrowitz (1995), The contributions of appearance to occupational outcomes in civilian and military settings. *Journal of Applied Social Psychology, 25,* 129–163.

60. M. Heilman (1983), Sex bias in work settings: The lack of fit model. *Research in Organizational Behavior, 5,* 269–298.

61. R. P. Abelson, D. R. Kinder, M. D. Peters, & S. T. Fiske (1982), Affective and semantic components in political person perception. *Journal of Personality and Social Psychology, 42,* 619-130. T. L. Budesheim & S. J. DePaola (1994), Beauty of the beast? The effects of appearance, personality, and issue information on evaluations of political candidates. *Personality and Social Psychology Bulletin, 20,* 339–348. D. R. Kinder, M. D. Peters, R. P. Abelson, & S. T. Fiske (1980), *Presidential prototypes. Political Behavior, 2,* 315-338.

62. M. G. Efran & E. W. Patterson (1974), Voters vote beautiful: The effect of physical appearance on a national election. *Canadian Journal of Behavioral Science, 6,* 352–356.

63. K. E. Lewis & M. Bierly (1990), Toward a profile of the female voter: Sex differences in perceived physical attractiveness and competence of political candidates. *Sex Roles, 22,* 1–12.

64. C. K. Sigelman, D. B. Thomas, L. Sigelman, & F. D. Ribich (1986), Gender, physical attractiveness, and electability: An experimental investigation of voter biases. *Journal of Applied Social Psychology, 16,* 229–248.

65. E. Walsh (1994, October 22), Putting the best face on an "ugly" charge. *The Washington Post,* p. A14.

66. For pertinent reviews, see the following: R. Bull & N. Rumsey (1988), *The social psychology of facial appearance* (Chapter 4). New York: Springer-Verlag. L. A. Jackson (1992), *Physical appearance and gender: Sociobiological and sociocultural perspectives* (chap. 5). Albany, NY: SUNY Press. L. Z. Zebrowitz & S. M. McDonald (1991), Impact of litigants' babyfacedness and attractiveness on judicial decisions in small claims court. *Law and Human Behavior, 15,* 603–623.

67. J. E. Stewart (1980), Defendant's attractiveness as a factor in the outcome of criminal trials. *Journal of Applied Social Psychology, 10,* 348–361.

68. Judge Harold Rothwax. Quoted in B. Gavzer (1996, July 28), We're in the fight for our lives. *Parade Magazine,* p. 6.

69. L. Berkowitz (1983), Aversively stimulated aggression: Some parallels and differences in research with animals and humans. *American Psychologist, 38,* 1135–1144.

70. Zebrowitz & McDonald (1991), Impact of litigants' babyfacedness and attractiveness.

71. A. M. Isen, M. Clark, & M. F. Schwartz (1976), Duration of the effect of good mood on helping: Footprints on the sands of time. *Journal of Personality and Social Psychology, 34,* 385–393. P. Salovey, J. D. Mayer, & D. L. Rosenhan (1991), Mood and healing: Mood as a motivator of helping and helping as a regulator of mood. In M. S. Clark (Ed.), *Prosocial behavior.* Newbury Park, CA: Sage.

72. G. L. Patzer (1985), *The attractiveness phenomenon* (pp. 70–78). New York: Plenum Press.

73. R. Barocas & F. L. Vance (1974), Physical appearance and personal adjustment counseling. *Journal of Counseling Psychology, 21,* 96–100. P. J. Martin, M. H. Friedmeyer, & J. E. Moore (1977), Pretty patient—healthy patient? A study of physical attractiveness and psychopathology. *Journal of Clinical Psychology, 33,* 990–994.

74. A. Farina, E. H. Fischer, S. Sherman, W. T. Smith, T. Grob, & P. Mermin (1977), Physical attractiveness and mental illness. *Journal of Abnormal Psychology, 86,* 510–517.

75. H. D. Hadjistavropoulos, M. A. Ross, & C. L. Von Baeyer (1990), Are physicians' ratings of pain affected by patients' physical attractiveness? *Social Science Medicine, 31,* 69–72.

76. M. R. Gilmore & C. T. Hill (1981), Reactions to patients who complain of pain: Effects of ambiguous diagnosis. *Journal of Applied Social Psychology, 11,* 14–22.

Chapter Eight

1. J. S. Hansen & D. S. Berry (1996), *Nonverbal correlates of facial maturity.* Unpublished manuscript, Southern Methodist University, Dallas, TX. L. A. Zebrowitz & J. M. Montepare (1992), Impressions of babyfaced males and females across the life span. *Developmental Psychology, 28,* 1143–1152. L. A. Zebrowitz & L. Voinescu (1993), *The effects of babyfaceness and smiling on trait impressions.* Unpublished manuscript, Brandeis University, Waltham, MA.

2. D. S. Berry & J. L. Finch-Wero (1993), Accuracy in face perception: A view from ecological psychology. *Journal of Personality, 61,* 497–520.

3. J. H. Langlois (1976), From the eye of the beholder to behavioral reality: The development of social behaviors and social relations as a function of physical attractiveness. In C. P. Herman, M. P. Zanna, & E. T. Higgins (Eds.), *Physical appearance, stigma, and social behavior: The Ontario Symposium* (Vol. 3, pp. 25–51). Hillsdale, NJ: Erlbaum.

4. J. H. Langlois, J. M. Ritter, R. J. Casey, & D. B. Sawin (1995), Infant attractiveness predicts maternal behavior and attitudes. *Developmental Psychology, 31,* 464–472.

5. C. Stephan & J. H. Langlois (1984), Baby beautiful: Adult attributions of infant competence as a function of infant attractiveness. *Child Development, 55,* 576–585. K. A. Hildebrandt & H. E. Fitzgerald (1983), The infant's physical attractiveness: Its effect on bonding and attachment. *Infant Mental Health Journal, 4,* 3–12.

6. J. Block, personal communication, February 20, 1996. G. Maruyama & N. Miller (1981), Physical attractiveness and personality. In B. A. Maher & W. B. Maher (Eds.), *Progress in experimental personality research* (Vol. 10, pp. 203–281). New York: Academic Press.

7. J. H. Langlois & L. Styczynski (1979), The effects of physical attractiveness on the behavioral attributions and peer preferences in acquainted children. *International Journal of Behavioral Development, 2,* 325–341. R. M. Lerner & J. V. Lerner (1977), Effects of age, sex, and physical attractiveness on child-peer relations, academic performance, and elementary school adjustment. *Developmental Psychology, 13,* 585–590.

8. R. E. Kleck, S. A. Richardson, & L. Ronald (1974), Physical appearance cues and interpersonal attraction in children. *Child Development, 45,* 305–310.

9. N. Cavior & P. R. Dokecki (1973), Physical attractiveness, perceived attitude similarity, and academic achievement as contributors to interpersonal attraction among adolescents. *Developmental Psychology, 9*, 44–54.

10. Langlois & Styczynski (1979), The effects of physical attractiveness. Lerner & Lerner (1977), Effects of age, sex, and physical attractiveness.

11. L. Lowenstein (1978), The bullied and non-bullied child. *Bulletin of the British Psychological Society, 31*, 316–318. G. J. Smith (1985), Facial and full-length ratings of attractiveness related to the social interactions of young children. *Sex Roles, 12*, 287–293.

12. K. H. Rubin & M. Wilkinson (1995), Peer rejection and social isolation in childhood: A conceptually inspired research agenda for children with craniofacial handicaps. In R. A. Eder (Ed.), *Developmental perspectives on craniofacial problems* (pp. 158–176). New York: Springer-Verlag.

13. L. A. Zebrowitz, S. Brownlow, & K. Olson (1992), Baby talk to the babyfaced. *Journal of Nonverbal Behavior, 16*, 143–158.

14. J. Bloomfield (1993), *Effects of children's facial appearance on teacher-student interactions in second grade classrooms.* Unpublished senior honors thesis, Brandeis University, Waltham, MA.

15. Quoted in E. Berscheid & E. Walster (Hatfield) (1974), Physical attractiveness. In L. Berkowitz (Ed.), *Advances in experimental social psychology* (Vol. 7, pp. 157–215), New York: Academic Press, p. 193.

16. K. K. Dion (1972), Physical attractiveness and evaluation of children's transgressions. *Journal of Personality and Social Psychology, 24*, 207–213.

17. Quoted in Berscheid & Walster (Hatfield) (1974), Physical attractiveness.

18. L. Berkowitz & A. Frodi (1979), Reactions to a child's mistakes as affected by her/his looks or speech. *Social Psychology Quarterly, 42*, 420–425.

19. K. Dion (1974), Children's physical attractiveness and sex as determinants of adult punitiveness. *Developmental Psychology, 10*, 772–778.

20. G. H. Elder, Jr., T. V. Nguyen, & A. Caspi (1985), Linking family hardship to children's lives. *Child Development, 56*, 361–375.

21. J. Rich (1975), Effects of children's physical attractiveness on teachers' evaluations. *Journal of Educational Psychology, 67*, 599–609.

22. L. A. Zebrowitz, K. Kendall-Tackett, & J. Fafel (1991), The influence of children's facial maturity on parental expectations and punishments. *Journal of Experimental Child Psychology, 52*, 221–238.

23. V. McCabe (1984), Abstract perceptual information for age level: A risk factor for maltreatment? *Child Development, 55*, 267–276.

24. K. L. Marwit, S. J. Marwit, & E. F. Walker (1978), Effects of student race and physical attractiveness on teachers' judgments of transgressions. *Journal of Educational Psychology, 70*, 911–915.

25. Zebrowitz et al. (1991), The influence of children's facial maturity.

26. J. E. Brophy & T. L. Good (1974), *Teacher-student relationships: Causes and consequences* (p. 26). New York: Holt, Rinehart & Winston.

27. M. Clifford & E. Walster (1973), Research note: The effects of physical attractiveness on teacher expectations. *Sociology of Education, 46*, 248–258. G. Adams & A. Cohen (1976), An examination of cumulative folder information used by teach-

ers in making differential judgments of children's abilities. *Alberta Journal of Educational Research, 22,* 216–225.

28. T. Kehle, W. Bramble, & E. Mason (1974), Teachers' expectations: Ratings of student performance. *Journal of Experimental Education, 43,* 54–60. D. Landy & H. Sigall (1974), Beauty is talent: Task evaluation as a function of the performer's physical attractiveness. *Journal of Personality and Social Psychology, 29,* 299–304. P. Morrow & J. McElroy (1984), The impact of physical attractiveness in evaluative contexts. *Basic and Applied Social Psychology, 5,* 171–182.

29. P. Kenealy, N. Frude, & W. Shaw (1988), Influence of children's physical attractiveness on teacher expectations. *The Journal of Social Psychology, 128,* 373–383. T. Martinek (1981), Physical attractiveness: Effects on teacher expectations and dyadic interactions in elementary age children. *Journal of Sport Psychology, 3,* 196–205.

30. G. Adams & A. Cohen (1974), Children's physical and interpersonal characteristics as they affect student-teacher interaction. *Journal of Experimental Education, 43,* 1–5. Brophy & Good (1974), *Teacher-student relationships.*

31. M. J. Harris & R. Rosenthal (1985), Mediation of interpersonal expectancy effects: 31 meta-analyses. *Psychological Bulletin, 97,* 363–386.

32. J. M. Ritter, J. Langlois, & R. J. Casey (1991), Adults' responses to infants varying in appearance of age and attractiveness. *Child Development, 62,* 68–82.

33. L. A. Zebrowitz & J. M. Montepare (1992), Impressions of babyfaced males and females across the lifespan. *Developmental Psychology, 28,* 1143–1152.

34. Zebrowitz et al. (1991), The influence of children's facial maturity.

35. Zebrowitz et al. (1992), Baby talk to the babyfaced.

36. J. LaVoie & G. Adams (1974), Teacher expectancy and its relation to physical and interpersonal characteristics of the child. *Alberta Journal of Educational Research, 20,* 122–132.

37. L. A. Zebrowitz, K. Olson, & K. Hoffman (1993), The stability of babyfaceness and attractiveness across the lifespan. *Journal of Personality and Social Psychology, 64,* 453–466.

38. L. A. Zebrowitz (1996), Unpublished data, Brandeis University, Waltham, MA.

39. M. Snyder, E. D. Tanke, & E. Berscheid (1977), Social perception and interpersonal behavior: On the self-fulfilling nature of social stereotypes. *Journal of Personality and Social Psychology, 35,* 656–666.

40. M. Snyder & W. B. Swann (1978), Hypothesis-testing processes in social interaction. *Journal of Personality and Social Psychology, 36,* 1202–1212.

41. J. L. Hilton & J. M. Darley (1985), Constructing other persons: A limit on the effect. *Journal of Experimental Social Psychology, 21,* 1–18. B. Major, C. Cozzarelli, M. Testa, & D. B. McFarlin (1988), Self-verification vs. expectancy confirmation in social interaction: The impact of self-focus. *Personality and Social Psychology Bulletin, 14,* 346–359.

42. M. Snyder (1992), Motivational foundations of behavioral confirmation. In M. P. Zanna (Ed.), *Advances in experimental social psychology* (Vol. 25, pp. 67–114). New York: Academic Press.

43. W. B. Swann, Jr. & R. J. Ely (1984), A battle of wills: Self-verification versus behavioral confirmation. *Journal of Personality and Social Psychology, 38*, 879–888.

44. M. H. Bond (1972), Effect of an impression set on subsequent behavior. *Journal of Personality and Social Psychology, 24*, 301–305. Hilton & Darley (1985), Constructing other persons.

45. M. H. Bond (1972), Effect of an impression set.

46. M. Snyder & J. A. Haugen (1994), Why does behavioral confirmation occur? A functional perspective on the role of the perceiver. *Journal of Experimental Social Psychology, 30*, 218–246.

47. L. Jussim (1989), Teacher expectations: Self-fulfilling prophecies, perceptual biases, and accuracy. *Journal of Personality and Social Psychology, 57*, 469–480.

48. Genetic or environmental factors that influence both appearance and behavior (Paths A and B in the model in Figure 3.1) provide one possible answer. Another possibility is that the covariation of appearance and behavior that is accurately reflected in perceivers' expectancies derives from earlier self-fulfilling prophecy effects or earlier Dorian Gray effects.

49. M. Shelley (1991), *Frankenstein* (p. 203. New York: Bantam Books. (Original work published 1818)

50. Shelley (1818), *Frankenstein*, p. 84.

51. R. J. Sampson & J. H. Laub (1993), *Crime in the making: Pathways and turning points through life* (p. 92). Cambridge, MA: Harvard University Press.

52. J. G. Parker & S. R. Asher (1987), Peer relations and later personal adjustment: Are low-accepted children at risk? *Psychological Bulletin, 102*, 357–389.

53. Sampson & Laub (1993), *Crime in the making*.

54. L. A. Zebrowitz, M. A. Collins, & R. Dutta (1996), *The relationship between appearance and personality across the lifespan.* Unpublished manuscript, Brandeis University, Waltham, MA.

55. H. Friedman & L. A. Zebrowitz (1992), The contribution of facial maturity to sex-role stereotypes. *Personality and Social Psychology Bulletin, 18*, 430–438.

56. K. K. Dion & S. Stein (1978), Physical attractiveness and interpersonal influence. *Journal of Experimental Social Psychology, 14*, 97–108. H. T. Reis, W. Spiegel, M. H. Kernis, J. Wezlek, & M. Perri (1982), Physical attractiveness and social interaction: II. Why does appearance affect social experience? *Journal of Personality and Social Psychology, 43*, 979–996.

57. J. Jacobs & J. S. Eccles (1992), The impact of mothers' gender-role stereotypic beliefs on mothers' and children's ability perceptions. *Journal of Personality and Social Psychology, 63*, 932–944.

58. R. Rosenthal & L. F. Jacobson (1968), Teacher expectations for the disadvantaged. *Scientific American, 218*, 19–23.

59. M. A. Collins & L. A. Zebrowitz (1996), *The relationship between appearance and intellectual outcomes across the lifespan.* Unpublished manuscript, Brandeis University, Waltham, MA.

60. Zebrowitz et al. (1992), Baby talk to the babyfaced.

61. A. Caspi, D. J. Bem, & G. H. Elder, Jr. (1988), Moving away from the world: Life-course patterns of shy children. *Developmental Psychology, 24*, 824–831.

62. A. Caspi, D. J. Bem, & G. H. Elder, Jr. (1987), Moving against the world: Life-course patterns of explosive children. *Developmental Psychology, 23*, 308–313.

63. P. T. Costa & R. R. McCrae (1988), Personality in adulthood: A six-year longitudinal study of self-reports and spouse ratings on the NEO personality inventory. *Journal of Personality and Social Psychology, 54,* 853–863. L. A. Zebrowitz et al. (1996), *The relationship between appearance and personality.*

64. C. Garcia-Coll, J. Kagan, & J. S. Reznick (1984), Behavioral inhibition in young children. *Child Development, 55,* 1005–1019. J. Kagan & N. Snidman (1991), Infant predictors of inhibited and uninhibited profiles. *Psychological Science, 2,* 40–44. J. Kagan, J. S. Reznick, C. Clarke, N. Snidman, & C. Garcia-Coll (1984), Behavioral inhibition to the unfamiliar. *Child Development, 55,* 2212–2225. J. S. Reznick, J. Kagan, N. Snidman, M. Gersten, K. Baak, & A. Rosenberg (1986), Inhibited and uninhibited children: A follow-up study. *Child Development, 57,* 660–680.

65. J. Block (1971), *Lives through time.* Berkeley: Bancroft. P. T. Costa & R. R. McCrae (1994), Set like plaster? Evidence for the stability of adult personality. In T. Heatherton & J. Weinberger (Eds.), *Can personality change?* Washington, DC: American Psychological Association. L. R. Huesmann, L. D. Eron, M. M. Lefkowitz, & L. O. Walder (1984), Stability of aggression over time and generations. *Developmental Psychology, 20,* 1120–1134. D. J. Ozer & P. F. Gjerde (1989), Patterns of personality consistency and change from childhood through adolescence. *Journal of Personality, 57,* 483–507.

66. C. Z. Malatesta, M. J. Fiore, & J. J. Messina (1987), Affect, personality, and facial expression characteristics of older people. *Psychology and Aging, 2,* 64–69.

67. Zebrowitz et al. (1996), *The relationship between appearance and personality.*

68. L. A. Zebrowitz, L. Voinescu, & M. Collins (1996), "Wide-eyed" and "crooked-faced": Determinants of perceived and real honesty across the lifespan. *Personality and Social Psychology Bulletin, 22,* 1258–1269.

69. C. F. Bond & M. Robinson (1988), The evolution of deception. *Journal of Nonverbal Behavior, 12,* 295–307.

70. For a review of research on the accuracy of the attractiveness stereotype in adolescents and adults, see A. Feingold (1992), Good-looking people are not what we think. *Psychological Bulletin, 111,* 304–341.

71. D. Krebs & A. A. Adolfini (1975), Physical attractiveness, social relations, and personality style. *Journal of Personality and Social Psychology, 31,* 245–253. Maruyama & Miller (1981), Physical attractiveness and personality. Collins & Zebrowitz (1996), *The relationship between appearance and intellectual outcomes.*

72. J. H. Langlois & A. C. Downs (1979), Peer relations as a function of physical attractiveness: The eye of the beholder or behavioral reality? *Child Development, 50,* 409–418. Langlois & Styczynski (1979), The effects of physical attractiveness. Lerner & Lerner (1977), Effects of age, sex, and physical attractiveness. Zebrowitz et al. (1996), *The relationship between appearance and personality.*

73. R. Agnew (1984), Appearance and delinquency. *Criminology: An interdisciplinary Journal, 22,* 421–440. N. Cavior & L. Howard (1973), Facial attractiveness and juvenile delinquency. *Journal of Abnormal Child Psychology, 1,* 202–213. H. Cavior, S. Hayes, & N. Cavior (1974), Physical attractiveness of female offenders. *Criminal Justice and Behavior, 1,* 321–331.

74. Feingold (1992), Good-looking people are not what we think.

75. P. Borkenau & A. Liebler (1993), Consensus and self-other agreement for trait inferences from minimal information. *Journal of Personality, 61*, 477–496. S. W. Gangestad, J. A. Simpson, K. DiGeronimo, & M. Biek (1992), Differential accuracy in person perception across traits: Examination of a functional hypothesis. *Journal of Personality and Social Psychology, 62*, 688–698. D. A. Kenny, C. Horner, D. A. Cashy, & L. Chu (1992), Consensus at zero acquaintance: Replication, behavioral cues, and stability. *Journal of Personality and Social Psychology, 62*, 88–97.

76. Feingold (1992), Good-looking people are not what we think.

77. Zebrowitz et al. (1996), *The relationship between appearance and personality.*

78. D. S. Berry & J. C. Landry (1997), *Social perception in the real world: Facial maturity and daily social interaction. Journal of Personality and Social Psychology,* in press.

79. P. Borkenau & A. Liebler (1995), Observable attributes as manifestations and cues of personality and intelligence. *Journal of Personality, 63*, 1–25.

80. D. S. Berry & S. Brownlow (1989), Were the physiognomists right? Personality correlates of facial babyishness. *Personality and Social Psychology Bulletin, 15*, 266–279. D. S. Berry (1990), Taking people at face value: Evidence for the kernel of truth hypothesis. *Social Cognition, 8*, 343–361. D. S. Berry (1991), Accuracy in social perception: Contributions of facial and vocal information. *Journal of Personality and Social Psychology, 61*, 298–307.

81. D. A. Kenny, C. Horner, D. A. Cashy, & L. Chu (1992), Consensus at zero acquaintance: Replication, behavioral cues, and stability. *Journal of Personality and Social Psychology, 62*, 88–97.

82. P. Borkenau & A. Liebler (1993), Consensus and self-other agreement.

83. Berry (1990), Taking people at face value. Berry (1991), Accuracy in social perception.

84. Zebrowitz et al. (1996), *The relationship between appearance and personality.*

85. Collins & Zebrowitz (1996), *The relationship between appearnace and intellectual outcomes.*

Chapter Nine

1. C. P. Gilman (1899), In this our world: An obstacle. Cited in J. Bartlett (1980), *Bartlett's familiar quotations* (15th ed., p. 695). Boston, Little, Brown.

2. Facial discrimination: Extending handicap law to employment discrimination on the basis of physical appearance. (1987). *Harvard Law Review, 100*, 2035–2052.

3. Effect sizes are reported in this chapter only for studies that directly investigated facial appearance.

4. M. H. Bond (1972), Effect of an impression set on subsequent behavior. *Journal of Personality and Social Psychology, 24*, 301–305. M. Snyder & J. A. Haugen (1994), Why does behavioral confirmation occur? A functional perspective on the role of the perceiver. *Journal of Experimental Social Psychology, 30*, 218–246.

5. V. Houston & R. Bull (1994), Do people avoid sitting next to someone who is facially disfigured? *European Journal of Social Psychology, 24*, 279–284.

6. A. Kruglanski & T. Freund (1983), The freezing and unfreezing of lay-inferences: Effects on impressional primacy, ethnic stereotyping, and numerical anchoring. *Journal of Experimental Social Psychology, 19*, 448–468.

7. S. L. Neuberg & S. T. Fiske (1987), Motivational influences on impression formation: Outcome dependency, accuracy-driven attention, and individuating processes. *Journal of Personality and Social Psychology, 53,* 431–444.

8. P. E. Tetlock (1985), Accountability: The neglected social context of judgment and choice. *Research in Organizational Behavior, 7,* 297–332. P. E. Tetlock & J. I. Kim (1987), Accountability and judgment processes in a personality prediction task. *Journal of Personality and Social Psychology, 52,* 700–709.

9. A. R. Harkness, K. G. DeBono, & E. Borgida (1985), Personal involvement and strategies for making contingency judgments: A stake in the dating game makes a difference. *Journal of Personality and Social Psychology, 49,* 22–32.

10. S. L. Neuberg & S. T. Fiske (1987), Motivational influences on impression formation: Outcome dependency, accuracy-driven attention, and individuating processes. *Journal of Personality and Social Psychology, 53,* 431–444.

11. E. Borgida & B. Howard-Pitney (1983), Personal involvement and the robustness of perceptual salience effects. *Journal of Personality and Social Psychology, 45,* 560–570.

12. A. Locksley, C. Hepburn, & V. Ortiz (1982), On the effects of social stereotypes on judgments of individuals: A comment on Grant and Holmes's "The integration of implicit personality theory schemas and stereotypic images." *Social Psychology Quarterly, 45,* 270–273.

13. C. A. Anderson (1982), Inoculation and counterexplanation: Debiasing techniques in the perseverance of social theories. *Social Cognition, 1,* 126–139.

14. J. M. Ritter & J. H. Langlois (1988), The role of physical attractiveness in the observation of adult-child interactions: Eye of the beholder or behavioral reality? *Developmental Psychology, 24,* 254–263.

15. D. T. Gilbert & D. S. Krull (1988), Seeing less and knowing more: The benefits of perceptual ignorance. *Journal of Personality and Social Psychology, 54,* 193–202.

16. G. C. Cupchik, J. C. Younger, & D. Klein (1979), The integration of physical and social information in social perception. In M. Cook & G. Wilson (Eds.), *Love and attraction: An international conference* (pp. 43–49). Oxford, England: Pergamon Press.

17. C. Hepburn & A. Locksley (1983), Subjective awareness of stereotyping: Do we know when our judgments are prejudiced? *Social Psychology Quarterly, 46,* 311–318.

18. R. E. Nisbett & N. Bellows (1977), Verbal reports about causal influences on social judgments: Private access to public theories. *Journal of Personality and Social Psychology, 35,* 613–624.

19. R. J. Ellis, J. M. Olson, & M. P. Zanna (1983), Stereotypic personality inferences following objective versus subjective judgments of beauty. *Canadian Journal of Behavioural Science, 15,* 35–42.

20. R. M. Friend & M. Vinson (1974), Leaning over backwards: Jurors' responses to defendants' attractiveness. *Journal of Communication, 24,* 124–129.

21. K. L. Dion & K. K. Dion (1987), Belief in a just world and physical attractiveness stereotyping. *Journal of Personality and Social Psychology, 52,* 775–780.

22. M. Snyder, E. Berscheid, & P. Glick (1985), Focusing on the exterior and the interior: Two investigations of the initiation of personal relationships. *Journal of Personality and Social Psychology, 48,* 1427–1439.

23. M. Snyder, E. Berscheid, & A. Matwychuk (1988), Orientations toward personnel selection: Differential reliance on appearance and personality. *Journal of Personality and Social Psychology, 54*, 972–979.

24. S. M. Andersen & S. L. Bem (1981), Sex typing and androgyny in dyadic interaction: Individual differences in responsiveness to physical attractiveness. *Journal of Personality and Social Psychology, 41*, 74–86. T. F. Cash & R. N. Kilcullen (1985), The eye of the beholder: Susceptibility to sexism and beautyism in the evaluation of managerial applicants. *Journal of Applied Social Psychology, 15*, 591–605.

25. Andersen & Bem (1981), Sex typing and androgyny in dyadic interaction. L. H. Janda, K. E. O'Grady, & S. A. Barnhart (1981), Effects of sexual attitudes and physical attractiveness on person perception of men and women. *Sex Roles, 7*, 189–199.

26. J. A. Graham & A. J. Jouhar (1981), The effects of cosmetics on person perception. *International Journal of Cosmetic Science, 3*, 199–210. P. Hamid (1972), Some effects of dress cues on observational accuracy, a perceptual estimate, and impression formation. *Journal of Social Psychology, 86*, 279–289.

27. T. Cash, K. Dawson, P. Davis, M. Bowen, & C. Galumbeck (1989), Effects of cosmetics use on the physical attractiveness and body image of American college women. *The Journal of Social Psychology, 129*, 349–355.

28. J. E. Workman & K. K. P. Johnson (1991), The role of cosmetics in impression formation. *Clothing and Textile Research Journal, 10*, 63–67.

29. Graham & Jouhar (1981), The effects of cosmetics on person perception. W. J. McKeachie (1952), Lipstick as a determiner of first impressions of personality: An experiment for the general psychology course. *Journal of Social Psychology, 36*, 241–244. Workman & Johnson (1991), The role of cosmetics in impression formation.

30. C. L. Cox & W. H. Glick (1986), Resume evaluations and cosmetics use: When more is not better. *Sex Roles, 14*, 51–58.

31. L. Grealy (1994), *Autobiography of a face* (pp. 177, 186, 188). Boston: Houghton Mifflin.

32. Graham & Jouhar (1981), The effects of cosmetics on person perception.

33. F. Muscarella & M. R. Cunningham (1996), The evolutionary significance and social perception of male pattern baldness and facial hair. *Ethology and Sociobiology, 17*, 99–117.

34. Muscarella & Cunningham (1996), The evolutionary significance and social perception of male pattern baldness and facial hair. S. M. Pancer & J. R. Meindl (1978), Length of hair and beardedness as determinants of personality impressions. *Perceptual and Motor Skills, 46*, 1328–1330. R. J. Pellegrini (1973), Impressions of the male personality as a function of beardedness. *Journal of Psychology, 10*, 29–33. J. A. Reed & E. M. Blunk (1990), The influence of facial hair on impression formation. *Social Behavior and Personality, 18*, 169–176. M. S. Wogalter & J. A. Hosie (1991), Effects of cranial and facial hair on perceptions of age and person. *Journal of Social Psychology, 131*, 589–591.

35. Pellegrini (1973), Impressions of the male personality as a function of beardedness.

36. Muscarella & Cunningham (1996), The evolutionary significance and social perception of male pattern baldness and facial hair.

37. Reed & Blunk (1990), The influence of facial hair on impression formation. Wogalter & Hosie (1991), Effects of cranial and facial hair.

38. L. A. Zebrowitz, D. R. Tenenbaum, & L. H. Goldstein (1991), The impact of job applicants' facial maturity, sex, and academic achievement on hiring recommendations. *Journal of Applied Social Psychology, 21,* 525–548.

39. H. T. Reis, I. M. Wilson, C. Monestere, S. Bernstein, K. Clark, E. Seidl, M. Franco, E. Gioioso, L. Freeman, & K. Radoane (1990), What is smiling is beautiful and good. *European Journal of Social Psychology, 20,* 259–267.

40. News release, August 8 1994.

41. L. A. Zebrowitz & L. Voinescu (1993), *The effects of babyfaceness and smiling on trait impressions.* Unpublished manuscript, Brandeis University, Waltham, MA.

42. K. A. Hildebrandt (1983), Effect of facial expression variations on ratings of infants' physical attractiveness. *Developmental Psychology, 19,* 414–417.

43. J. P. Forgas (1987), The role of physical attractiveness in the interpretation of facial expression cues. *Personality and Social Psychology Bulletin, 13,* 478–489.

44. Reis et al. (1990), What is smiling is beautiful and good. Zebrowitz & Voinescu (1993), *The effects of babyfaceness and smiling.*

45. Reis et al. (1990), What is smiling is beautiful and good. Zebrowitz & Voinescu (1993), *The effects of babyfaceness and smiling.*

46. S. L. Ellyson & J. F. Dovidio (1985), *Power, dominance, and nonverbal behavior.* New York: Springer-Verlag. R. Gifford (1994), A lens-mapping framework for understanding the encoding and decoding of interpersonal dispositions in nonverbal behavior. *Journal of Personality and Social Psychology, 66,* 398–412.

47. J. M. Montepare & L. Zebrowitz-McArthur (1988), Impressions of people created by age-related qualities of their gaits. *Journal of Personality and Social Psychology, 55,* 547–556.

48. A. S. Imada & M. D. Hakel (1977), Influence of nonverbal communication and rater proximity on impressions and decisions in simulated employment interviews. *Journal of Applied Psychology, 62,* 295–300.

49. R. E. Riggio, K. F. Widaman, J. S. Tucker, & C. Salinas (1991), Beauty is more than skin deep: Components of attractiveness. *Basic and Applied Social Psychology, 12,* 423–439. R. E. Riggio & H. S. Friedman (1986), Impression formation: The role of expressive behavior. *Journal of Personality and Social Psychology, 50,* 421–427. R. M. Sabatelli & M. Rubin (1986), Nonverbal expressiveness and physical attractiveness as mediators of interpersonal perceptions. *Journal of Nonverbal Behavior, 10,* 120–133.

50. For a pertinent review, see L. A. Zebrowitz (1990), *Social perception* (chap. 3). Pacific Grove, CA: Brooks/Cole.

51. R. Gifford, C. F. Ng, & M. Wilkinson (1985), Nonverbal cues in the employment interview: Links between applicant qualities and interviewer judgments. *Journal of Applied Social Psychology, 70,* 729–736.

52. D. S. Berry, J. W. Pennebaker, J. S. Mueller, & W. S. Hiller (1995), *Language and social perception.* Unpublished manuscript, Southern Methodist University, Dallas, TX.

53. L. Zebrowitz-McArthur & J. M. Montepare (1989), Contributions of a baby-face and a childlike voice to impressions of moving and talking faces. *Journal of Nonverbal Behavior, 13*, 189–203.

54. R. E. Geiselman, N. A. Haight, & L. G. Kimata, (1984), Context effects on the perceived physical attractiveness of faces. *Journal of Experimental Social Psychology, 20*, 409–424.

55. D. H. Wedell, A. Parducci, & R. E. Geiselman (1987), A formal analysis of ratings of physical attractiveness: Successive contrast and simultaneous assimila-tion. *Journal of Experimental Social Psychology, 23*, 230–249.

56. Geiselman et al. (1984), Context effects.

57. K. Edwards (1987), Effects of sex and glasses on attitudes toward intelli-gence and attractiveness. *Psychological Reports, 60*, 590. M. B. Harris, R. J. Harris, & S. Bochner (1982), Fat, four-eyed, and female: Stereotypes of obesity, glasses, and gender. *Journal of Applied Social Psychology, 12*, 503–516. G. R. Thornton (1944), The effect of wearing glasses upon judgments of personality traits of persons seen briefly. *Journal of Applied Psychology, 28*, 203–207. R. L. Terry & R. J. Macy (1991), Children's social judgments of other children who wear eyeglasses. *Journal of So-cial Behavior and Personality, 6*, 965–974.

58. Edwards (1987), Effects of sex and glasses on attitudes. Thornton (1944), The effect of wearing glasses. P. N. Hamid (1968), Style of dress as a perceptual cue in impression formation. *Perceptual and Motor Skills, 26*, 904–906.

59. M. Argyle & R. McHenry (1971), Do spectacles really affect judgments of in-telligence? *British Journal of Social and Clinical Psychology, 10*, 27–29.

60. S. Brownlow (1992, March), *Putting the best face forward: Facial babyishness, types of glasses, and perceptions of faces.* Poster presented at the annual meeting of the Southeastern Psychological Association, Knoxville, TN.

61. K. Gibbins (1969), Communication aspects of women's clothes and their re-lation to fashionability. *British Journal of Social and Clinical Psychology, 8*, 301–312. Hamid (1968), Style of dress. M. R. Solomon (Ed.), (1985), *The psychology of fashion.* Lexington, MA: Lexington Books.

62. S. J. Sweat & M. A. Zentner (1985), Attributions toward female appearance styles (pp. 321–335), In Solomon (Ed.), *The psychology of fashion.*

63. J. E. Driskell & B. Mullen (1990), Status, expectations, and behavior: A meta-analytic review and test of the theory. *Personality and Social Psychology Bulletin, 16*, 541–553. B. Mullen, C. Copper, & J. E. Driskell (1990), Jaywalking as a function of model behavior. *Personality and Social Psychology Bulletin, 16*, 320–330. M. Walker, S. Harriman, & S. Costello (1980), The influence of appearance on compliance with a request. *Journal of Social Psychology, 112*, 159–160.

64. J. E. Copley, & S. Brownlow (1995), The interactive effects of facial maturity and name warmth on perceptions of job candidates. *Basic and Applied Social Psy-chology, 16*, 251–265.

65. D. S. Berry & S. Brownlow (1989), Were the physiognomists right? Personal-ity correlates of facial babyishness. *Personality and Social Psychology Bulletin, 15*, 266–279. A. C. Downs (1991), Objective and subjective physical attractiveness cor-relates of adult social interactions. *Psychology: A Journal of Human Behavior, 28*, 11–16. G. L. Patzer (1985), *The physical attractiveness phenomena* (pp. 23–26). New York: Plenum Press.

66. D. A. Kenny & B. M. DePaulo (1993), Do people know how others view them? An empirical and theoretical account. *Psychological Bulletin, 114*, 145–161.

67. A. Feingold (1992), Good-looking people are not what we think. *Psychological Bulletin, 111*, 304–341.

68. Berry & Brownlow (1989), Were the physiognomists right?

69. K. K. Dion (1986), Stereotyping based on physical attractiveness: Issues and conceptual perspectives. In C. P. Herman, M. P. Zanna, & E. T. Higgins (Eds.), *Physical appearance, stigma, and social behavior: The Ontario Symposium* (Vol. 3, pp. 7–22). Hillsdale, NJ: Erlbaum.

70. G. R. Adams, M. Hicken, & M. Salehi (1988), Socialization of the physical attractiveness stereotype: Parental expectations and verbal behaviors. *International Journal of Psychology, 23*, 137–149.

71. Feingold (1992), Good-looking people are not what we think.

72. S. Coopersmith (1967), *The antecedents of self-esteem.* San Francisco: Freeman.

73. K. A. Brattesani, R. W. Weinstein, & H. H. Marshall (1984), Student perceptions of differential teacher treatment as moderators of teacher expectation effects. *Journal of Educational Psychology, 76*, 236–247. R. S. Weinstein, H. H. Marshall, L. Sharp, & M. Botkin (1987), Pygmalion and the student: Age and classroom differences in children's awareness of teacher expectations. *Child Development, 58*, 1079–1093.

74. D. A. Byrnes (1987), The physically unattractive child. *Childhood Education, 64*, 80–85.

75. A. C. Downs & S. K. Harrison (1985), Embarrassing age spots or just plain ugly? Physical attractiveness stereotyping as an instrument of sexism on American television commercials. *Sex Roles, 13*, 9–19.

76. D. T. Kenrick & S. E. Gutierres (1980), Contrast effects and judgments of physical attractiveness: When beauty becomes a social problem. *Journal of Personality and Social Psychology, 38*, 131–140.

77. D. T. Kenrick, S. E. Gutierres, & L. I. Goldberg (1989), Influence of popular erotica on judgments of strangers and mates. *Journal of Experimental Social Psychology, 25*, 159–167.

78. M. Baker & G. Churchill (1977), The impact of physically attractive models on advertising evaluations. *Journal of Marketing Research, 14*, 538–555. G. E. Belch, M. A. Belch, & A. Villarreal (1987), Effects of advertising communications: Review of research. *Research in Marketing, 9*, 59–117.

79. L. Wheeler & Y. Kim (1996), *The physical attractiveness stereotype has different content in collectivist cultures.* Unpublished manuscript, Department of Clinical and Social Sciences in Psychology, Rochester University, Rochester, NY.

80. L. Albright, Q. Dong, T. E. Malloy, D. A. Kenny, & D. Yu (1996), *Interpersonal perception at zero acquaintance in Chinese culture.* Unpublished manuscript, Westfield State College, Westfield, MA. L. Albright, T. E. Malloy, Q. Dong, X. Fang, L. Winquist, & D. A. Kenny (1996), *Cross-cultural consensus in personality judgments.* Unpublished manuscript, Westfield State College, Westfield, MA. M. H. Bond (1991), *Beyond the Chinese face.* Hong Kong: Oxford University Press.

81. K. K. Dion, A. W. P. Pak, & K. L. Dion (1990), Stereotyping based on physical attractiveness: A sociocultural perspective. *Journal of Cross-Cultural Psychology, 21*, 378–398.

About the Book and Author

Do we read character in faces? What information do faces actually provide? What are the social and psychological consequences of reading character in faces? Zebrowitz unmasks the face and provides the first systematic, scientific account of our tendency to judge people by their appearance. Offering an in-depth discussion of two appearance qualities that influence our impressions of others—"baby-faceness" and "attractiveness"—and an analysis of these impressions, Zebrowitz has written an accessible and valuable book for professionals and general readers alike.

Leslie A. Zebrowitz is Manuel Yellen Professor of Social Relations and professor of psychology at Brandeis University.

Index

DA